THEN & NOW

GEORGETOWN

OPPOSITE: George Price Sr. came to Georgetown in the late 1800s. He farmed this property just west of Wilbarger Point, a high promontory on the eastern edge of town. Pictured near an outbuilding on the property in this c. 1910 photograph are two of his children, Katherine and George Jr., their mother, Margaret, and John, who was a freed slave. John and his wife helped take care of the Price children. This remote location remains sparsely populated today, as it rests quietly between Wilbarger Point on the east, Southwestern University on the west, Highway 29 to the south, and the San Gabriel River to the north. (Image by George Price Sr.; courtesy John S. Lesesne.)

THEN & NOW

GEORGETOWN

Donna Scarbrough Josey

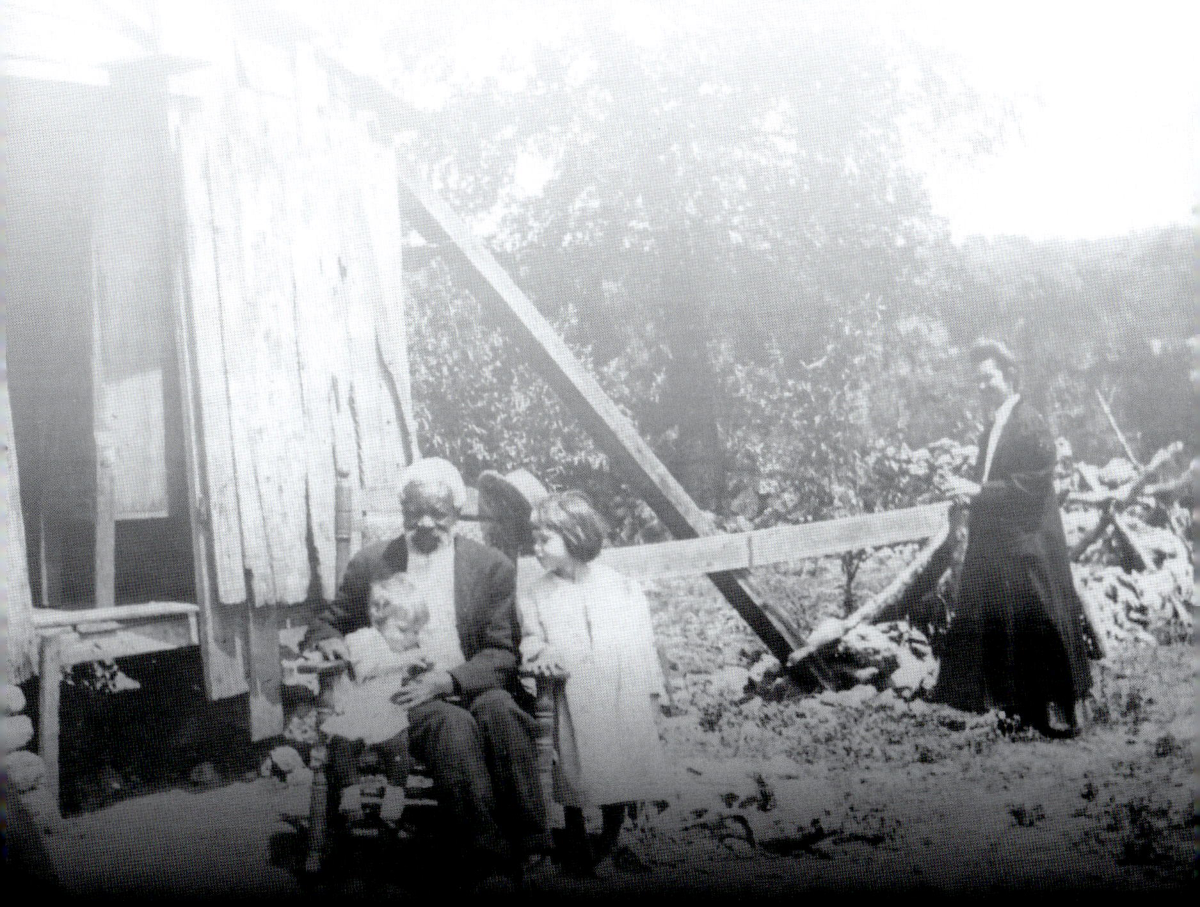

For Grace, Jared, and Auburn.

ISBN 978-1-4671-3160-5

Library of Congress Control Number: 2013955450

Published by Arcadia Publishing
Charleston, South Carolina

Printed in the United States of America

For all general information, please contact Arcadia Publishing:
Telephone 843-853-2070
Fax 843-853-0044
E-mail sales@arcadiapublishing.com
For customer service and orders:
Toll-Free 1-888-313-2665

Visit us on the Internet at www.arcadiapublishing.com

On the Front Cover: Georgetown firefighters pose with their parade float on the west side of the 800 block of Main Street. The two-story 1884 Stone-Lesesne building on the right is the only structure shown in both the historical image and today's streetscape. The Victorian courthouse was replaced by the current Neoclassical facility in 1911. The frame buildings were replaced around 1920 by more-substantial structures. (Courtesy Georgetown Heritage Society.)

On the Back Cover: This early-1900s photograph shows the corner of Ninth and Main Streets humming with activity on parade day. Participants rode bicycles, tricycles, horses, and elaborate floats in festive celebrations such as May Fete and the Firemen's Picnic. This corner building was constructed around 1892 and housed city offices, the jail, and the firehouse. Today, it is home to the Georgetown Art Center. (Courtesy Georgetown Heritage Society.)

Contents

Acknowledgments vii

Introduction ix

1. A Splendid Downtown Square 11

2. The Evolution of the Railroad District 25

3. River Vistas and Landmarks 37

4. Old-Town Neighborhoods 49

5. Southwestern University 65

6. Over the River and Around the Town 77

ACKNOWLEDGMENTS

Writing this book certainly put my history "sleuthing skills" to the test. I no doubt owe this passion to my maternal grandmother, who passed down her love for puzzles, and my mother, who had the tenacity to follow a history clue all the way to an answer.

Many people assisted me in researching this book, and I heartily thank every one of them. Numerous pictures were gathered from the Georgetown Heritage Society, *Williamson County Sun* newspaper, and Southwestern University. These historical photographs were vital in telling the story of Georgetown, and I am very grateful to be able to use them.

I want to thank several people who allowed me multiple interviews over the past year, including Dr. Doug and Nell Benold, J.C. Johnson, Paulette Taylor, Grace King Conlee, John Lesesne, William Atlee, and Don and Donnell Bishop. Many of their memories and stories are contained in this book. I also owe thanks to many others who contributed historical photographs, history, or both, including Esther Weir, Liz Mealy, Virginia Mitchell, Barry Chamberlin, Lori Mitchell, Russell Ramsey, Dan Utley, Johnny Brummett, Judy Wolf Hindelang, Jean Odom, Glynn Buie, Jo Beth Johnson Carter, Wayne and Betty Kuehn, Genie and Mike Vogler, Mark Dixon, James Draeger, Dr. Richard and Barbara Pearce, Drs. Mark and Jane Shepherd, Dan Thomasson with the Army Corp of Engineers, and Carolyn Nelson and David Boone, both with the Texas Department of Transportation. Thanks also to Eric Lashley and Robert Barber at the Georgetown Public Library, Doreen Prevots and Kathryn Stallard at Southwestern University, and to Georgetown Parks and Recreation director Kimberly Garrett.

I owe very special thanks to my sweet family for their support and patience and to my "hiking" partner, Mike D'Amelio, who accompanied me on many river explorations and helped with photographs that took more athleticism than I could muster.

Lastly, I especially want to honor the memory of Wiggy Shell, Ralph Dixon Love, and Tommie Williams, who passed away during the process of researching this book. These three individuals eagerly helped me, and their love of Georgetown was evident in every story they told.

Unless credited otherwise, all of the "now" images are courtesy of the author.

Introduction

Travelling downstream over the high banks and rough terrain of the North San Gabriel River in 1853, diarist J.H. Kuykendall recorded his thoughts as he made his way to the region where Georgetown had been established in 1848. Noting the abundant natural resources, he wrote, "This is an admirable section and must soon attract attention. There are but two or three settlements hereabout, where there is room for a hundred." Indeed, this area along the Balcones Fault and Edwards Aquifer is rich in water resources, timber, stone, wildlife, and good soil for farming.

Georgetown's original 173 acres was donated by land developers in exchange for naming the town after one of the owners, George Washington Glasscock. This tiny town was nestled in a scenic crook of the South San Gabriel River, where early industries such as mills, gins, farms, and orchards were established and supported by the waterway. It was a good place for a town to grow.

From the mid-1860s, cattle drives on South Texas trails came through the center of Georgetown on their way north to the Chisholm Trail. It was a rough cowboy town filled with saloons, a few stores and inns, blacksmith shops, and log or frame dwellings. The local economy revolved around farming and cattle, but two developments in the 1870s ultimately shaped Georgetown's growth and personality. First, the Methodist Church consolidated four colleges to form Southwestern University in 1873. Soon after, in 1878, Georgetown's first rail line was built, linking the town to important points across the country.

Georgetown grew quickly in size and sophistication from 1880 to 1920. But like many small towns, for a few decades in the mid-1900s, it stagnated and declined. Railroads eventually disappeared, and Interstate 35 was completed in the 1960s, bypassing downtown. Many businesses closed, and buildings were left vacant as traffic through downtown dwindled. Fortunately, many of these badly deteriorated buildings were restored during Georgetown's participation in the Main Street Project, which began in 1982. Today, the Georgetown Square is considered one of the finest and best preserved in Texas.

Georgetown, a little village in the 1850s, has evolved into a dynamic small city with a population of over 50,000. There have been many changes along the way, but the downtown area, Old-Town neighborhoods, Southwestern University, and beautiful, natural areas along the river are visible treasures that link us to the community's colorful history.

CHAPTER 1

A Splendid Downtown Square

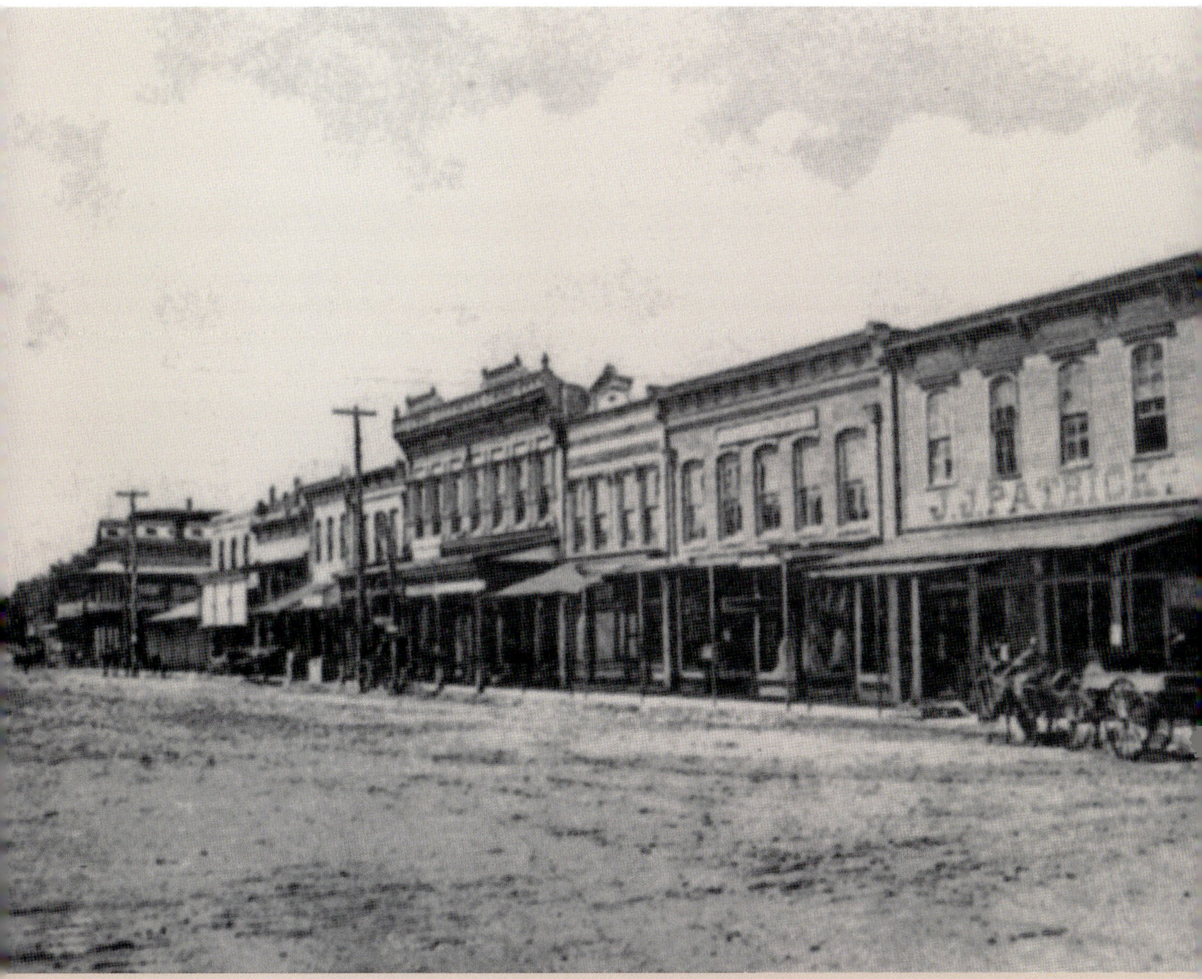

When this photograph was taken prior to 1910, Brushy Street, now Austin Avenue, still looked like a cattle trail, while downtown businesses flourished within stylish storefronts. By 1960, these Victorian buildings had fallen into bad repair, but they began a spectacular turnaround in 1982 when Georgetown participated in the Main Street program. (Author's collection.)

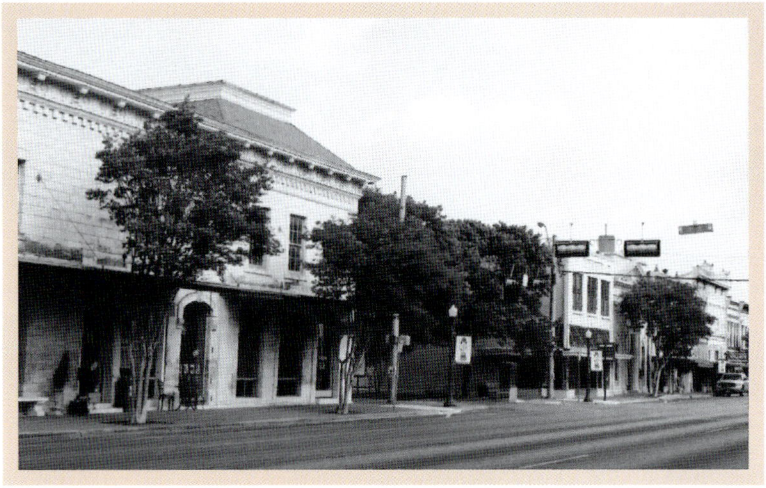

From the 1850s to the mid-1900s, the 800 block of Austin Avenue was home to inns or hotels, including the Ake, Dewey, City Hotel, and Makemson Hotel, pictured here around 1926 with its ornate balcony rail. This old cattle trail eventually became Highway 81, the main north-south artery between San Antonio and Dallas until Interstate 35 was built. Today, downtown hotels are a thing of the past. (Then image by Luis W. Atlee; courtesy *Williamson County Sun*.)

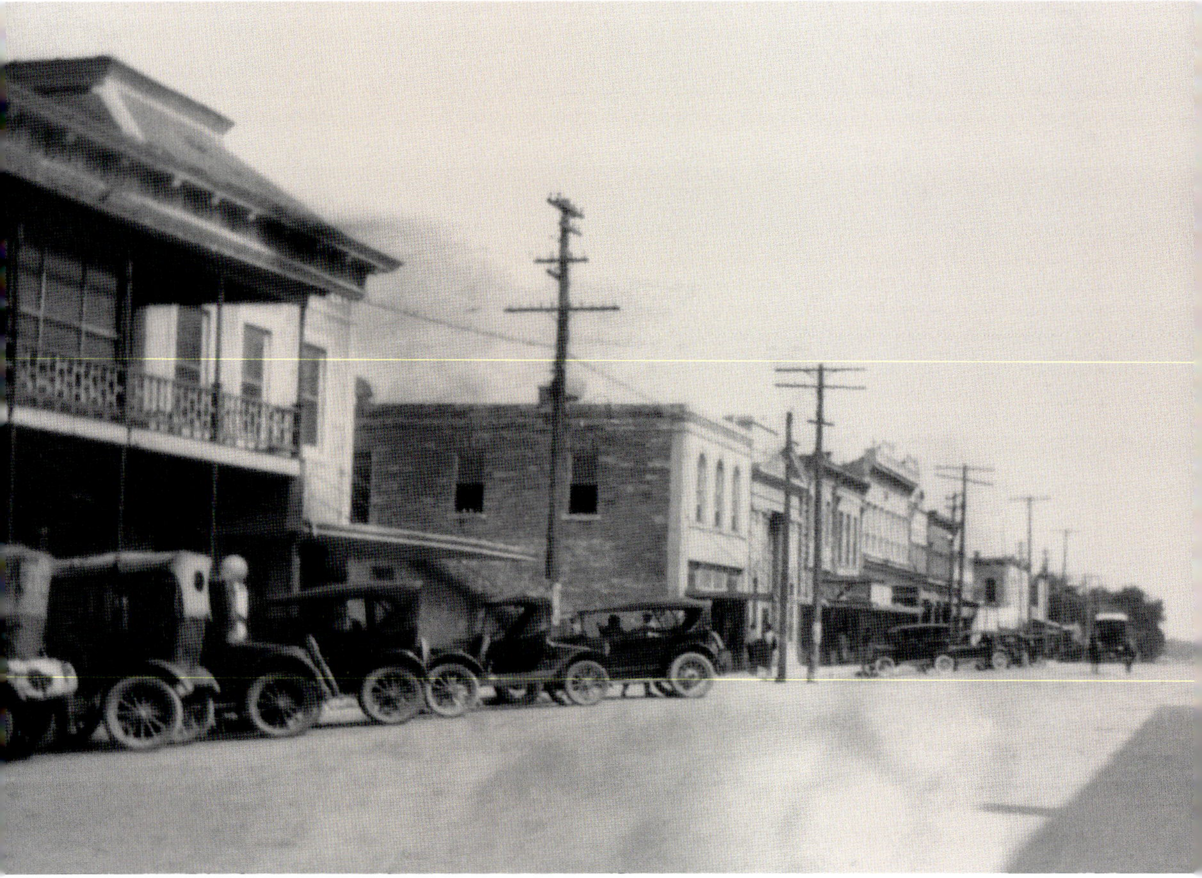

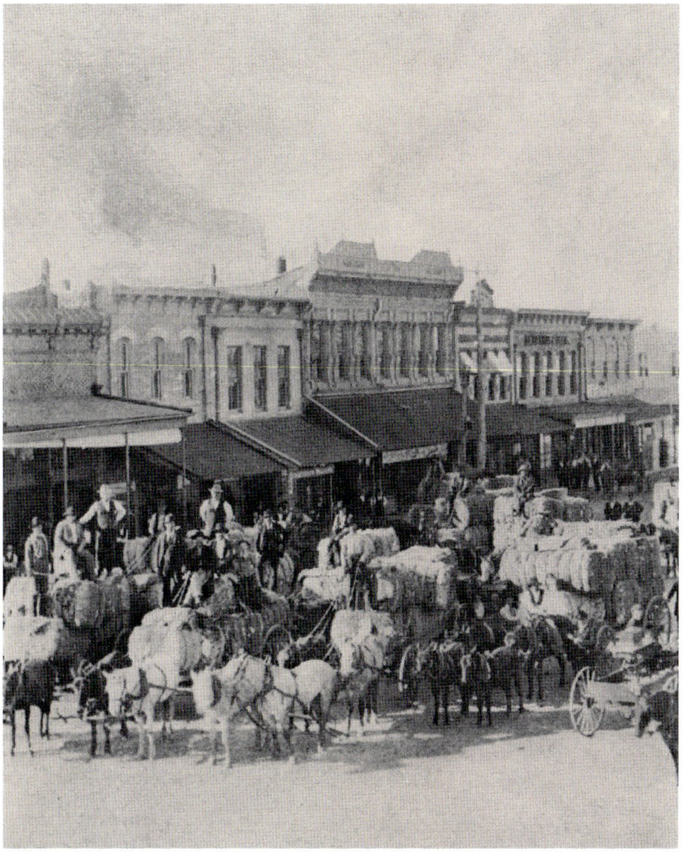

This classic photograph of the square appeared on the cover of a c. 1910 brochure and was titled "Cotton Crop of One Farmer." Agriculture, especially cotton production, was a major force in the local economy. Despite its early date, the image brings home the high level of architectural sophistication achieved on the square before 1910. Today's photograph shows the same block of buildings, west of the courthouse. (Then image courtesy author's collection.)

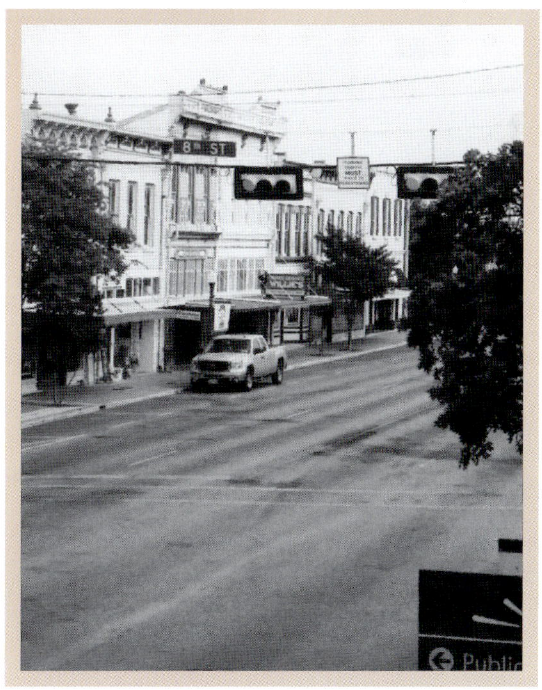

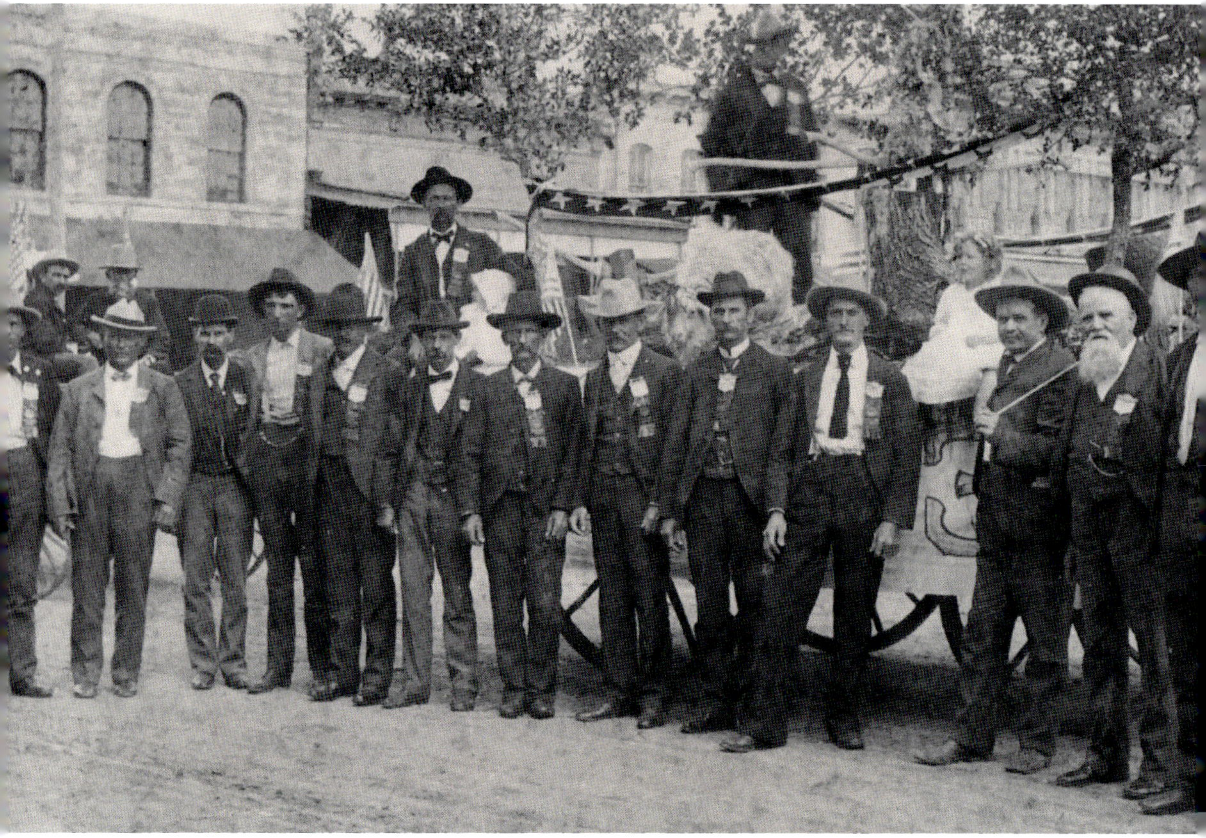

Tree stumps with embedded axes on this wagon and the Angora goat mascot identify the group in this vintage photograph as Woodmen of the World. Behind them is the 700 block of Austin Avenue. The second building from the left shows the pre-1910 appearance of the bank building. To its left, the corner building has been remodeled several times and was recently reverted to its 1926 facade. (Then image courtesy author's collection.)

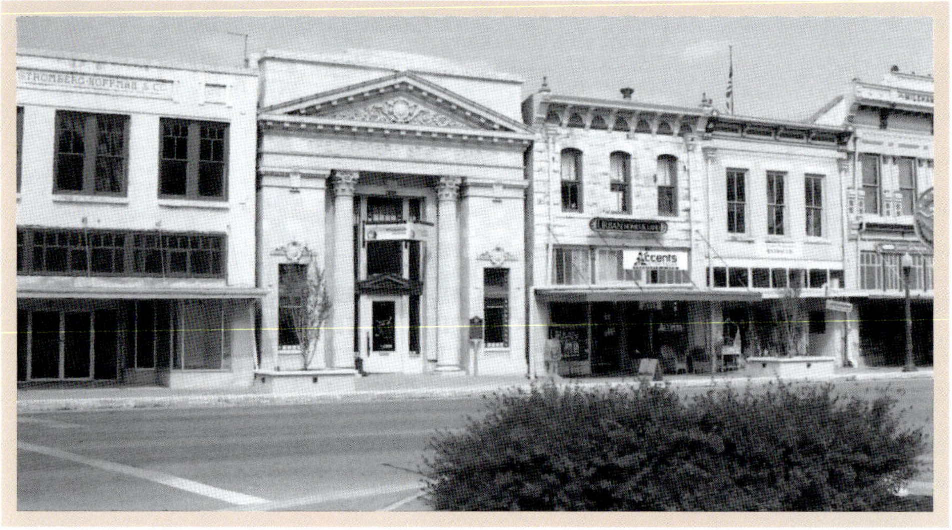

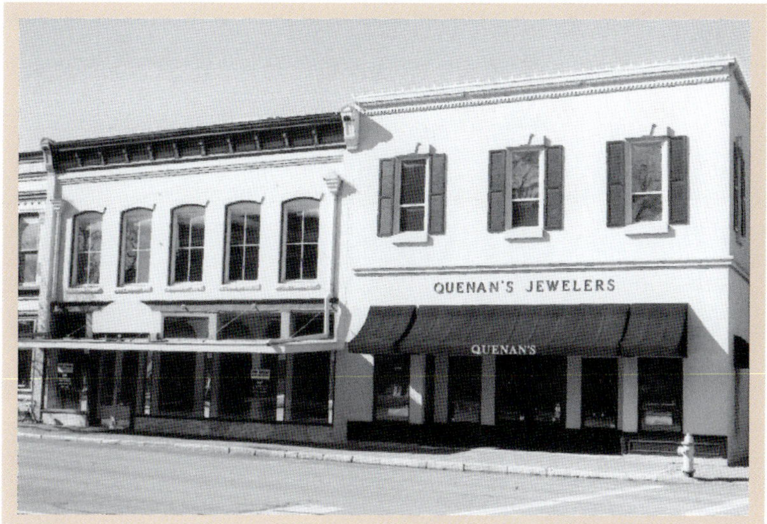

An 1880s saloon and, later, the J.J. Patrick Grocery, operated from a two-story wood structure on this corner at 700 South Austin Avenue. It was replaced in 1913 by the Rouser Building (far right), which housed various businesses, including a dry goods store and a hat factory. Pictured around 1915, Annie Maude Cheek is the second woman from the right. A recent, comprehensive remodel has added a second story to the building. (Then image courtesy Grace Anna King Conlee.)

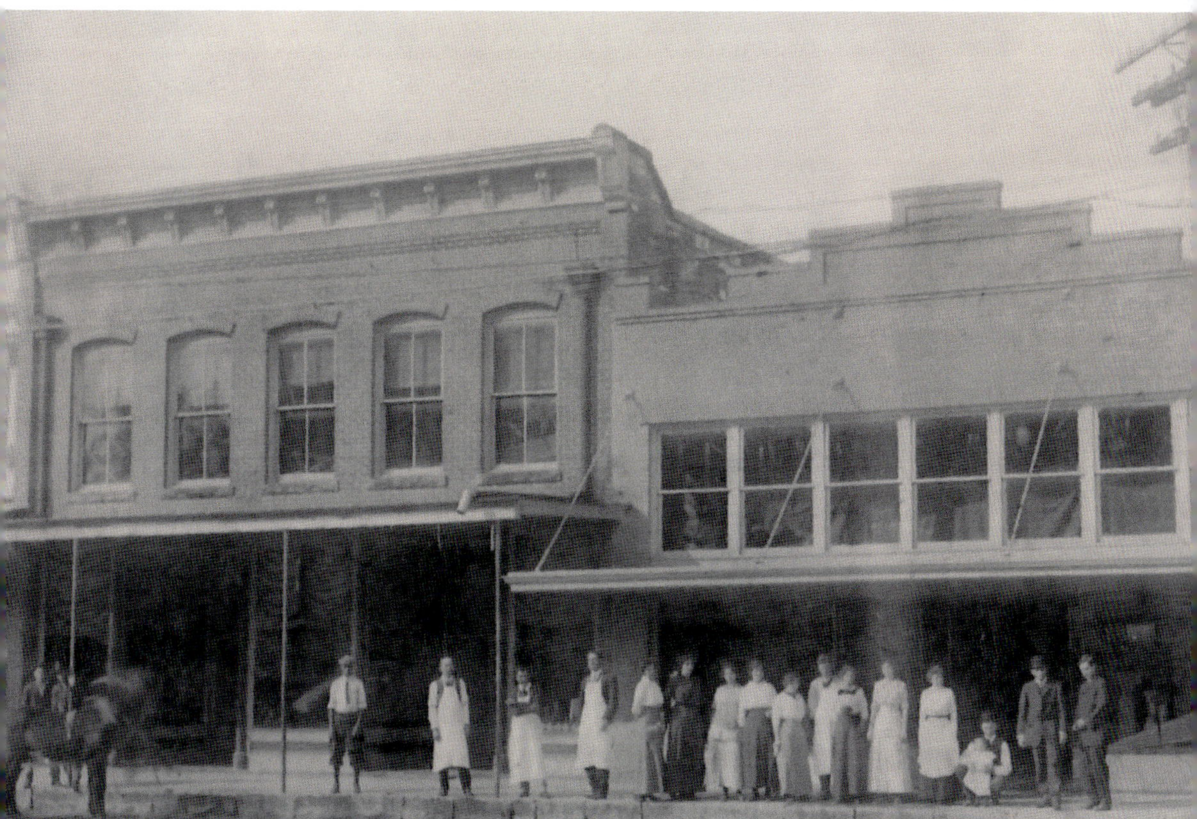

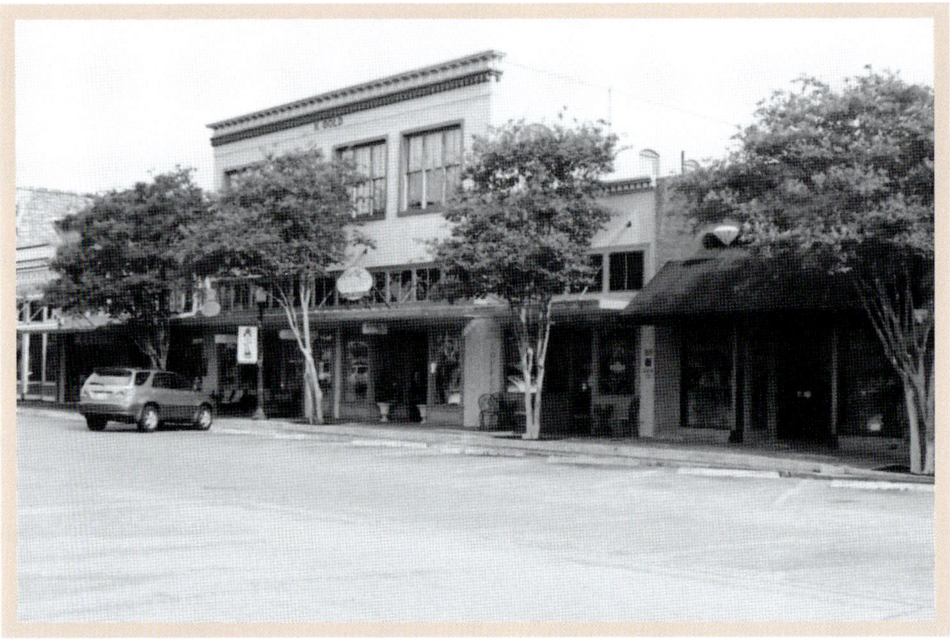

Stylishly modernized for the 1960s, Gold's Department Store at 105 West Seventh Street was the undisputed anchor of Georgetown retailers for several decades. Opening in Georgetown in 1936, it was first located on the west side of the square, moving to the north side in 1949. Today's photograph shows the building after a complete renovation. (Then image courtesy *Williamson County Sun*.)

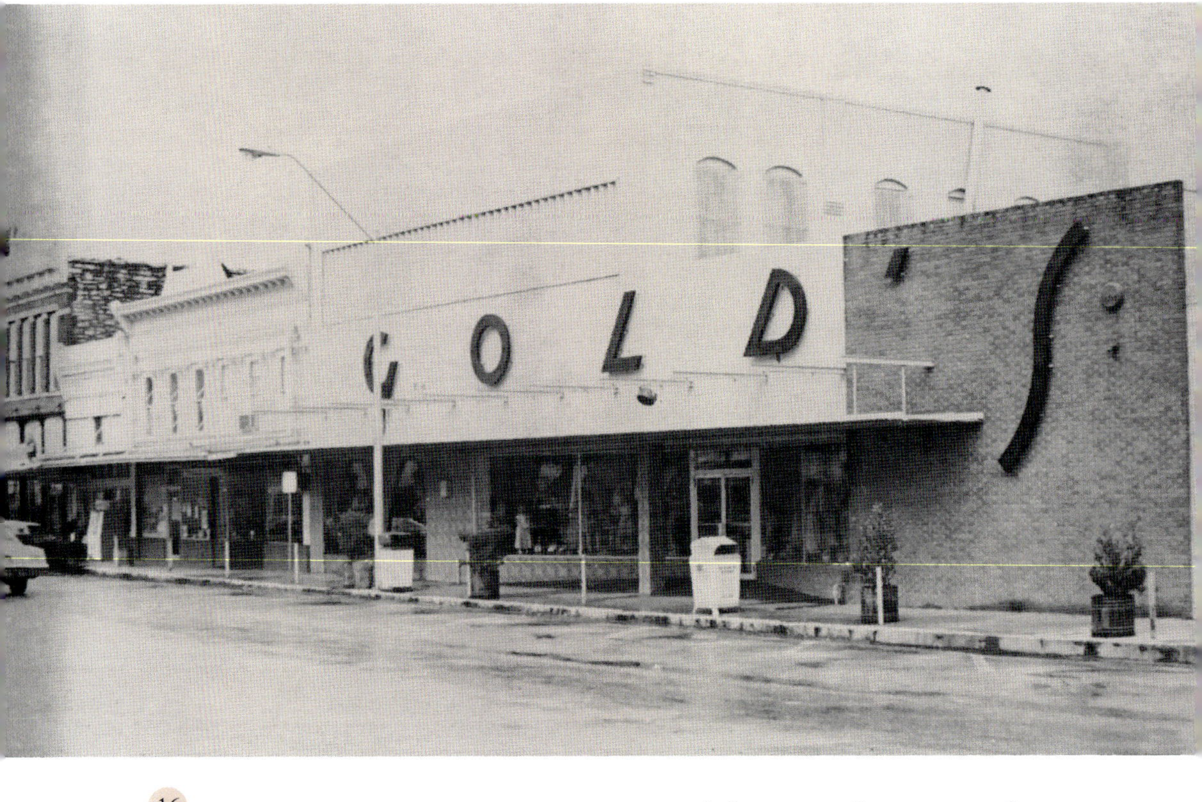

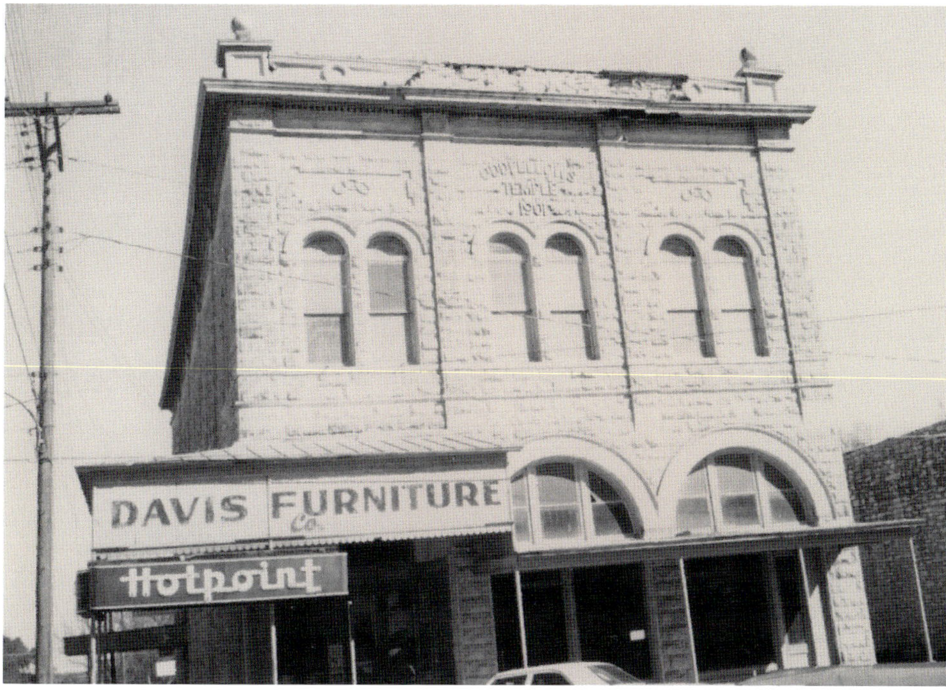

By the 1960s, many structures, including the Odd Fellows Building at the northeast corner of Seventh and Main Streets, were badly deteriorated. A casualty of the prevalent attitude at the time that "new is better," this building was demolished. The new structure first housed the Georgetown Public Library. Today's view shows the results of a 2003 renovation by the city, which added architectural elements that blend seamlessly with the square as a whole. (Then image courtesy City of Georgetown.)

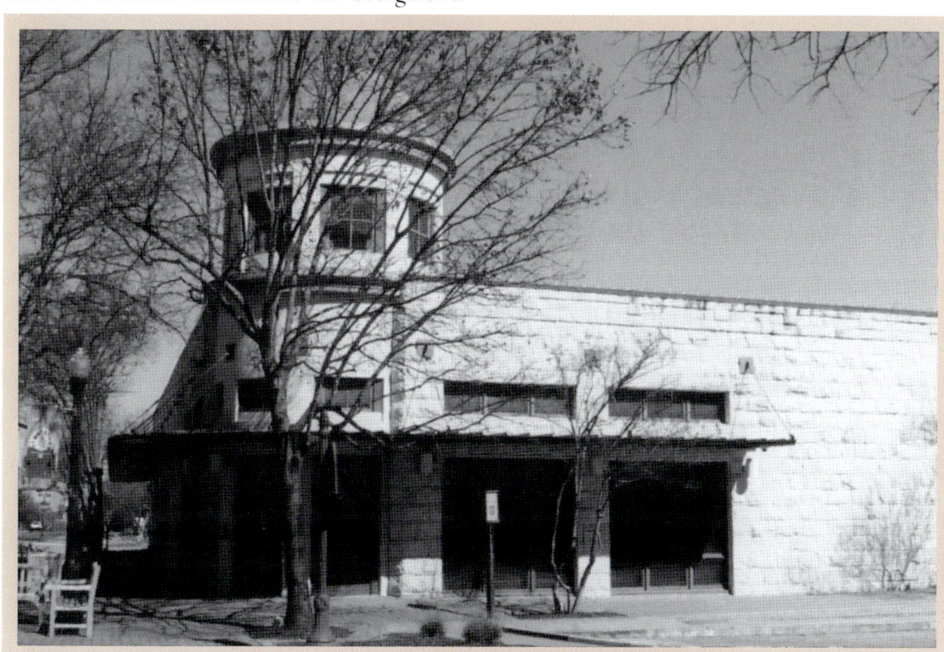

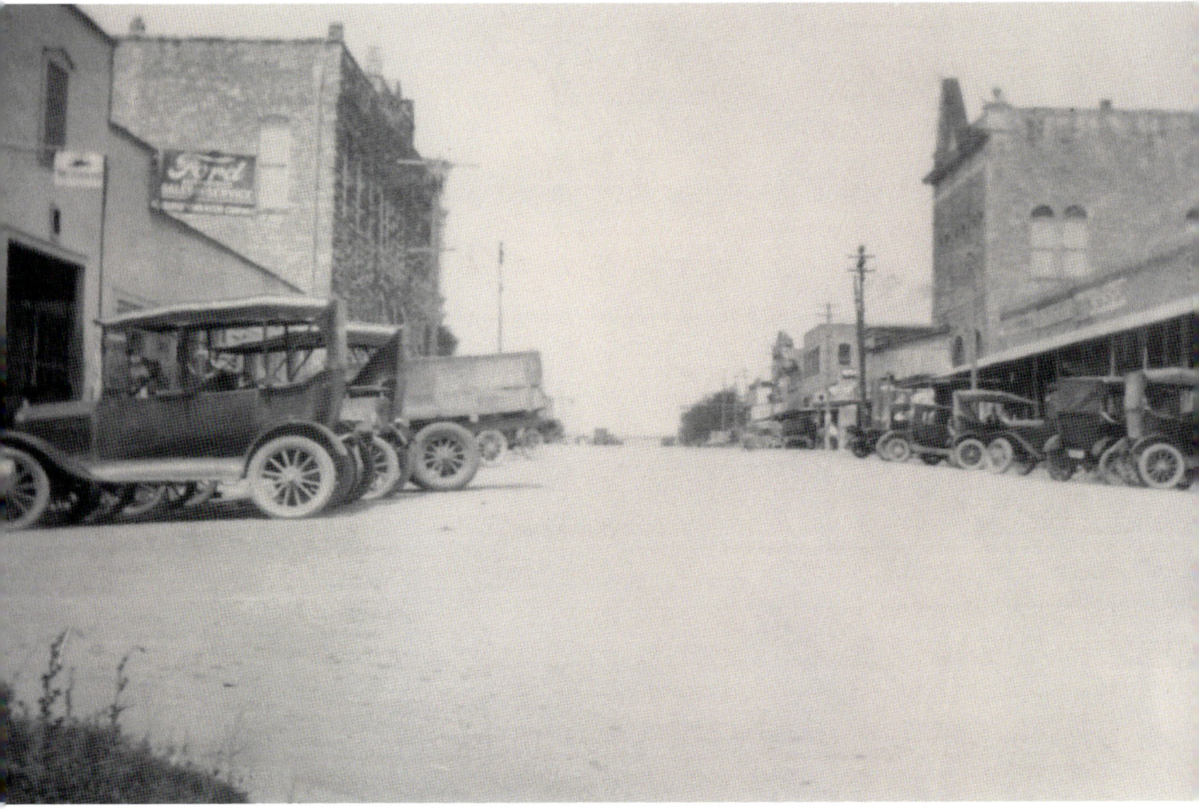

Looking west on Seventh Street from Church Street, the two-story Odd Fellows Building and the Glasscock Block are visible on the right in this mid-1920s photograph. At left, the Masonic Building and the Ford dealership fill the whole block. Four of the seven c. 1907 buildings named for George W. Glasscock Jr., son of Georgetown's namesake, were destroyed by fire, leaving gaps in the block that are still present today. (Then image by Luis W. Atlee; courtesy *Williamson County Sun*.)

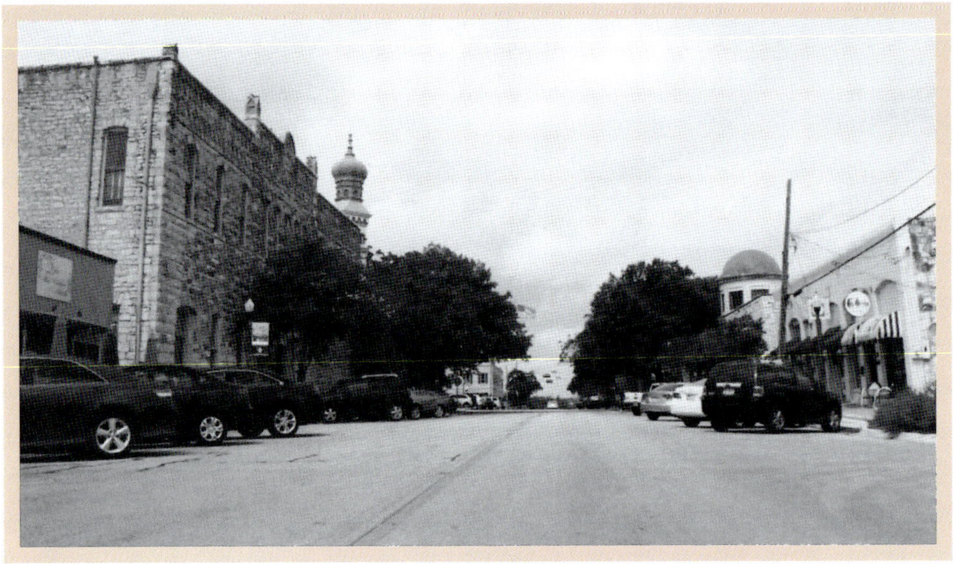

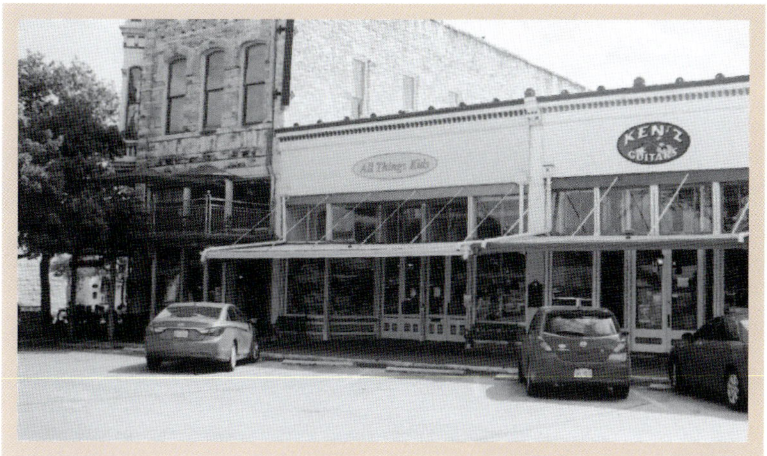

The corner of Main and Seventh Streets is pictured in the early 1950s. At the far left is the now-demolished Odd Fellows Building. Santa Claus is in the middle of the large crowd. A young boy stands on the Georgetown Fire Department truck that brought Santa to the square. It is interesting to note that there were three different furniture stores on just this corner alone. (Then image courtesy Georgetown Heritage Society.)

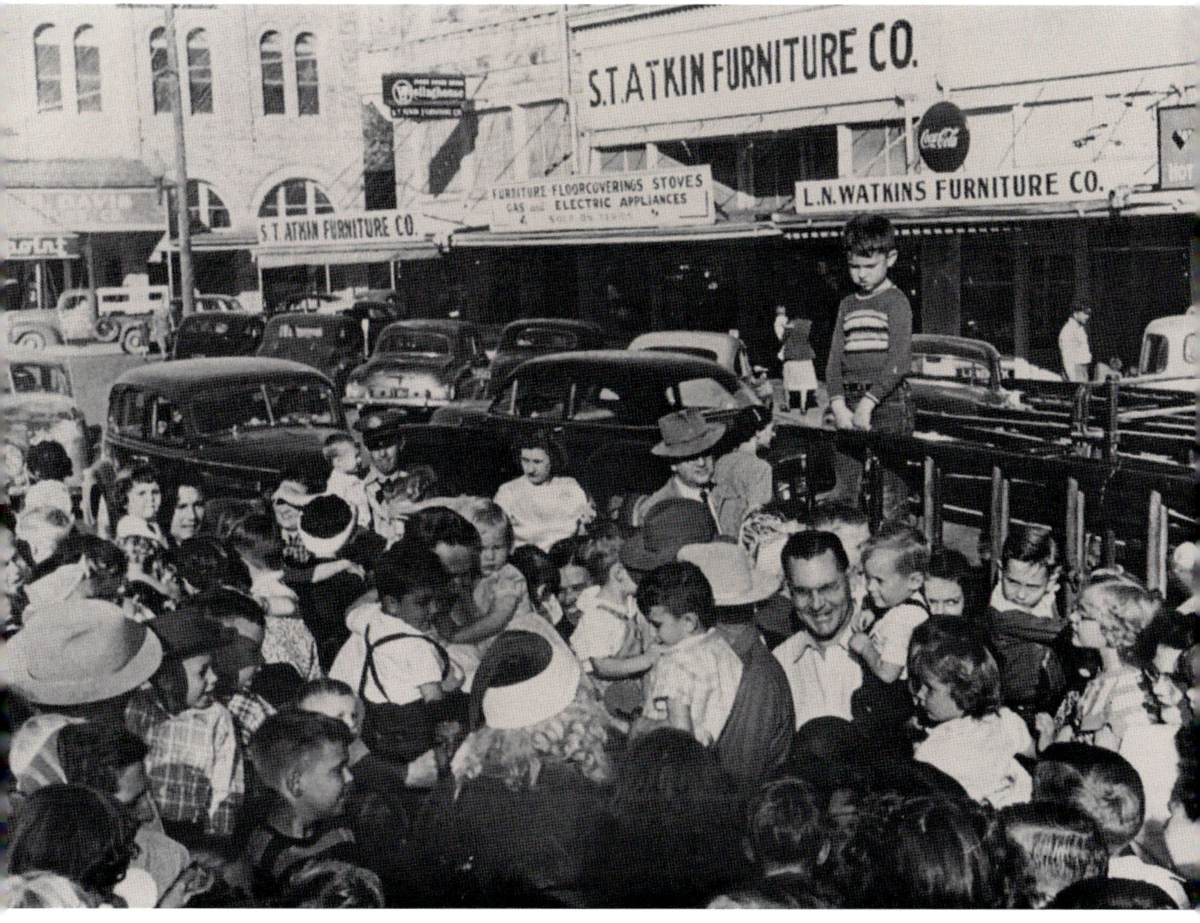

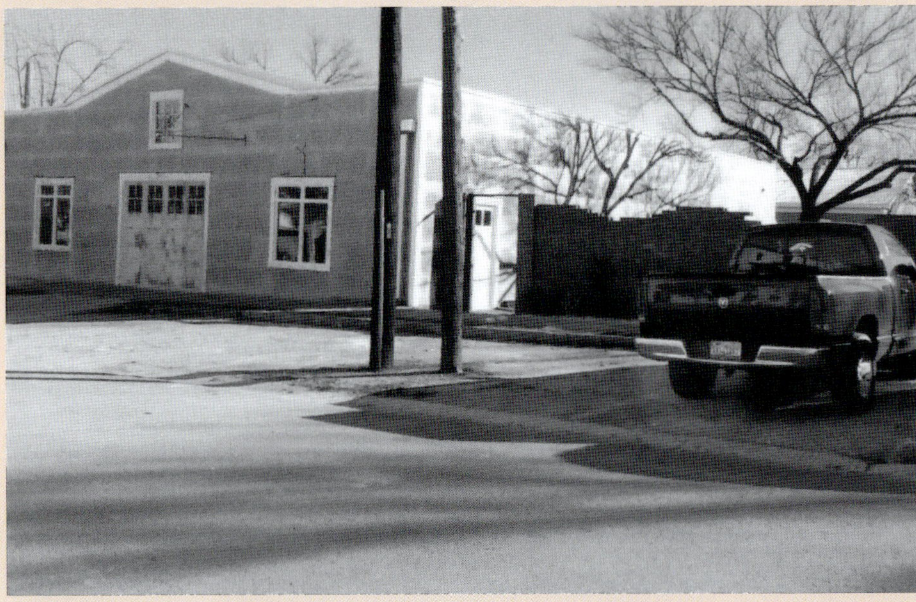

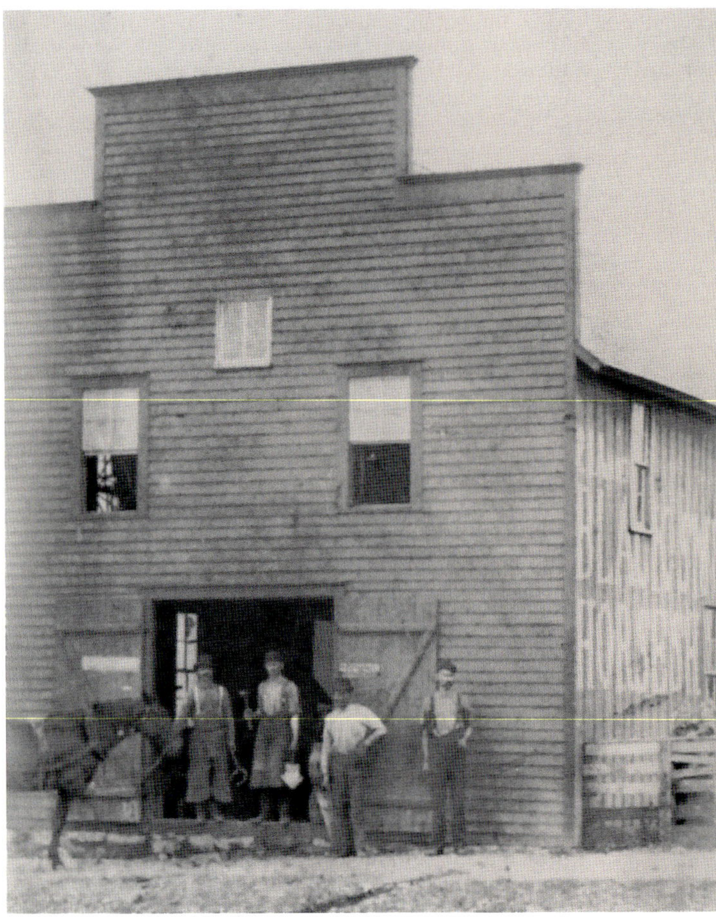

P.J. Anderson's blacksmith building stood at 206 East Eighth Street until the late 1960s. Pictured are P.J. Anderson, Emil Anderson, J.M. Oman, and T.J. Caswell. Caswell operated a buggy shop on the second floor. A fire destroyed the upper part of the building, so it was rebuilt as a one-story structure. A brick-walled courtyard was built on the site of the blacksmith shop in 2013. The courtyard adjoins the business in the old Anderson Garage to the east. (Then image courtesy author's collection.)

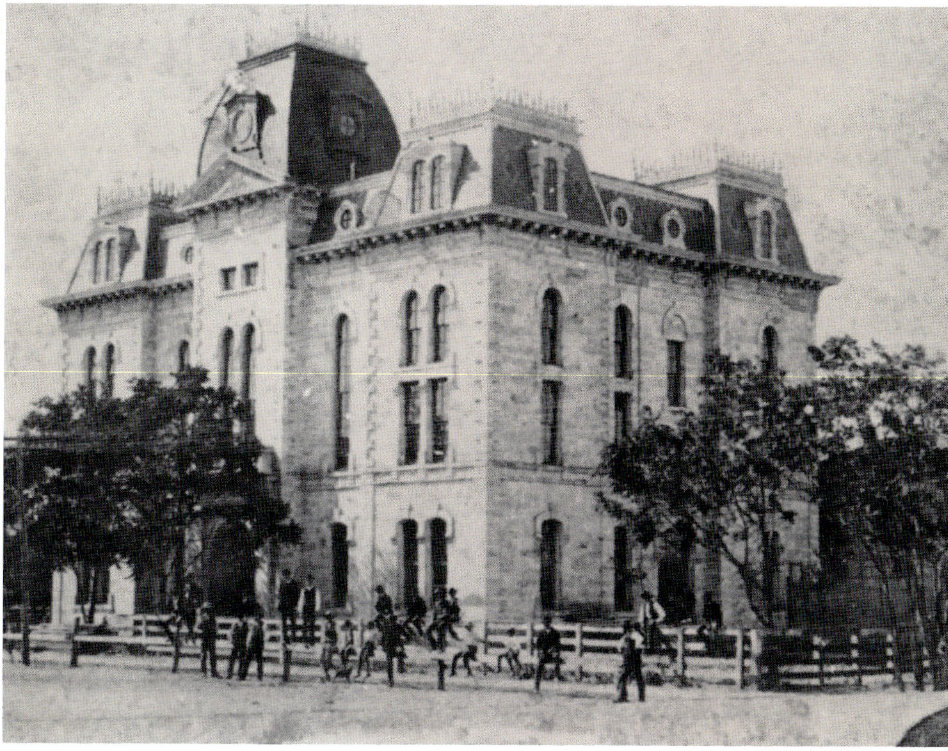

The Victorian era was in full swing when Williamson County built this larger and more elegant courthouse in 1877. It was in the center of the square, with the front facing on Eighth Street. It served the county just over 30 years before it was deemed too small, and it was demolished and replaced by the current Neoclassical Revival–style courthouse in 1911. The current structure underwent an award-winning $9 million restoration in 2007. (Then image courtesy author's collection.)

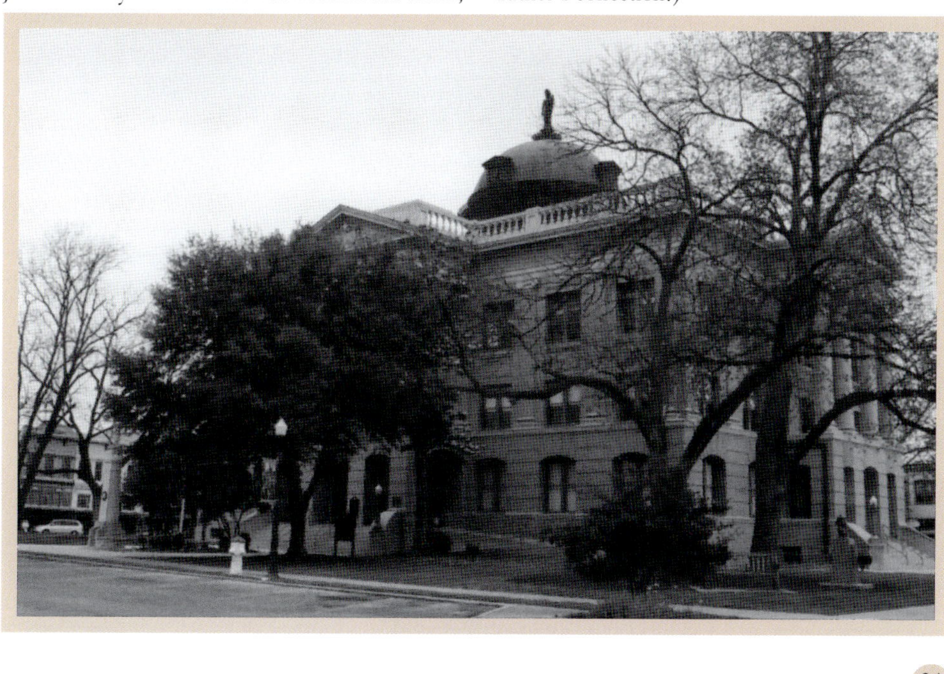

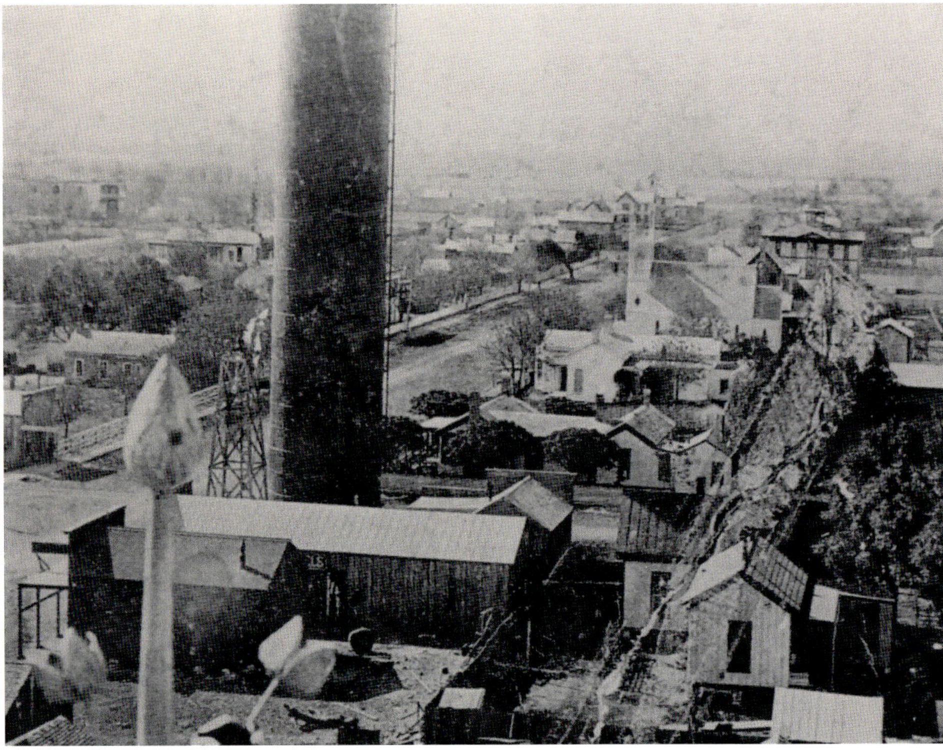

This remarkable view was likely taken around 1890, before the ell-shaped city hall was built around the huge standpipe containing Georgetown's water supply. To its left is the fire bell. Farther down South Main Street, Grace Episcopal Church appears ghostly, and Southwestern University's first women's building, with the central tower, is visible. Today's view shows Grace Episcopal (Grace Heritage Center) in its new location on the opposite side of Main Street, and the 1926 Main Street Baptist Church beyond. (Then image courtesy author's collection.)

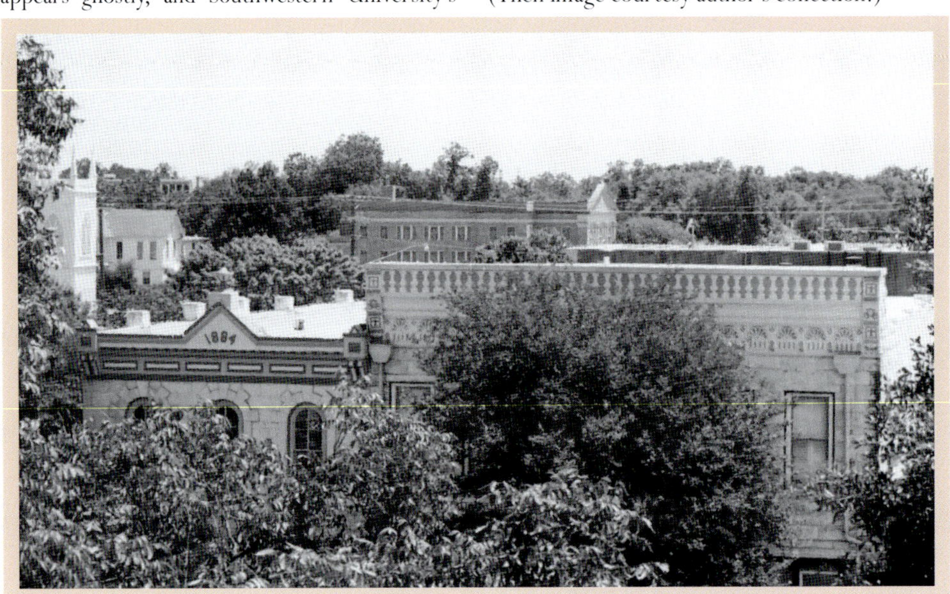

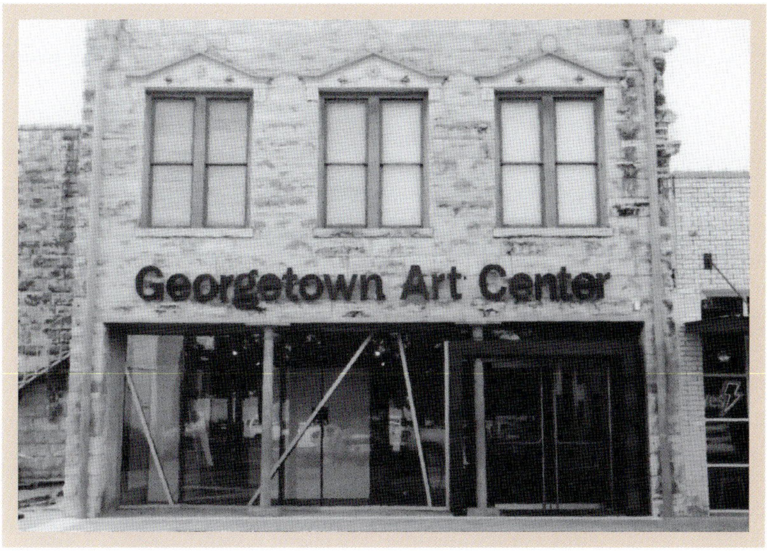

Behind the buggy, pictured around 1900, is the front of the Georgetown Municipal Building at 816 South Main Street. The ornate iron gates adorned the fire department bays. Today, the building houses the Georgetown Art Center, which opened in 2013. The structure dates to around 1892 and housed not only the firehouse, but also city hall and the city jail. The fire department maintained offices here until 2012. (Then image courtesy Georgetown Heritage Society.)

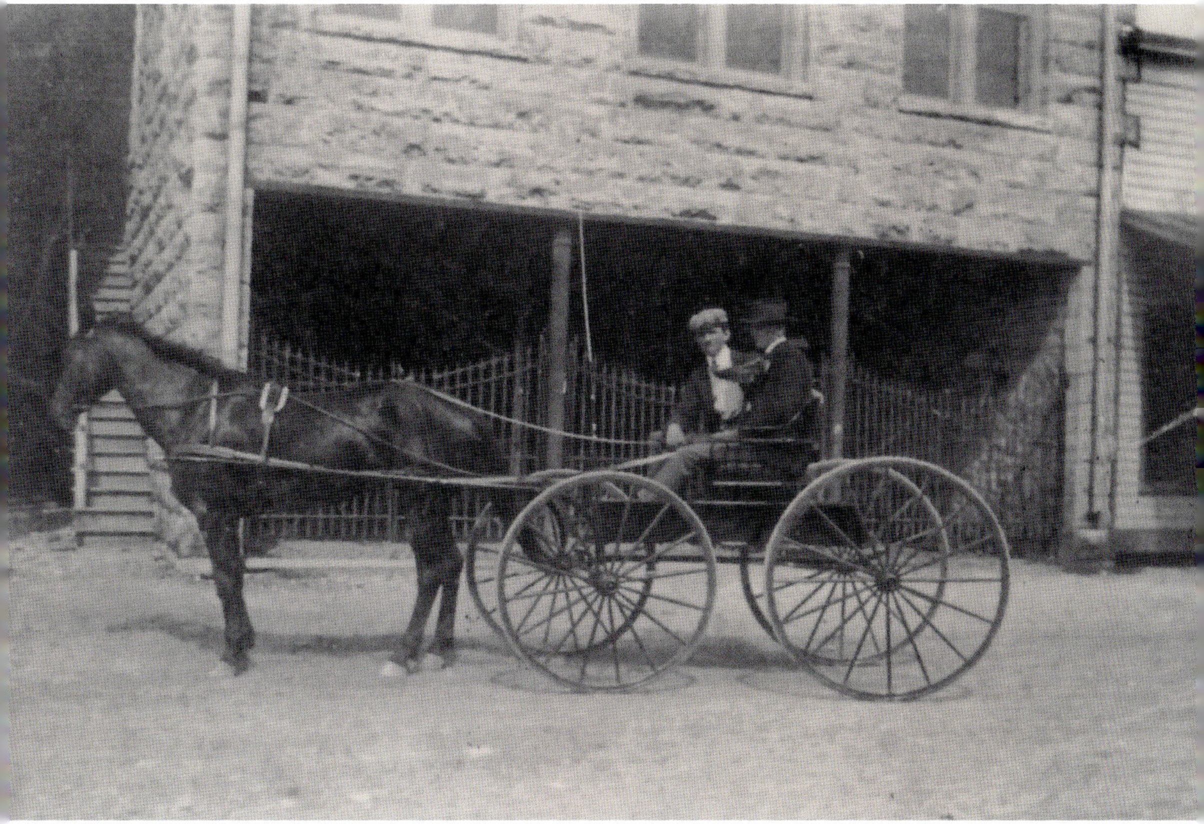

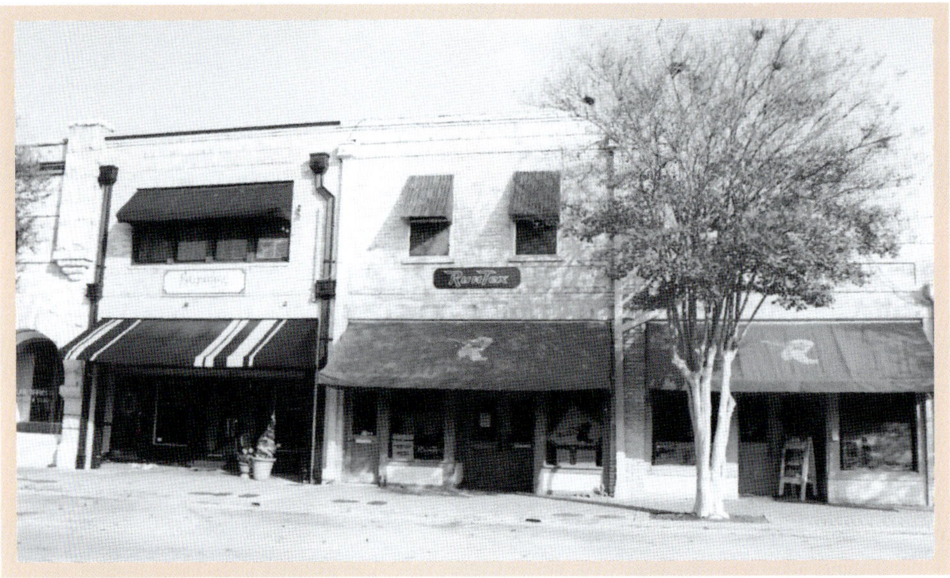

In the earlier image, Mary Mann, left, and a friend await the Firemen's Picnic celebration before 1910. They have paused in front of the Texas Bakery, located on the east side of Main Street, just around the corner from Henry and James Price's grocery on West Eighth Street. The Firemen's Picnic was one of the most anticipated social events each year. Today's photograph shows the same block, just south of the P.H. Dimmitt Building on South Main Street. (Then image courtesy author's collection.)

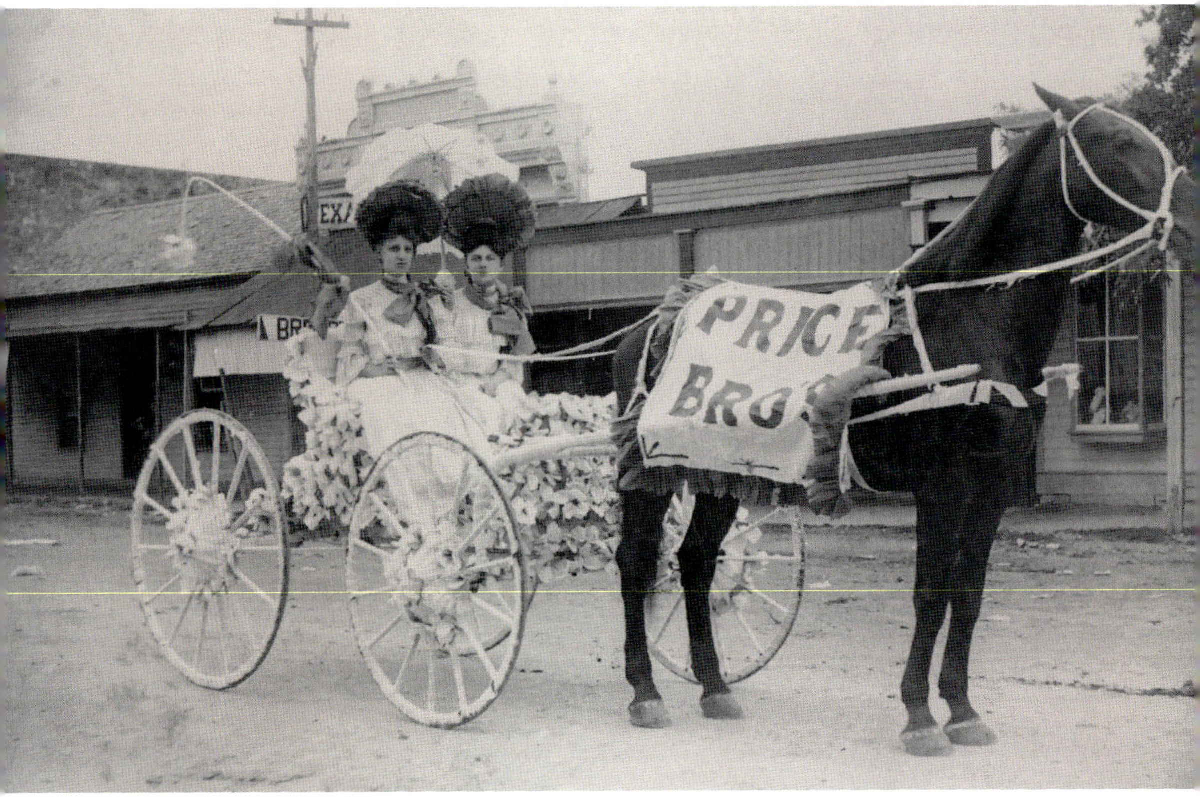

CHAPTER 2

The Evolution of the Railroad District

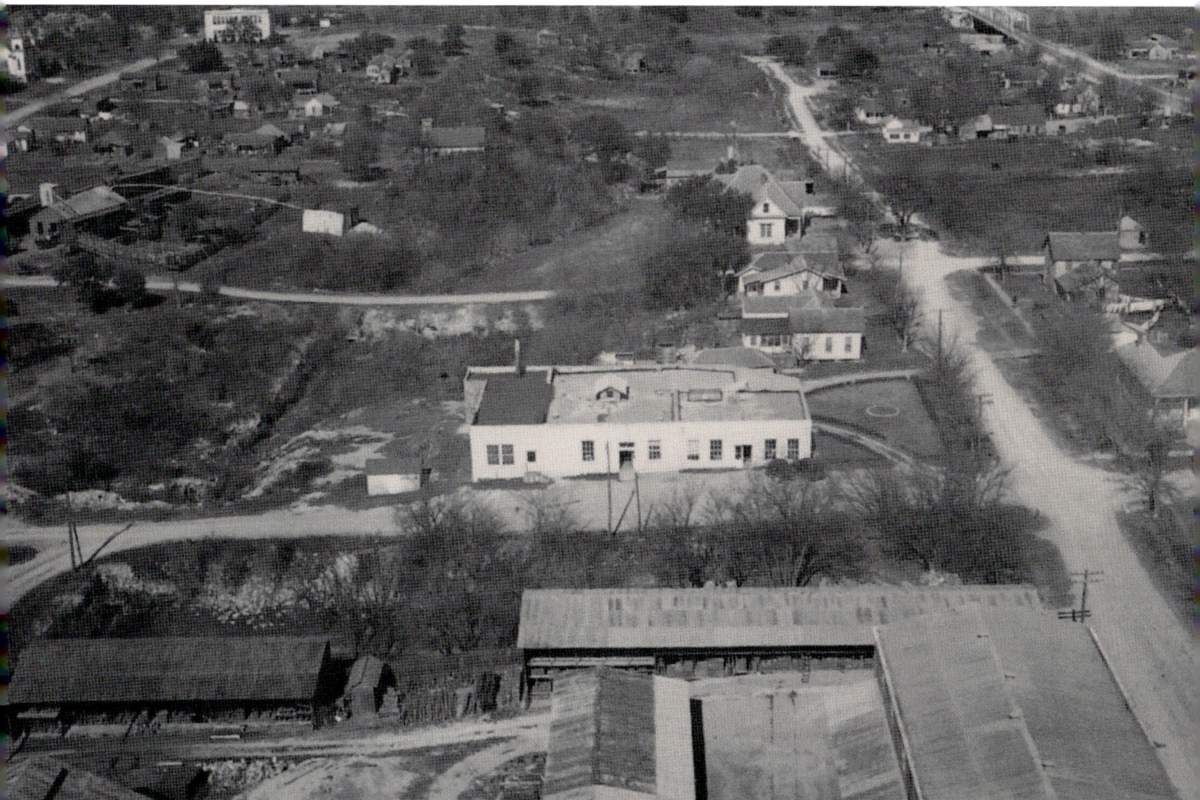

Belford Lumber's rooftops dominate this c. 1930 aerial, with Troy Laundry just beyond the lumber sheds and West Sixth Street. Clockwise are train-yard animal pens, Macedonia Baptist Church, Marshall-Carver School, and the 1924 Austin Avenue South San Gabriel Bridge (top right). Today, most of this area is covered by the County's Criminal Justice Complex. (Courtesy Southwestern University, Special Collections, Georgetown, Texas.)

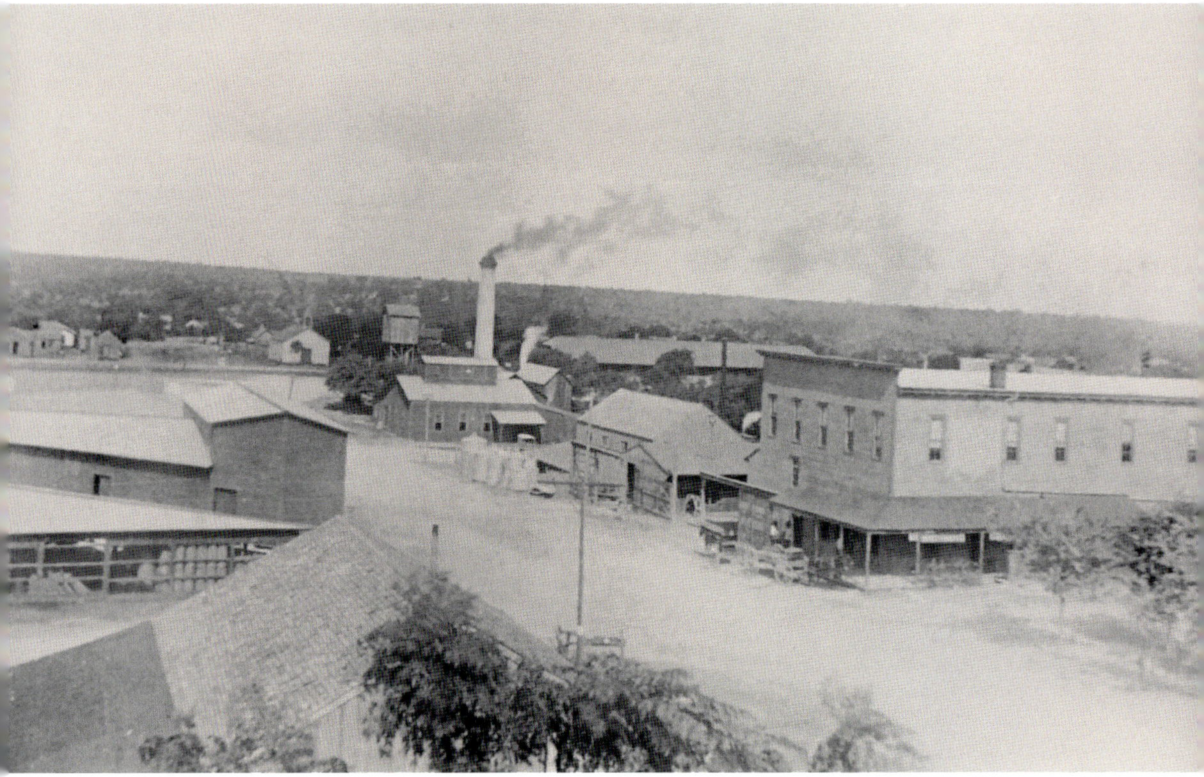

In this view west down Seventh Street around 1900 is the heart of the Railroad District in its heyday. Belford Lumber's two-story office is located on the right, and due west is the icehouse, with its smokestack and water tower. To its right is the roof of the railroad depot. Outlasting all of these iconic places is St. Paul Methodist Church, visible across the tracks. Organized in 1873, it is still active today. (Then image courtesy Georgetown Heritage Society.)

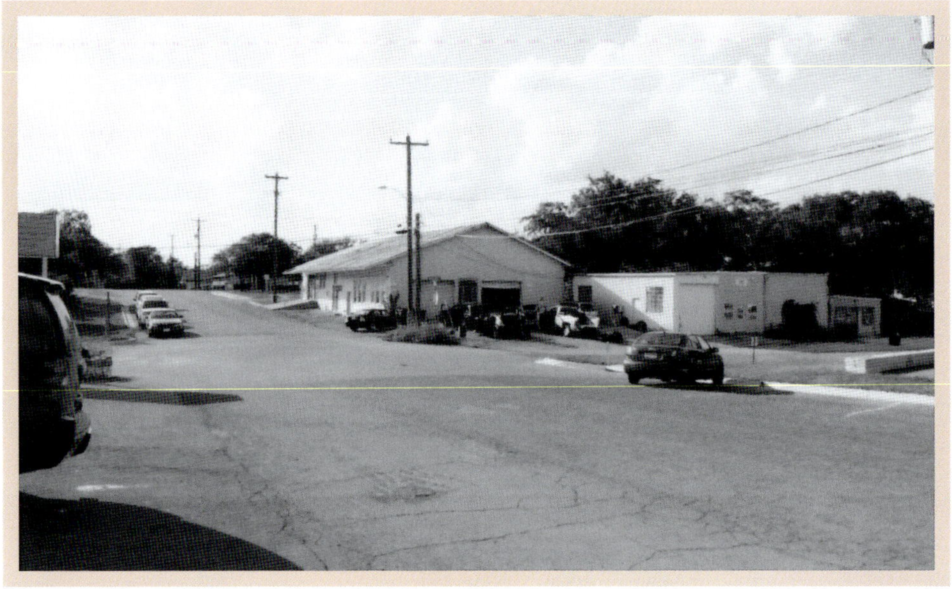

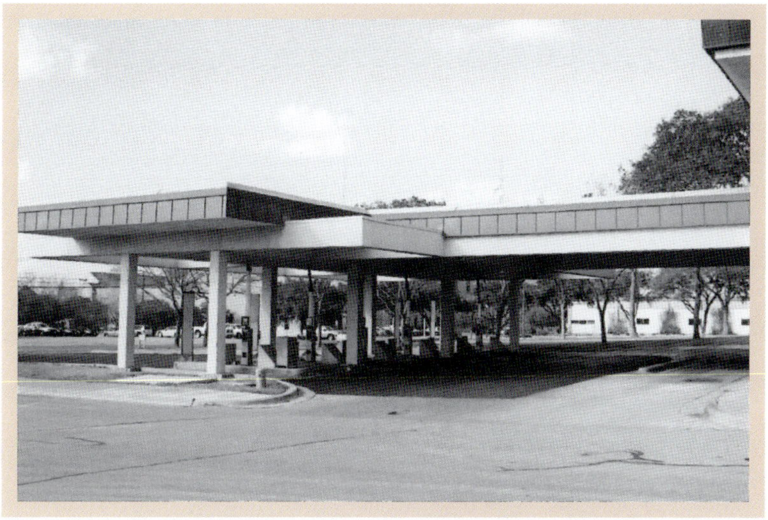

Georgetown's Commercial Hotel at Seventh and Rock Streets was often described as "palatial" or "hoity-toity." A favorite stop for travelling salesmen, called "drummers," the hotel was renowned for its wonderful food. Sisters Ella Hemphill and Mrs. L.H. Wright ran the hotel and always demanded proper attire and behavior from patrons. The hotel burned to the ground in 1930. Today, Bank of America's drive-through lanes occupy the site of the hotel. (Then image courtesy Georgetown Heritage Society.)

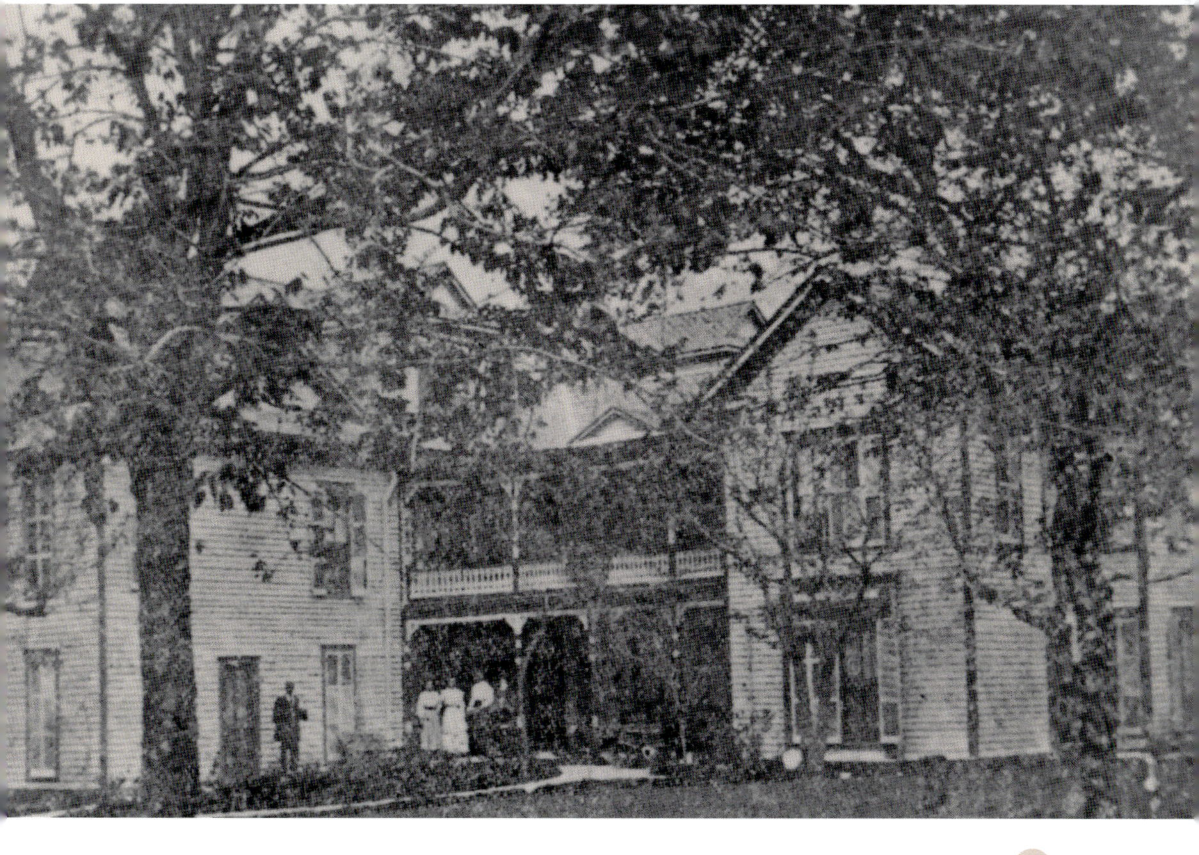

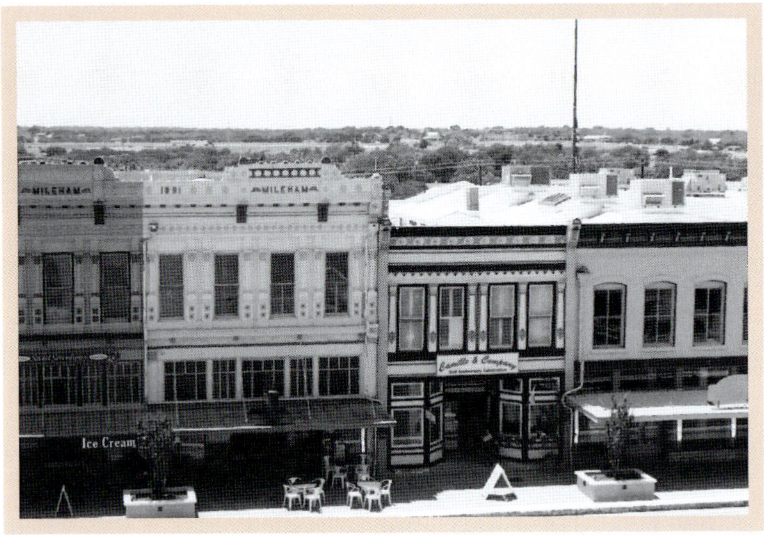

This intriguing image, dating to around 1890, shows the impact of the railroads on Georgetown's original residential neighborhood west of the square. After 1878, railroad tracks and numerous spurs crossed the area, and warehouses, wagon yards, gins, mills, lumberyards, hotels, and other businesses soon proliferated. Today's view is partly obstructed by taller buildings and courthouse columns. In the distance, a wide swath devoid of trees marks the interstate beyond the river. (Then image courtesy author's collection.)

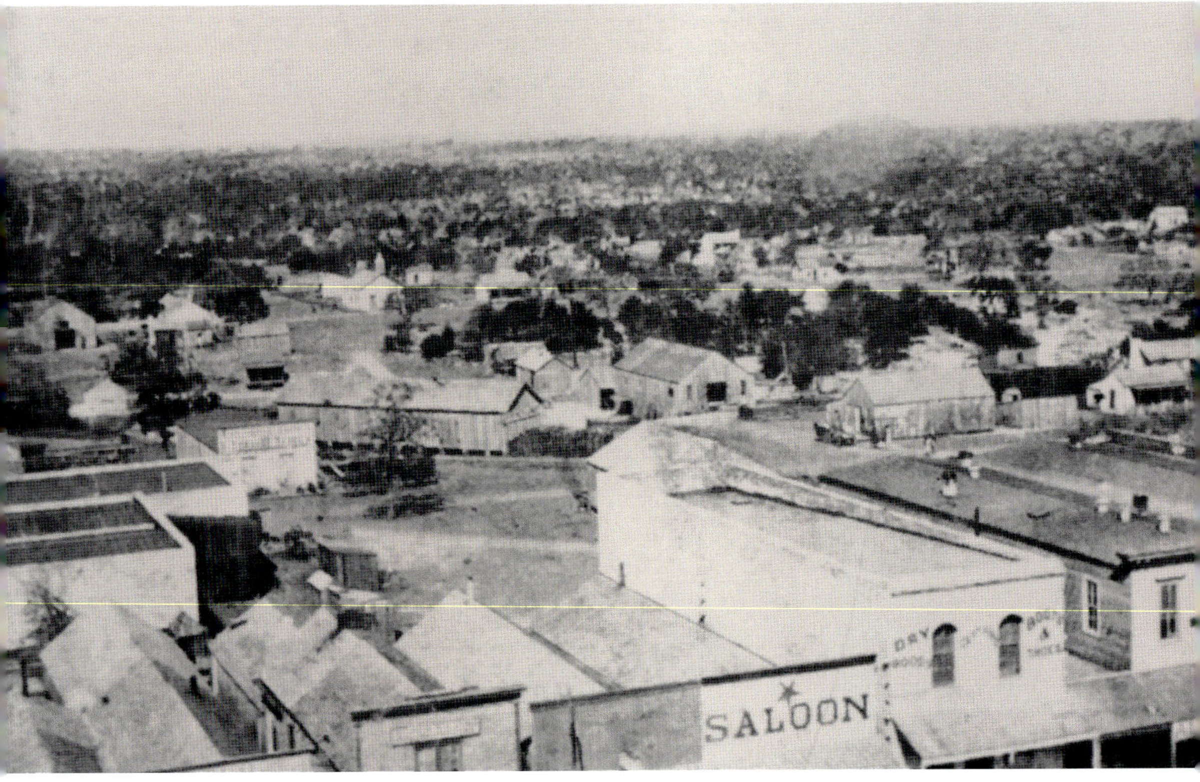

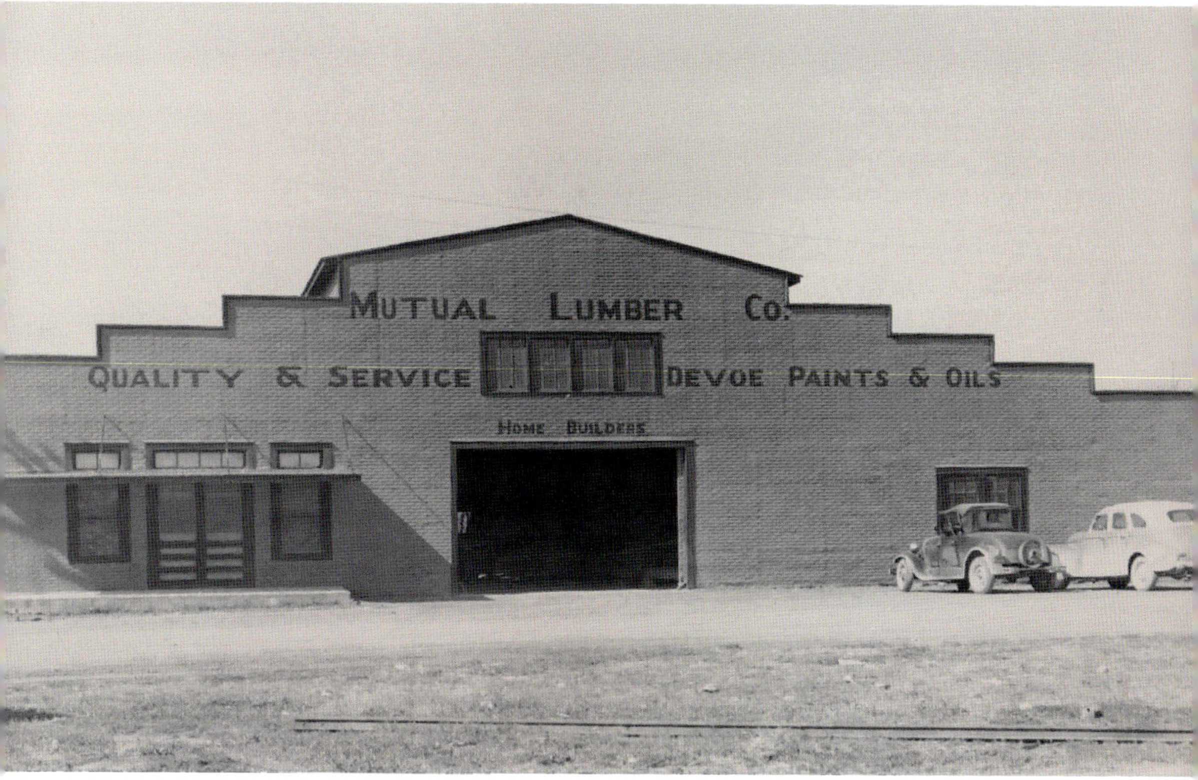

This neighborhood attracted numerous African American families by 1900, and they quickly built churches, an early school, and fraternal lodges. The business district was generally located between the square and Timber (now Martin Luther King) Street. The northwest corner of Timber and Eighth Streets was home to Griffith Lumber before 1900. At the same spot, this unique structure housed Wm. Cameron & Co. in the 1930s and, later, Mutual Lumber. This lot is now residential. (Then image courtesy *Williamson County Sun*.)

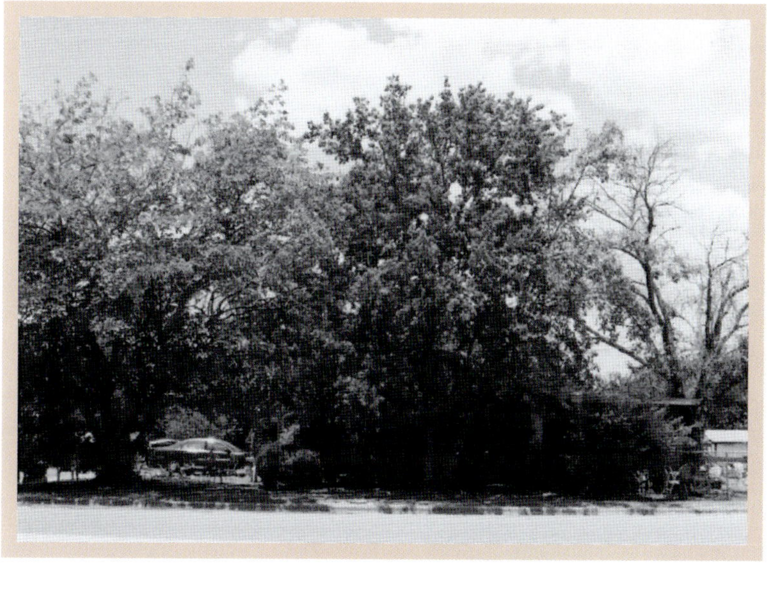

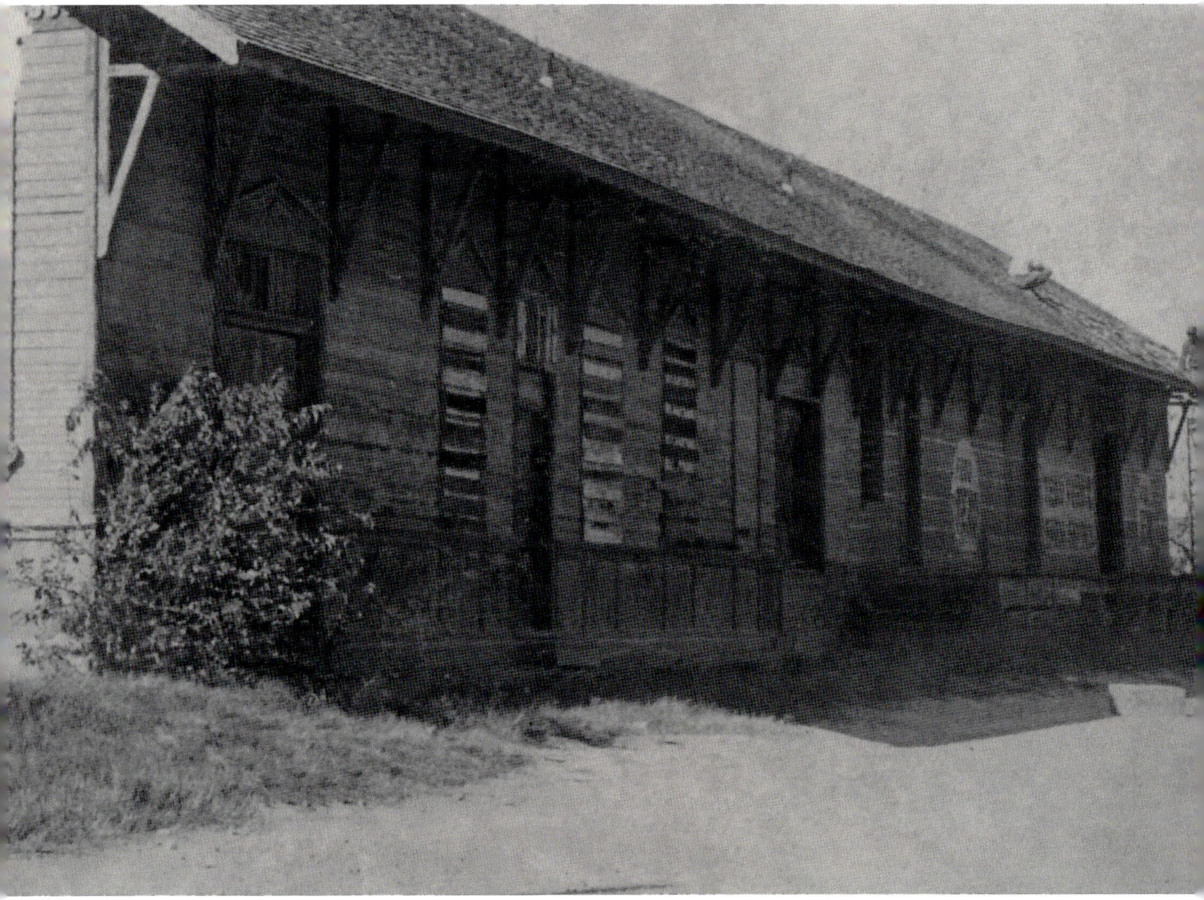

By the 1880s, the cattle business and the cotton industry had impacted the Railroad District, where mills, gins, and related businesses were thriving. When the railroad era declined in the 1900s, many of these commercial buildings sat vacant and decaying for decades. This 1960s photograph shows the Missouri-Pacific train depot east of Martin Luther King Street, just south of Sixth Street. The depot was removed around 1970, and the location where it stood is now a parking lot. (Then image courtesy author's collection.)

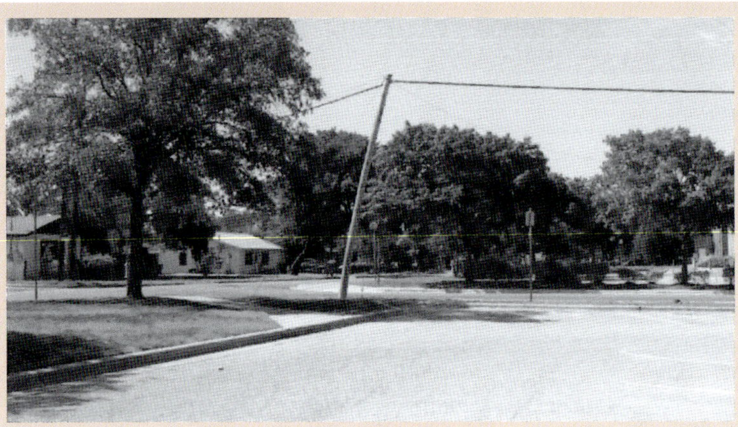

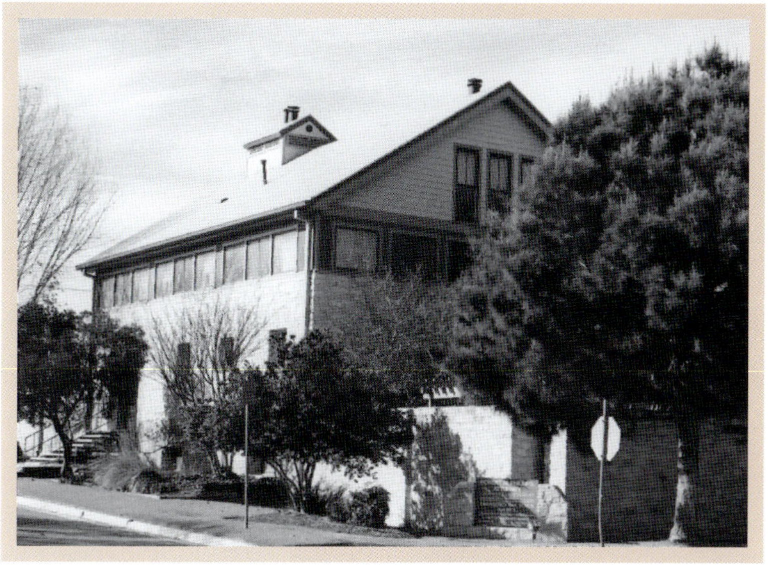

One business dependent on the river and the railroad was the 1904 produce warehouse at 401 West Sixth Street. River water was piped under the floor, and giant fans created a water-cooled space for produce. One of the few structures remaining from the railroad era, the building was saved from demolition and beautifully restored in 1996. Today, it is an attractive office building. (Then image courtesy *Williamson County Sun*.)

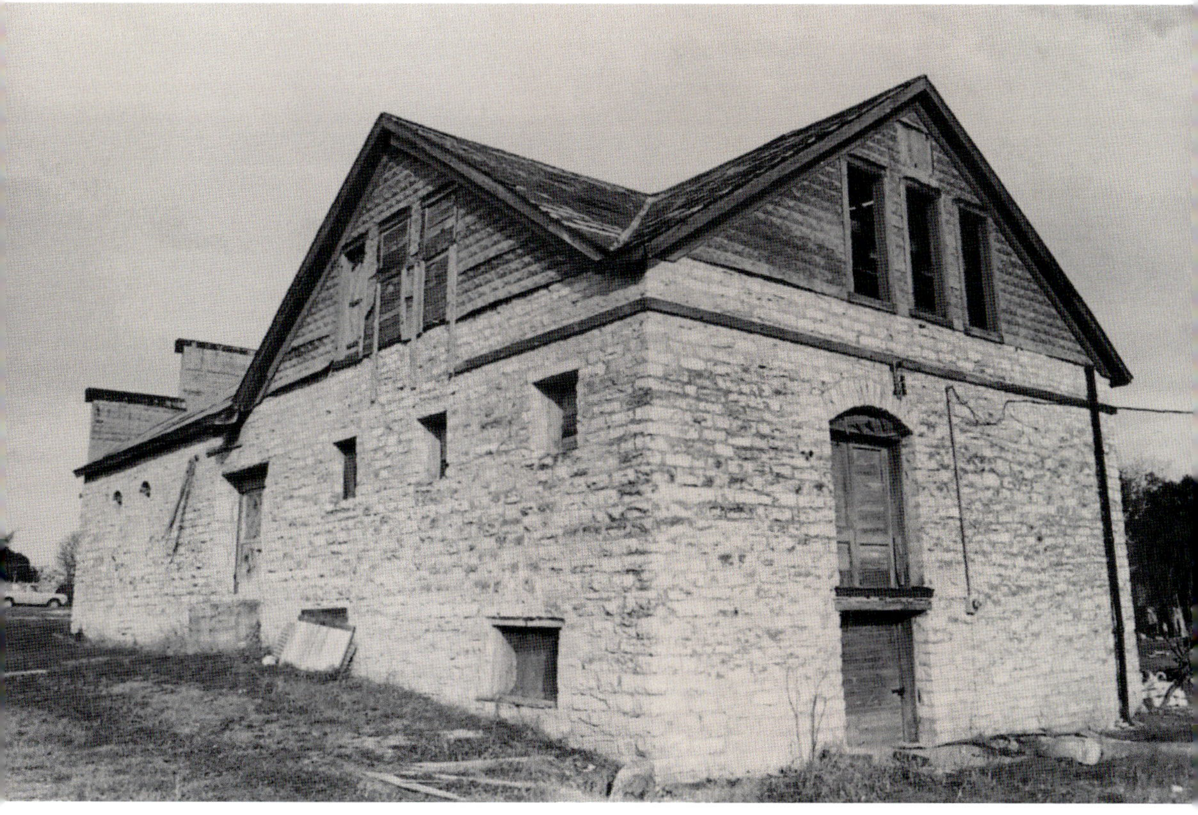

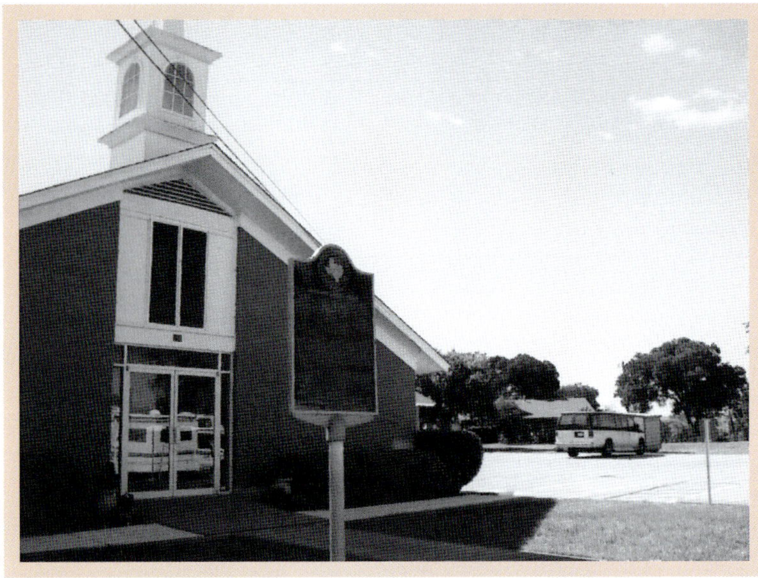

This historic structure, built by Belford Lumber Company, was the 1914 Macedonia Baptist Church. A new sanctuary, shown in today's photograph, was built alongside the old church in 1975 at 206 Martin Luther King Street. The old building was described in the *Williamson County Sun* as one of the most "popular structures in Georgetown" among photographers, architects, and artists. Several groups attempted to save and restore the building, but it was ultimately demolished. (Then image courtesy *Williamson County Sun*.)

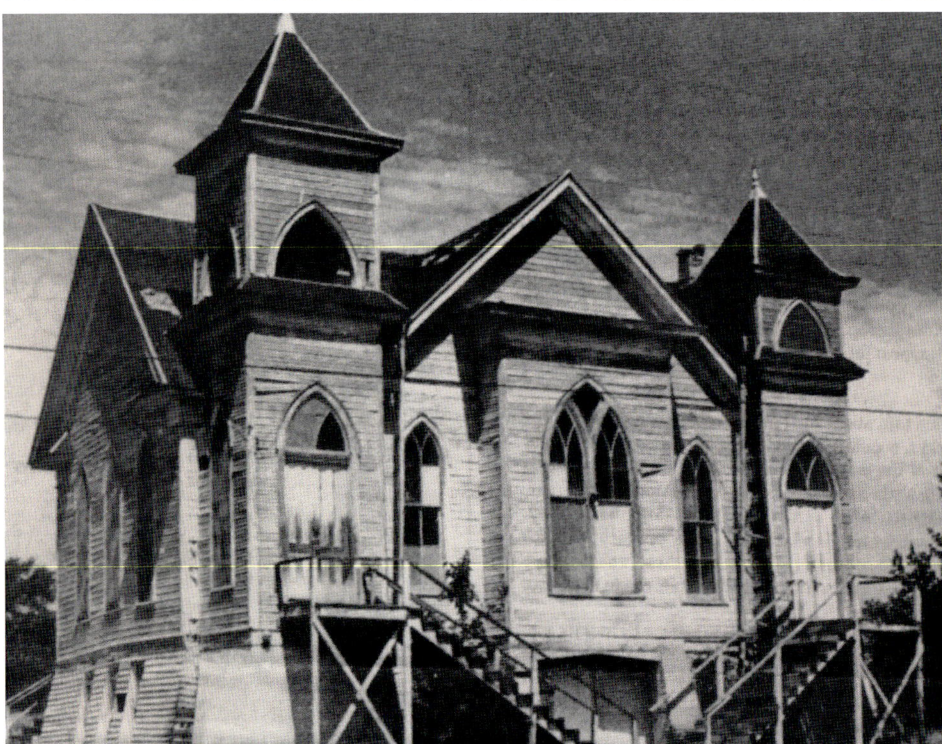

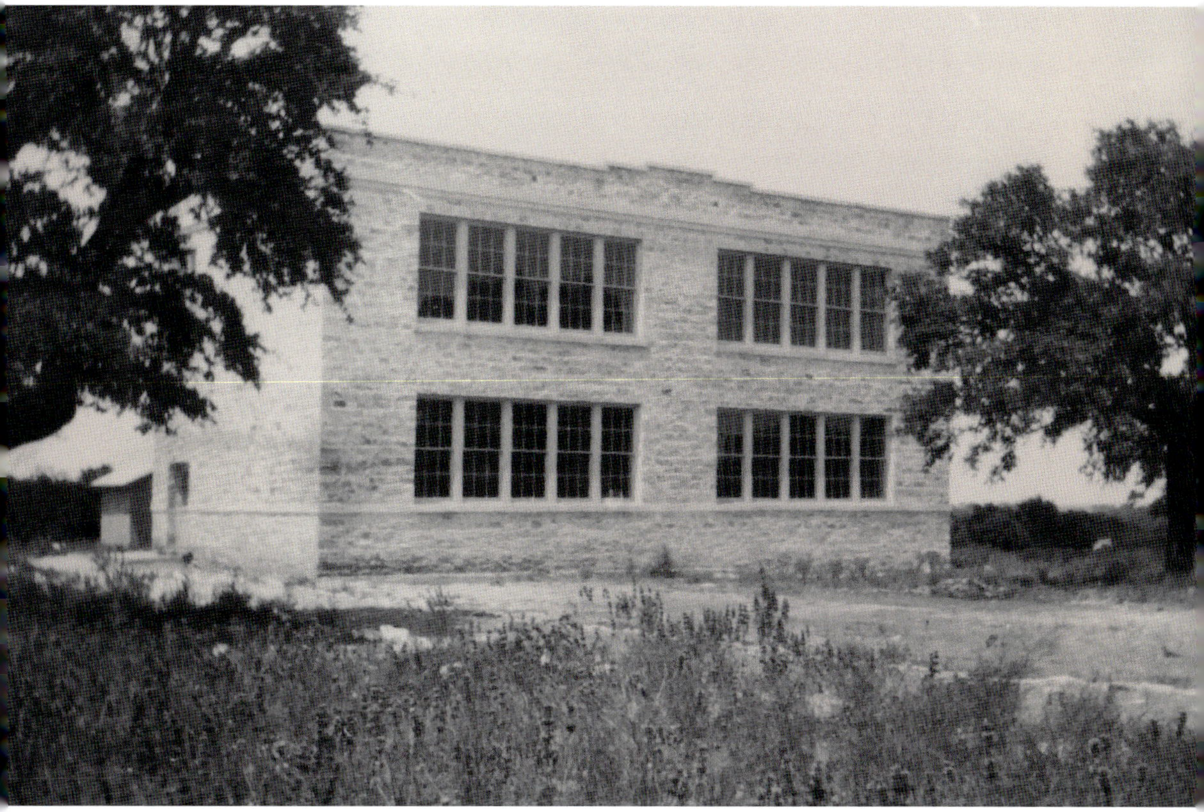

Marshall-Carver School was built at today's Martin Luther King and Second Streets in 1923, replacing a three-room school for African American students. The new school was originally named for principal and teacher S.C. Marshall. This new building created a much-improved environment for learning, but it was torn down after full integration was completed in 1965. The school was situated behind and between the two large oak trees in today's photograph. (Then image by Luis W. Atlee; courtesy *Williamson County Sun*.)

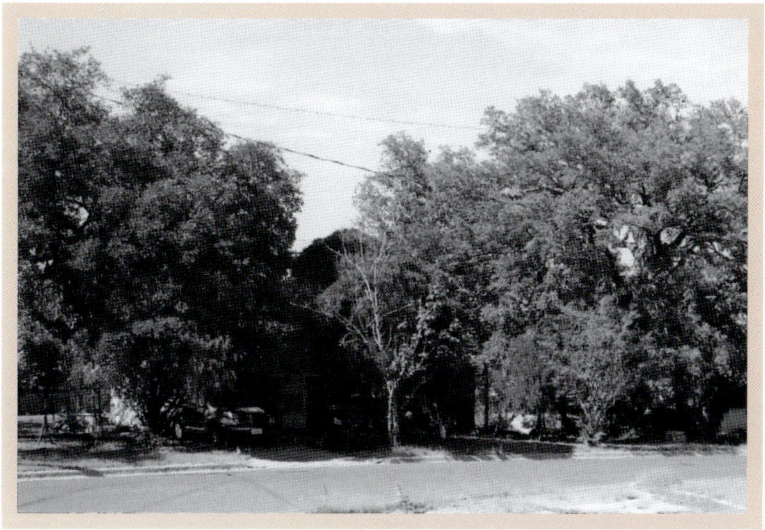

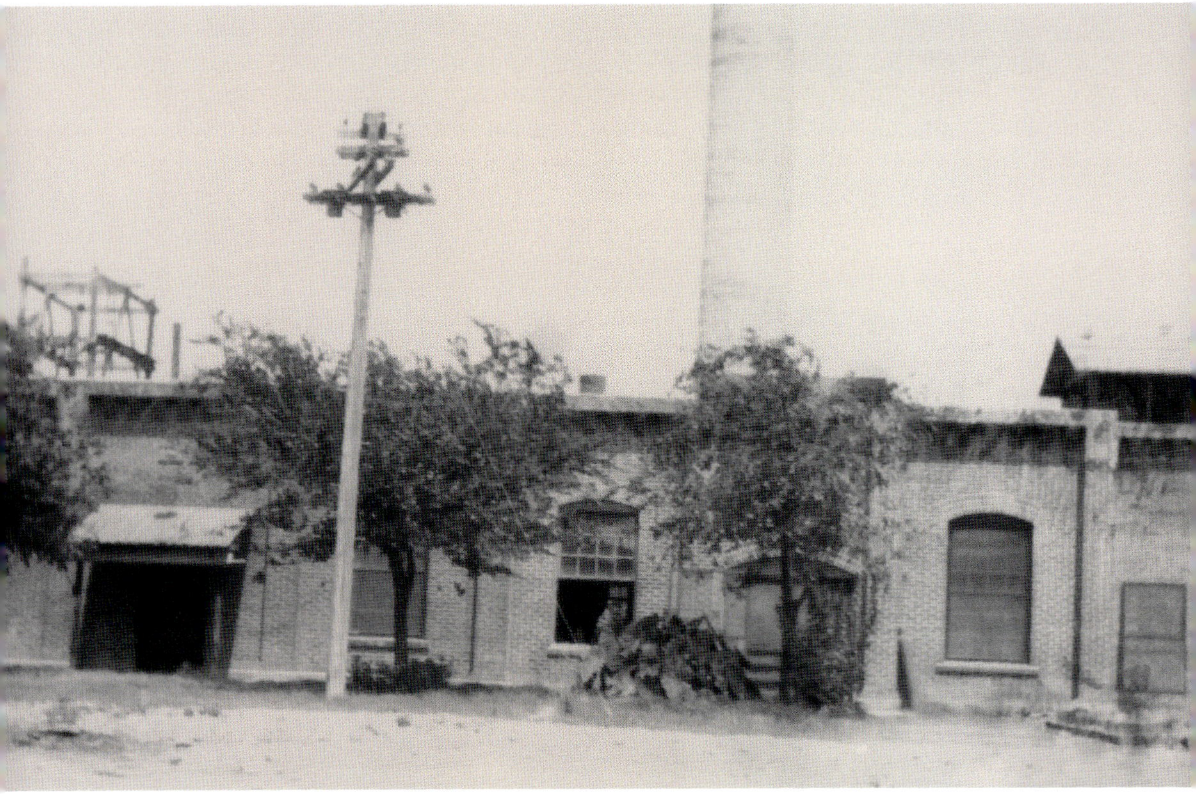

In 1911, the City of Georgetown purchased the private company that had supplied water to residents since 1884. By 1916, the city had built a new water plant in the Railroad District. The water plant, at 809 Martin Luther King Street, appears quite new in this mid-1920s photograph and was enlarged over the years. A 1986 restoration by the city transformed the badly deteriorated structure into new police department offices. (Then image by Luis W. Atlee; courtesy *Williamson County Sun*.)

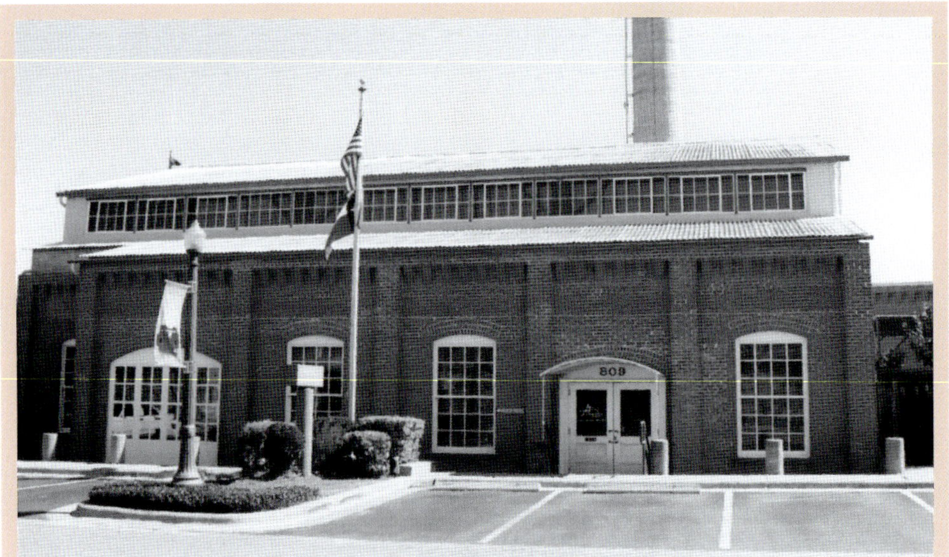

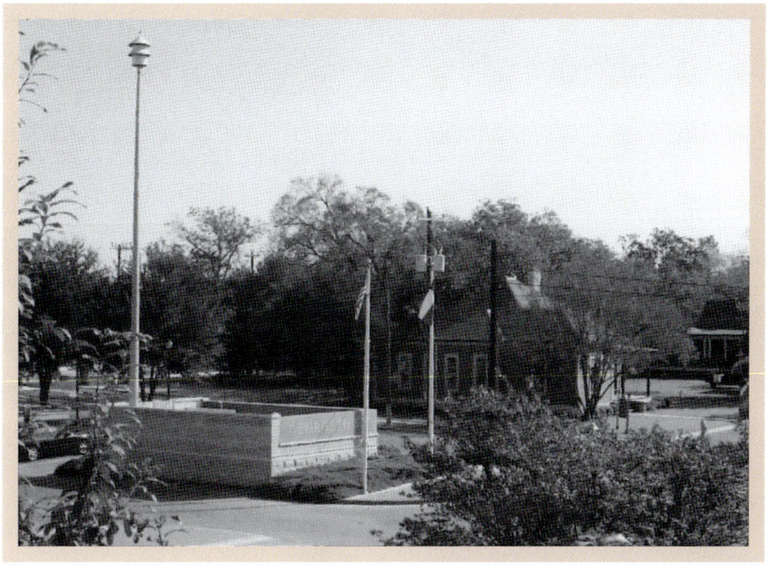

This stunning image of the cotton yard dates to around 1900. Viewed from the corner of Ninth and Forest Streets, the back of the Central Baptist Church is visible at the far left. The large building in the distance is the 1895 Georgetown Public School. The steeple is that of the Christian Church, which became the Church of Christ, at 1102 South Austin Avenue. Today's view, taken from the Georgetown Public Library, shows the same block. (Then image courtesy author's collection.)

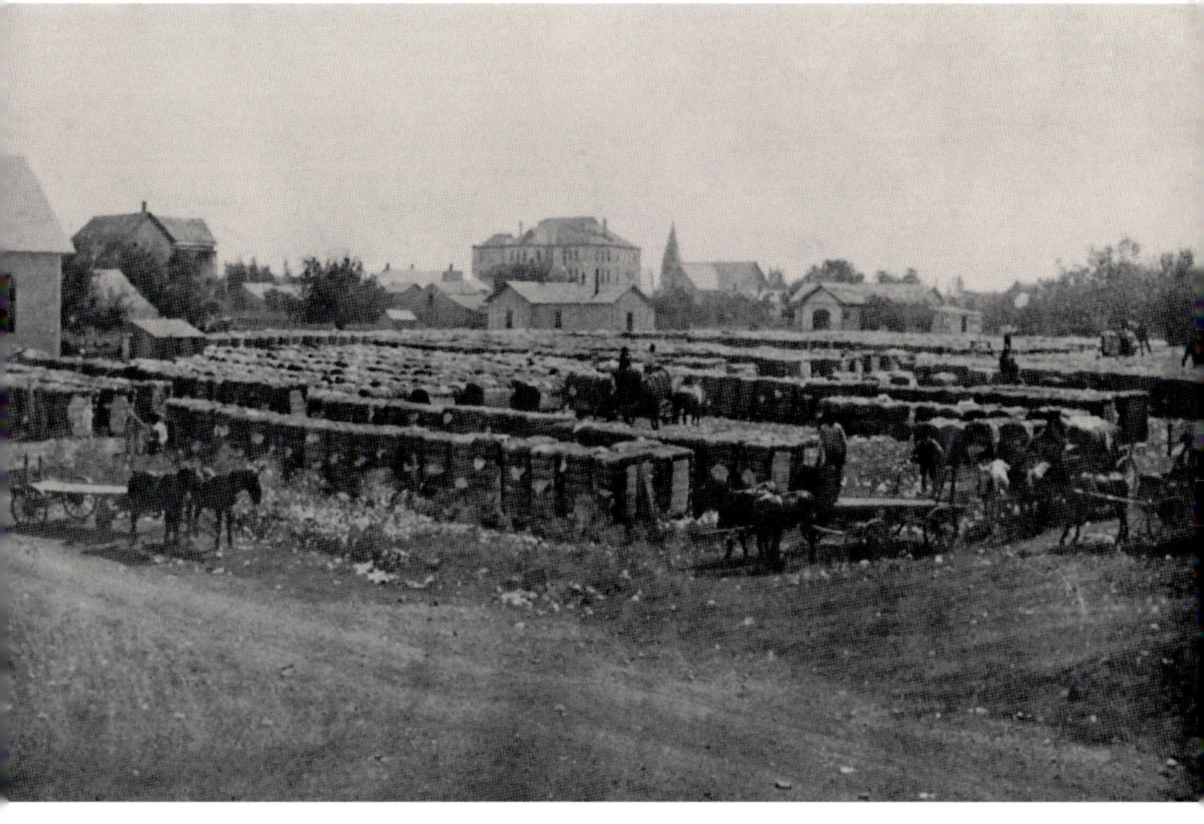

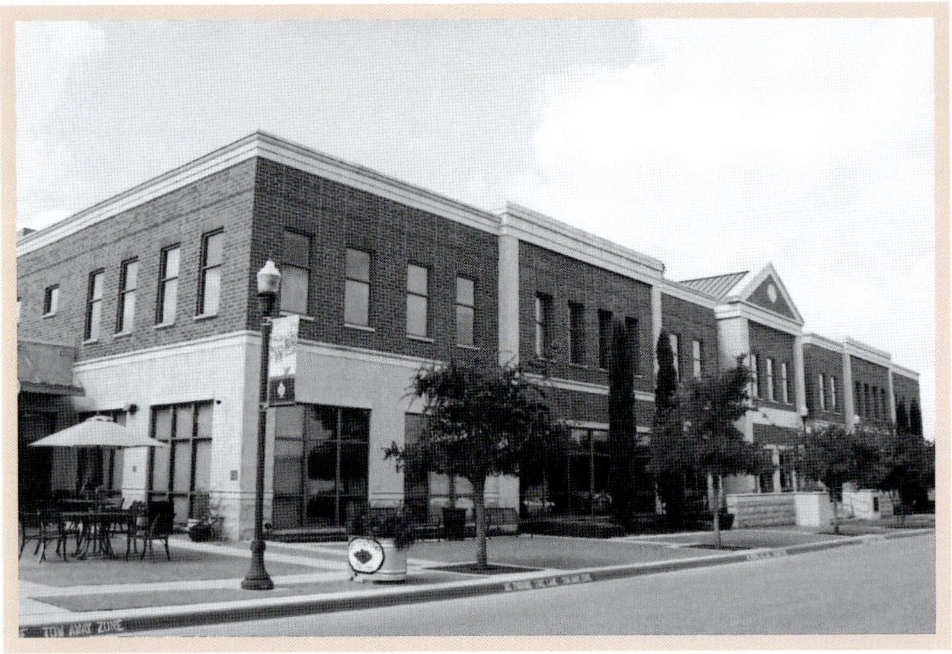

The 49,500-square-foot Georgetown Public Library opened in 2007, reviving almost an entire block, which contained metal buildings, a wooden storage shed, and a city water reservoir. Georgetown's first railroad depot was located just across Eighth Street from today's library and was a hub of activity in the 1880s, just as the library is today. Pictured is the Eighth Street side of today's library and the metal building formerly on this part of the block. (Then image courtesy Lori Mitchell, Atkins NA.)

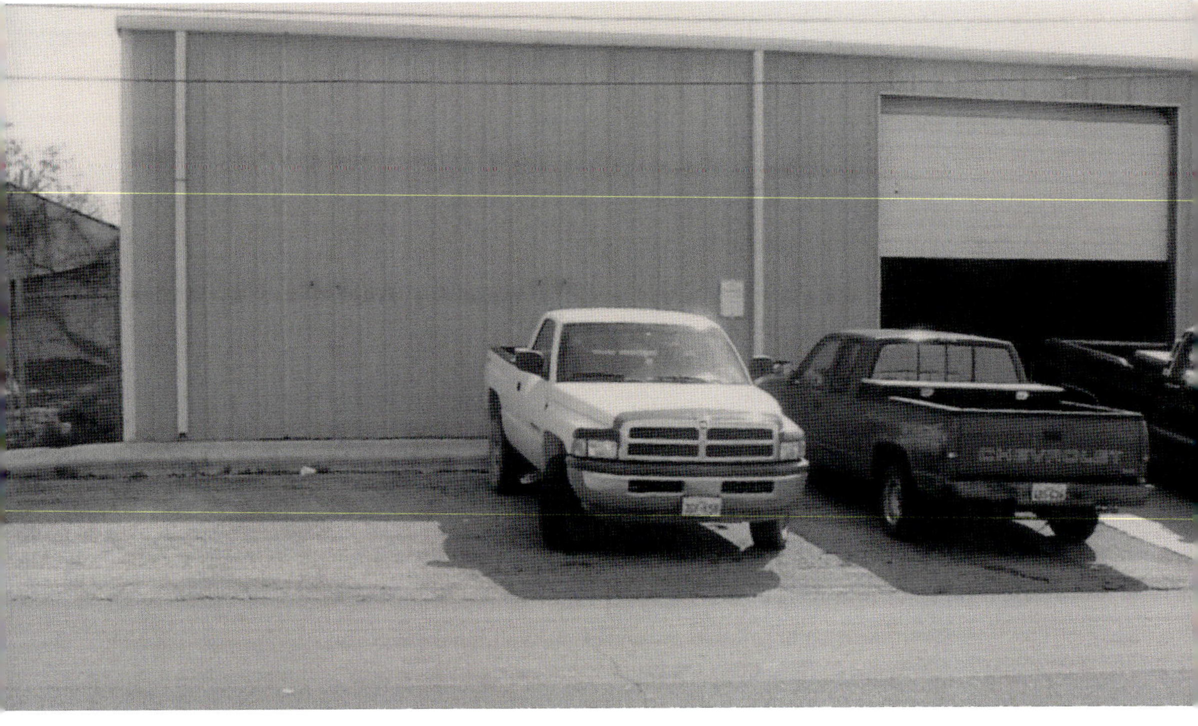

CHAPTER 3

RIVER VISTAS AND LANDMARKS

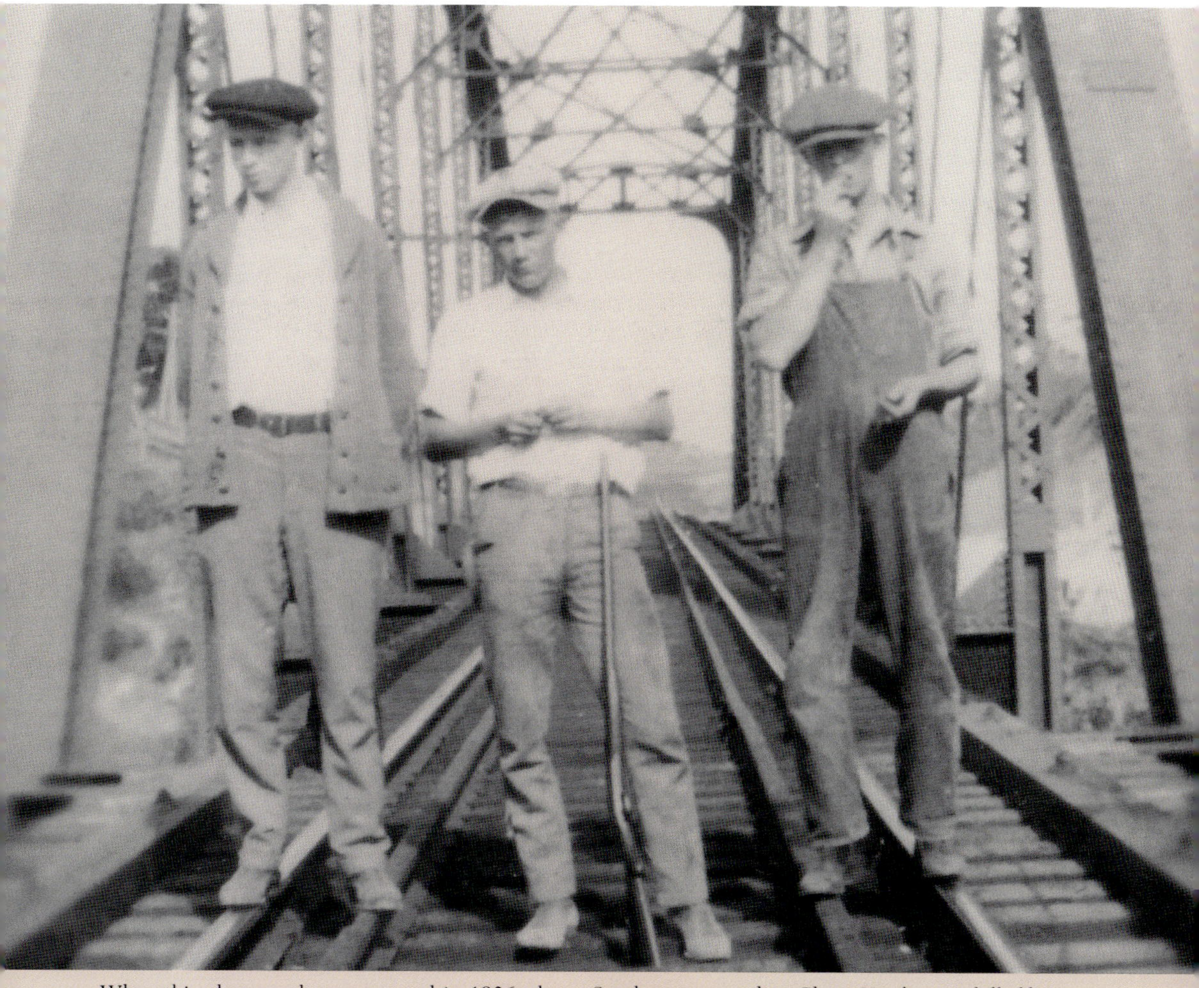

When this photograph was snapped in 1926, the Katy Railroad Bridge was easily accessible, and the area became a popular recreational spot. The bridge brought tragedy as well. Around 1940, Southwestern student Gloria Hawker was killed by an unexpected train as she tried to flee the bridge with friends. (Image by George Price Jr.; courtesy John S. Lesesne.)

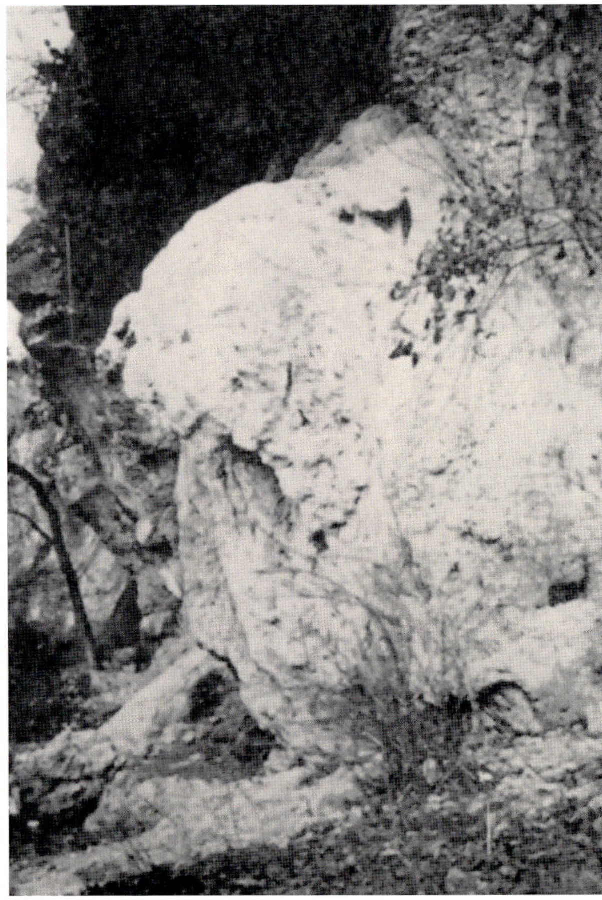

Lion's Head, near Rivery Park, was formerly part of Shell family property and the setting for legendary foxhunts, campouts, and picnics. Owners generously shared this wild and exotic locale named for the large rock formation with Georgetown and Southwestern University. Today, Lion's Head is not publicly accessible. The spring that waters the lion's mossy neck is less constant, but otherwise the area remains relatively unchanged. (Then image courtesy Southwestern University, Special Collections, Georgetown, Texas; now image courtesy Wayne Kuehn.)

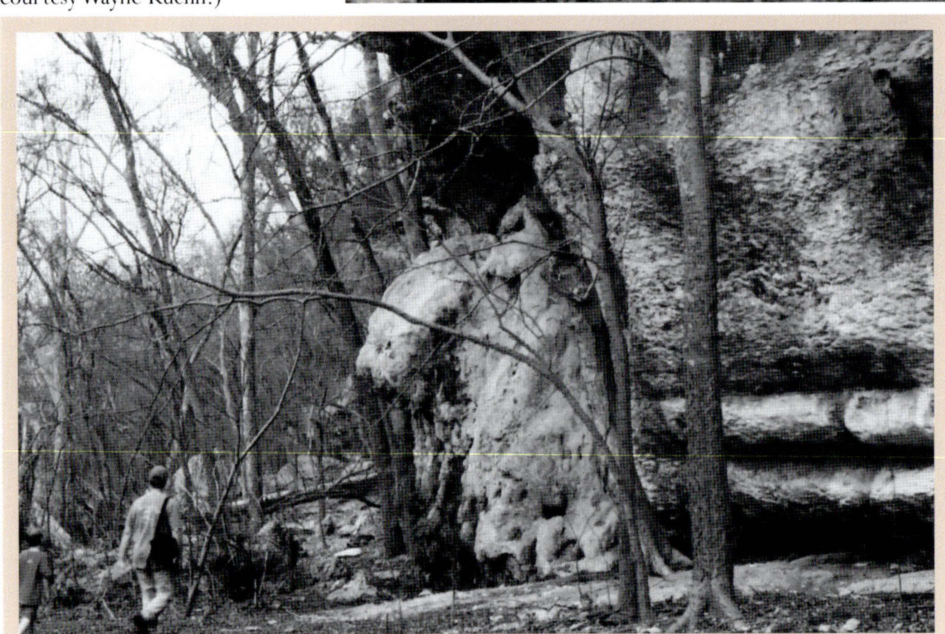

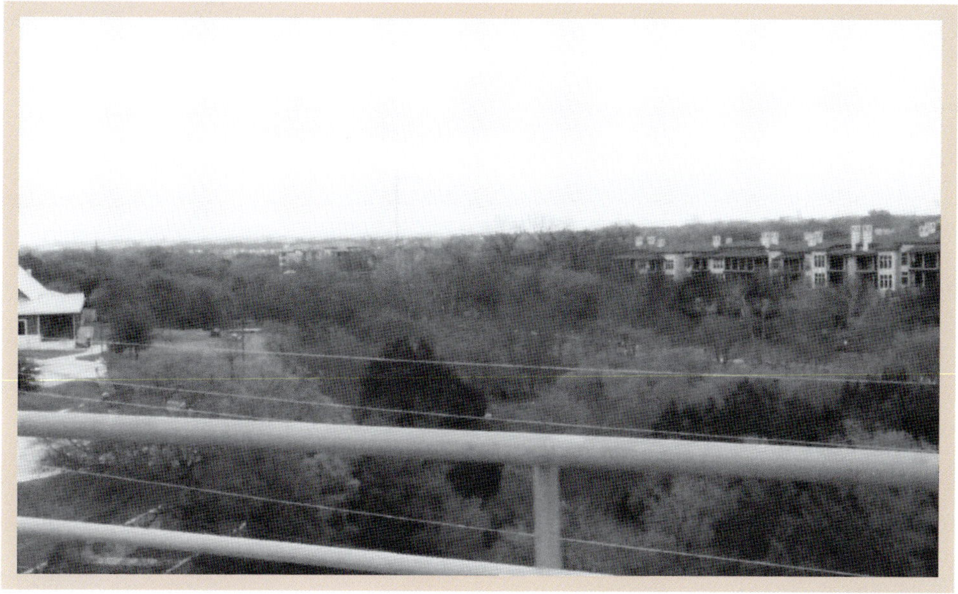

This old image was taken in the mid-1920s from a high vantage point over the North San Gabriel River near today's Interstate 35. Looking downstream, the image shows a wide-open view of the 1924 Highway 81 Bridge. Today's river, vastly changed due to controlled water releases from Lake Georgetown, is crowded with trees, with cliff-top condominiums peering over the scene and the hike and bike trail snaking alongside the water. (Then image by Luis W. Atlee; courtesy *Williamson County Sun*.)

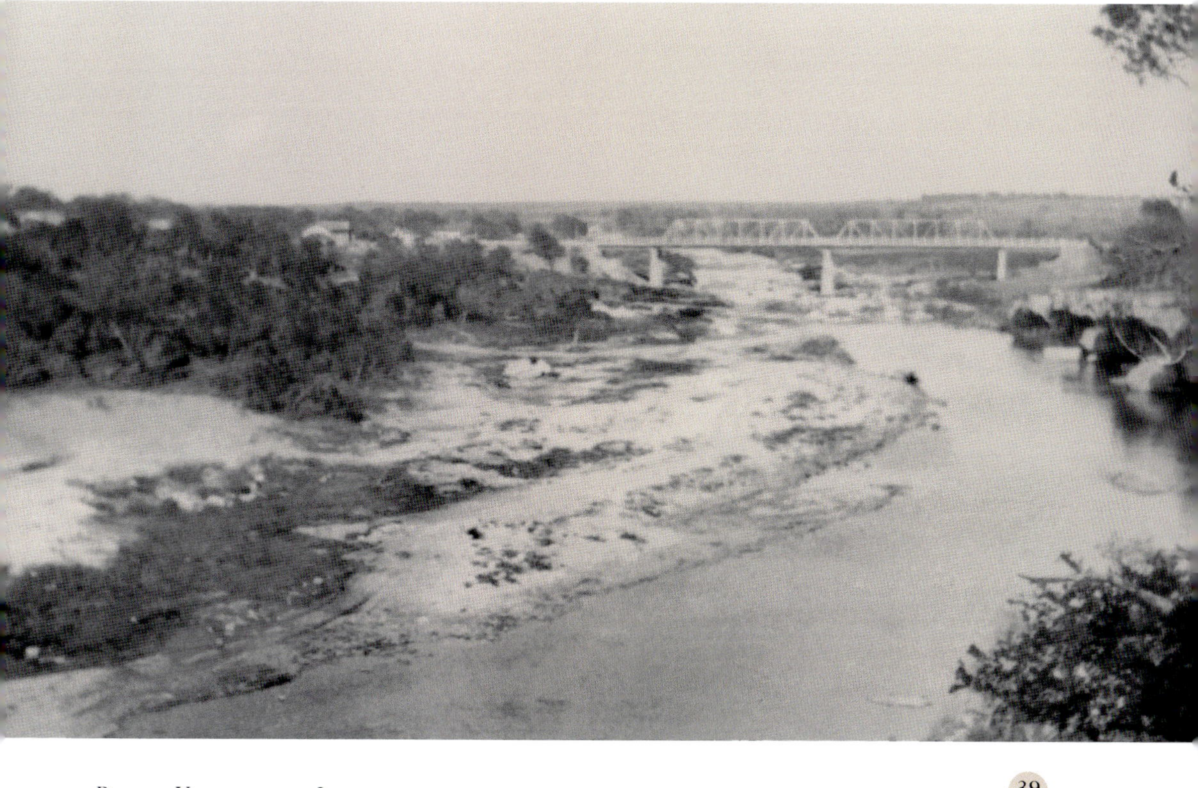

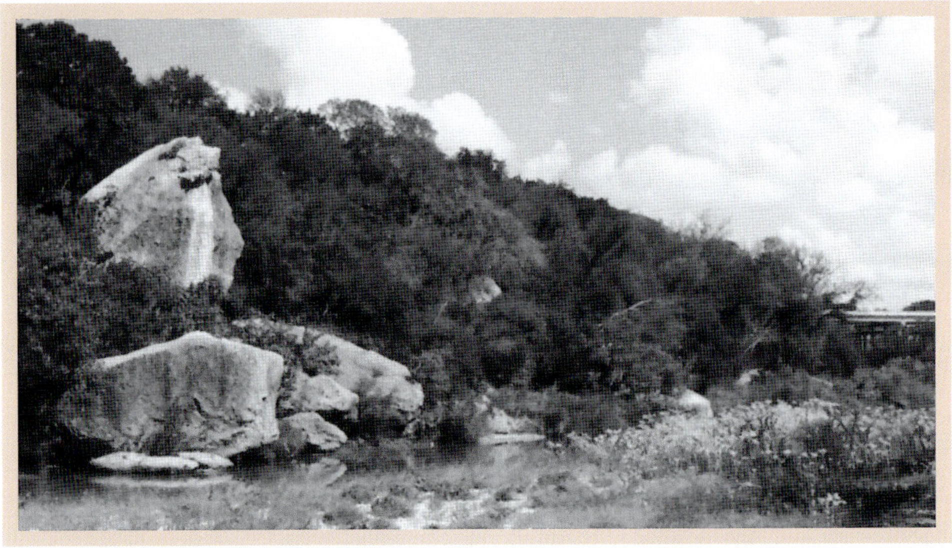

This c. 1910 photograph shows the Ellyson family and horse Dolly paused in front of an enormous rock "near Bear's Den" (according to the photographer's notes) along the South San Gabriel River. This formation still stands facing south toward the old Page-Weir Ranch, upstream from the interstate. Recent explorations reveal at least one small cave behind the monolith. According to Georgetown's Esther Weir, a nearby rock fence dates from an early-1900s turkey farm. (Then image courtesy Johnson/Ellyson Estate.)

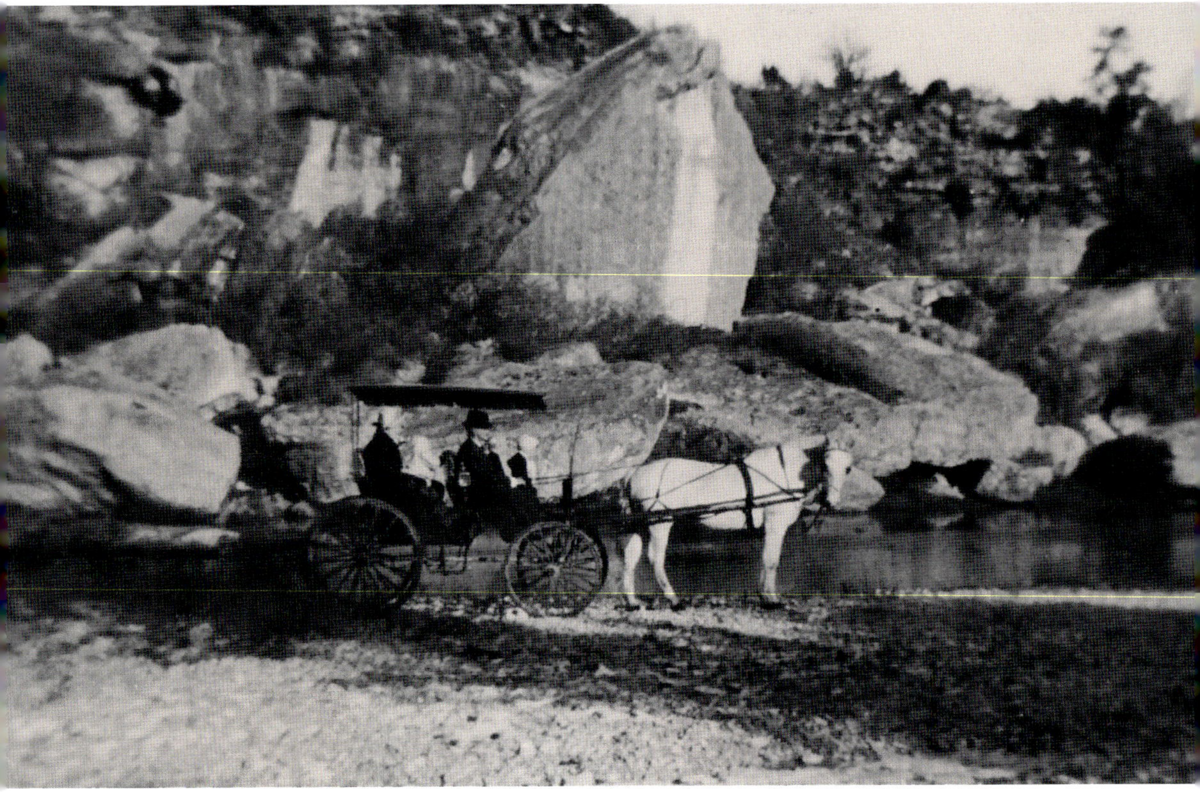

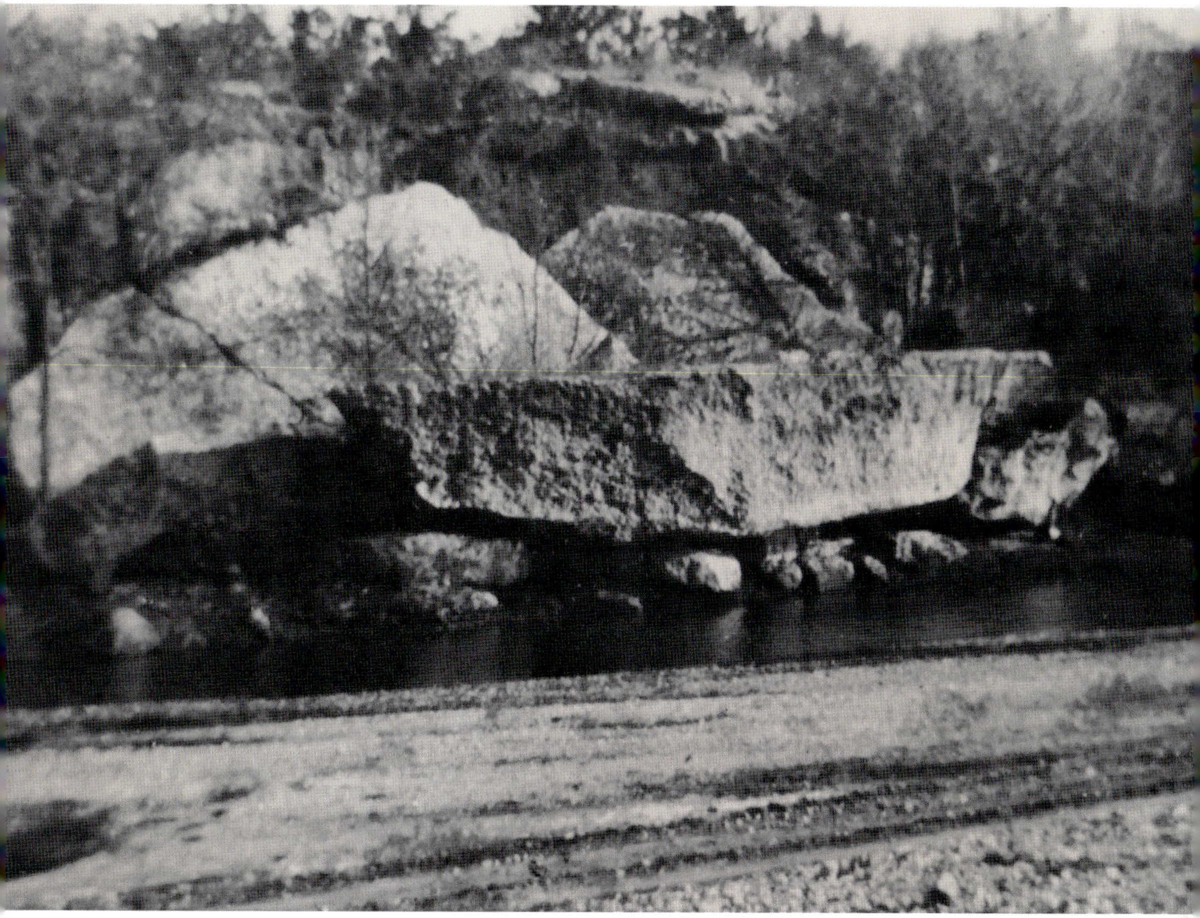

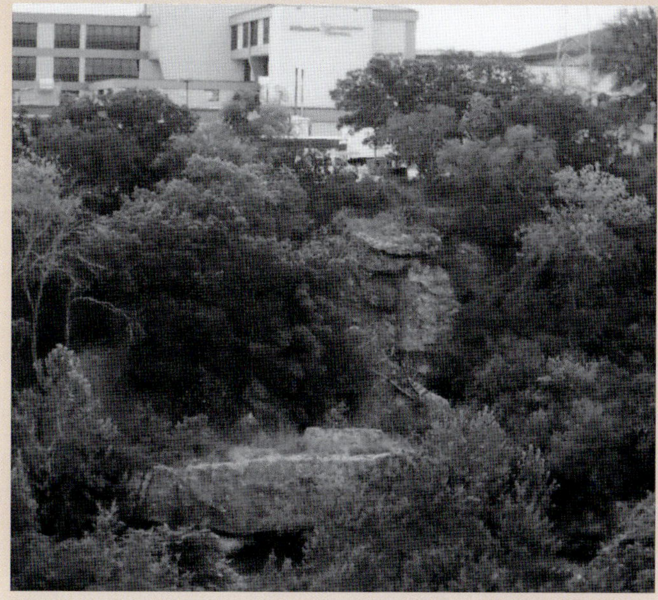

This huge rock in the South San Gabriel River is known as "Ship-Rock" or "Boat-Rock." It is pictured in many Southwestern University yearbooks, often with a number of students on top. It was a well-known landmark through most of the 20th century. When the river is up, this massive formation appears to float like a ship in the water. It is just downstream from the interstate, below St. David's Georgetown Hospital. (Then image courtesy Johnson/Ellyson Estate.)

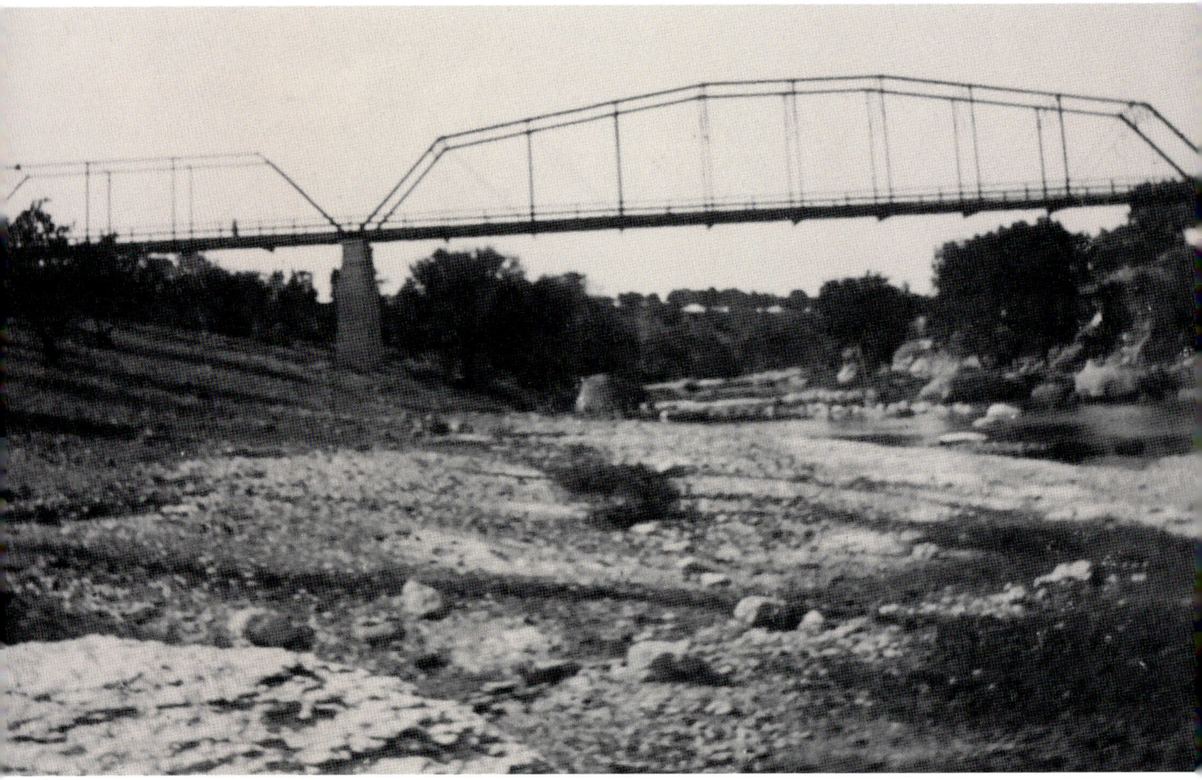

This 1908 image, described by the photographer as showing the "new bridge," captures the Tenth Street bridge over the South San Gabriel River. Automobile traffic shared early bridges with mule- and horse-drawn buggies and wagons, riders on horseback, and livestock being moved to the railroads or pastures. Extensive regulations were enacted to reduce the number of accidents caused by spooking animals on roads and bridges. Today's image shows the present Highway 29 bridge, which replaced the old crossing. (Then image courtesy Johnson/Ellyson Estate.)

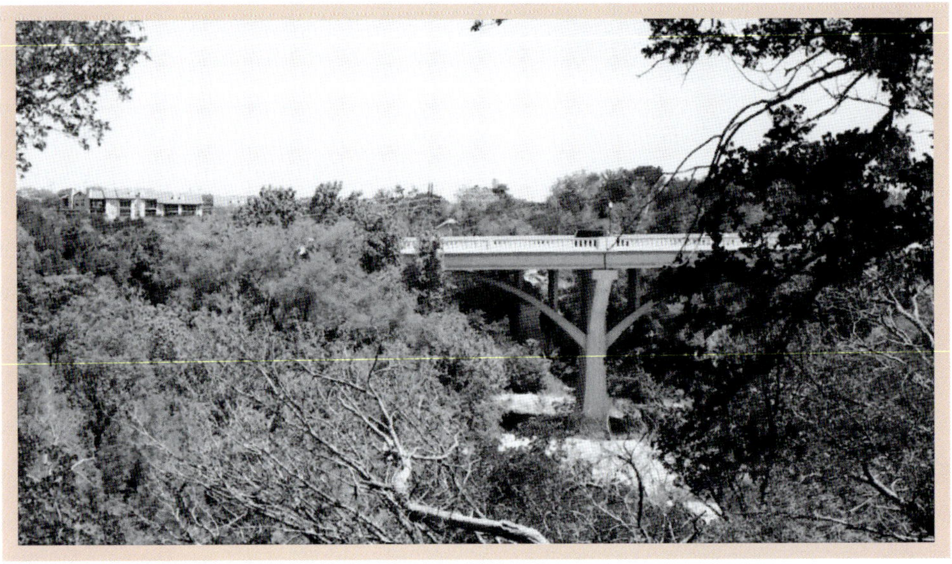

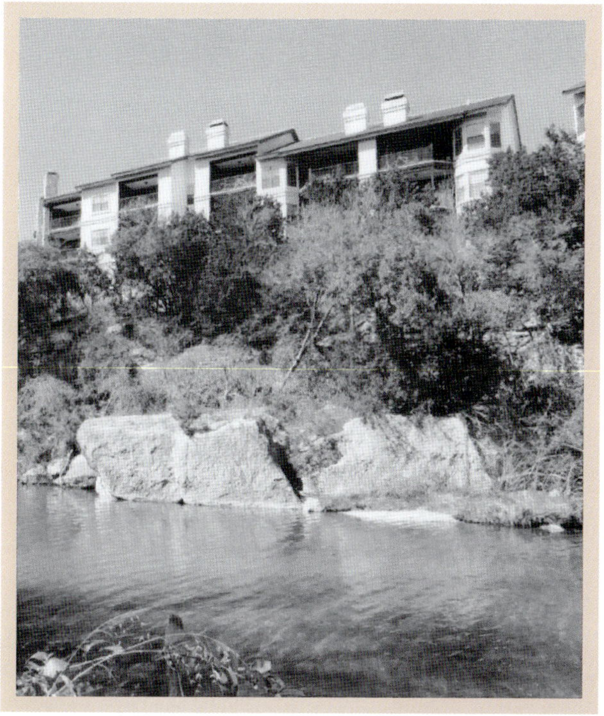

The Chautauqua movement of the 1880s spread like wildfire across the country. Georgetown's assembly was supported by the town's most prominent citizens. Several wealthy families built summerhouses on the north bank of the South San Gabriel River near the Chautauqua grounds. The best-known structure, Steele's Castle, pictured here around 1900, was built by M.E. Steele, a successful dry goods merchant. Today, the "castle" would sit to the right of this apartment building. (Then image courtesy Special Collections, Southwestern University, Georgetown, Texas.)

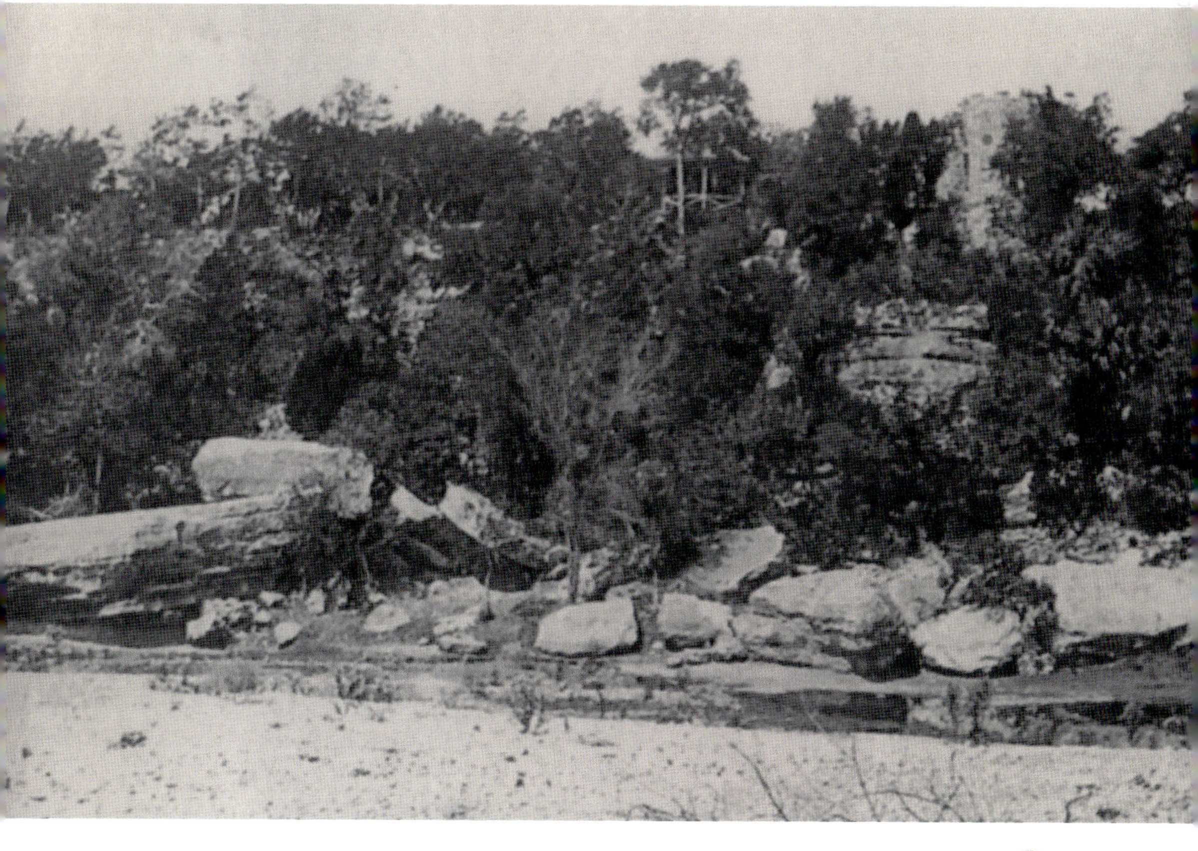

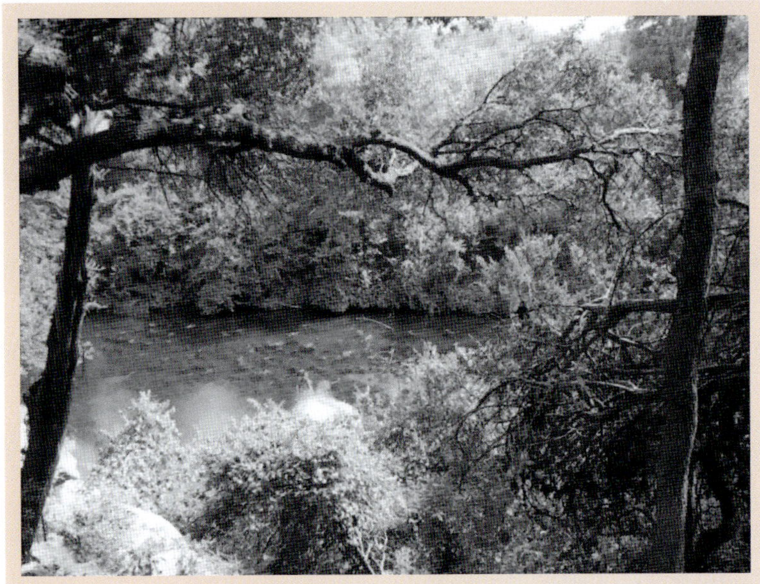

Described in the 1893 history *The Lone Star State* as a "magnificent suspension bridge," it was built in the early 1890s over the South San Gabriel River for easier access to Georgetown's Chautauqua grounds north of the river. It joined a long wooden stairway, which ascended the steep north bluff. Today, this stairway would rise between the first and second apartment buildings on River Oaks Cove. A sign at Chautauqua Park marks where the bridge was fastened to the ground. (Then image courtesy author's collection.)

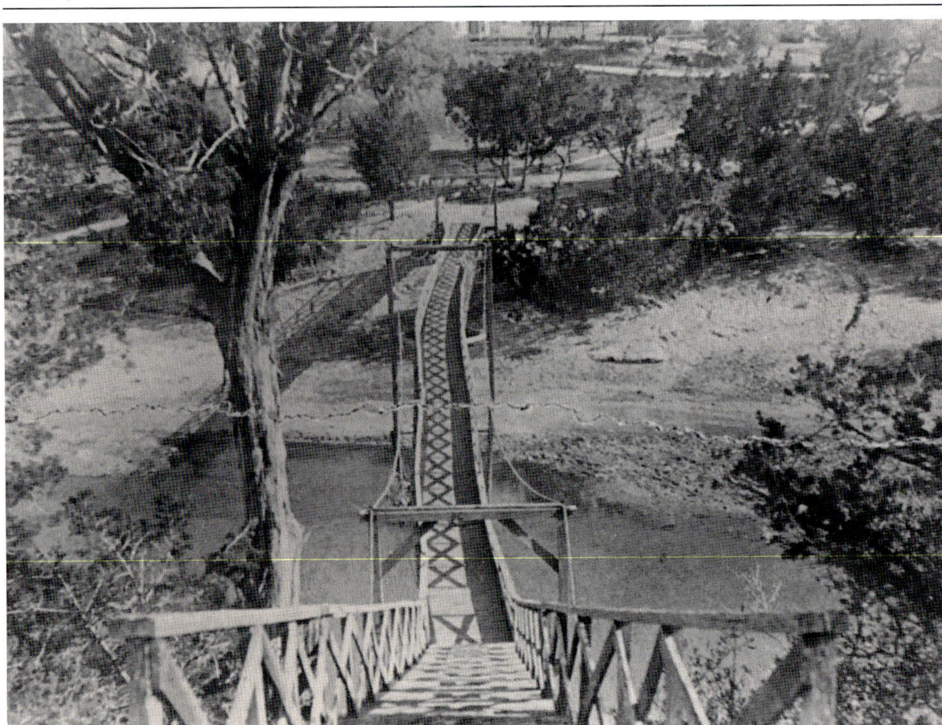

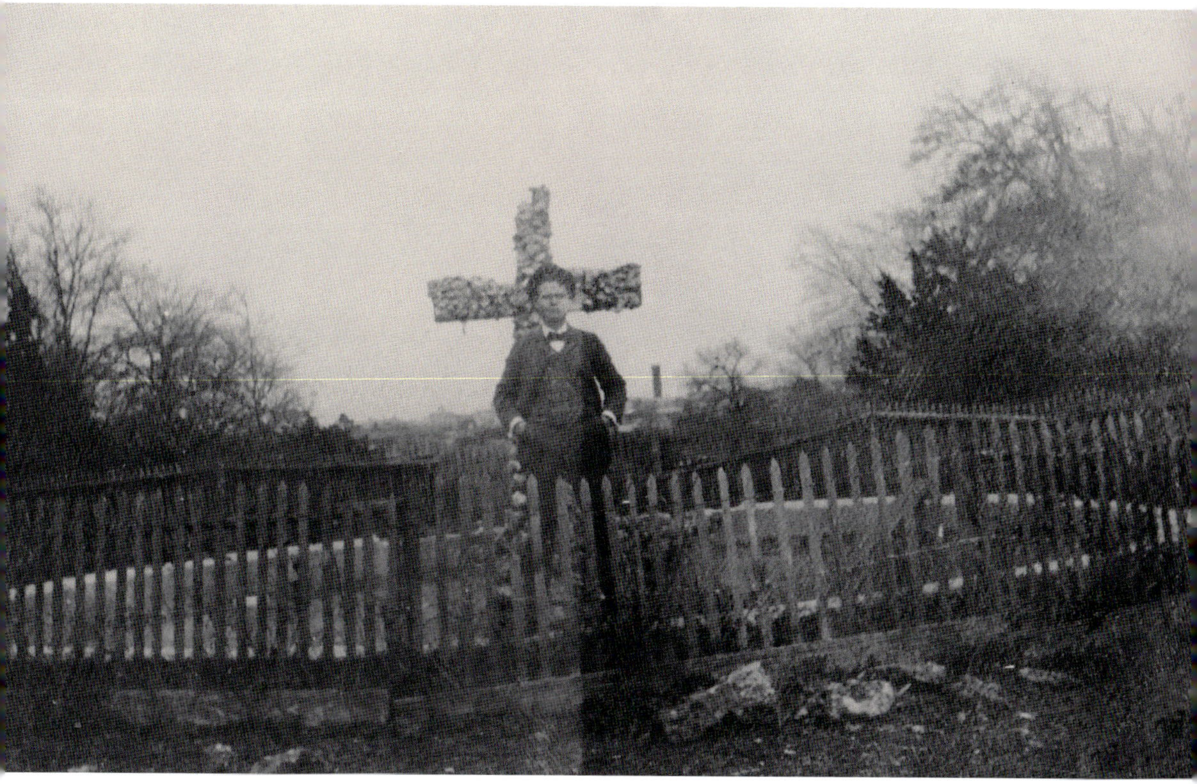

This cross and fountain once stood on Georgetown's Chautauqua grounds behind today's Burger King on the northbound access road of Interstate 35. In the background, downtown Georgetown is visible. In the old photograph, downtown and the standpipe are to the right of the cross. The 2013 image shows the Waters Edge Apartments and the courthouse. Historian J.C. Johnson notes that the Chautauqua Tabernacle was near today's northbound Interstate 35. (Then image courtesy Johnson/Ellyson Estate.)

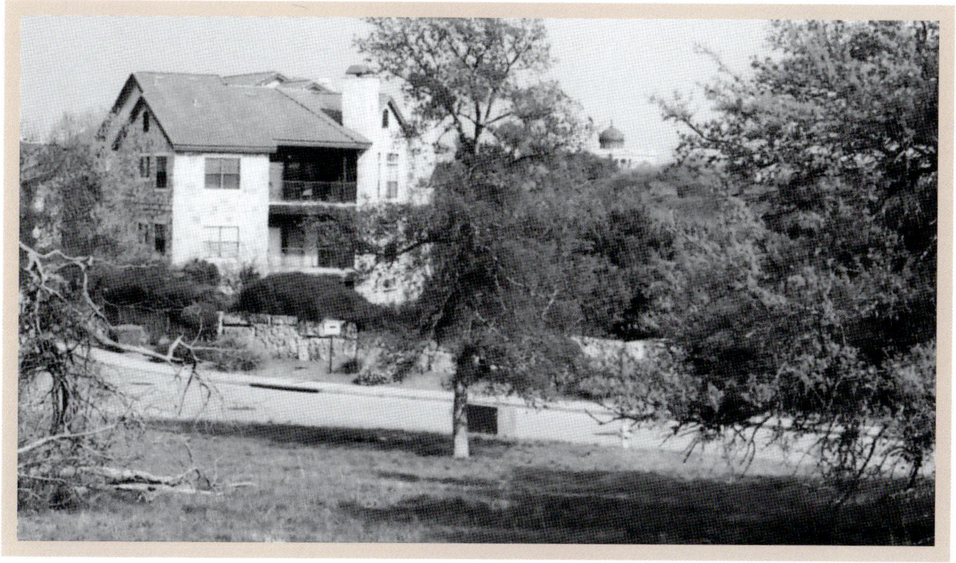

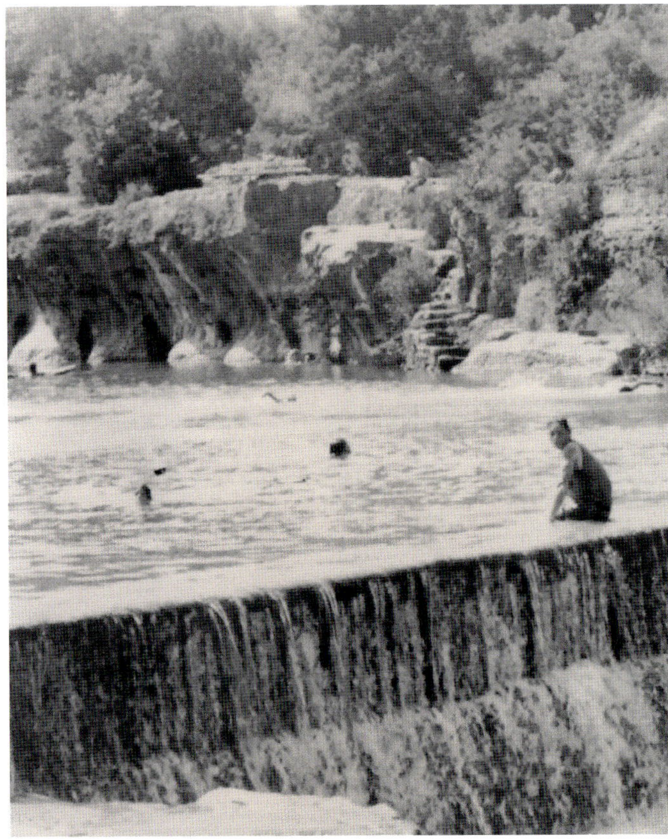

Downstream from the Chautauqua grounds, Blue Hole is just below Georgetown's oldest cemetery. The dam is named for L.P. Imhoff, a machinist who helped construct it in 1932. Boys attending Marshall-Carver High School loved to climb down the cliffs behind campus for an after-school swim. Photographed in the present day from the Austin Avenue Bridge, this beautiful and mysterious deep water attracts large crowds almost every summer day. (Then image courtesy *Williamson County Sun*.)

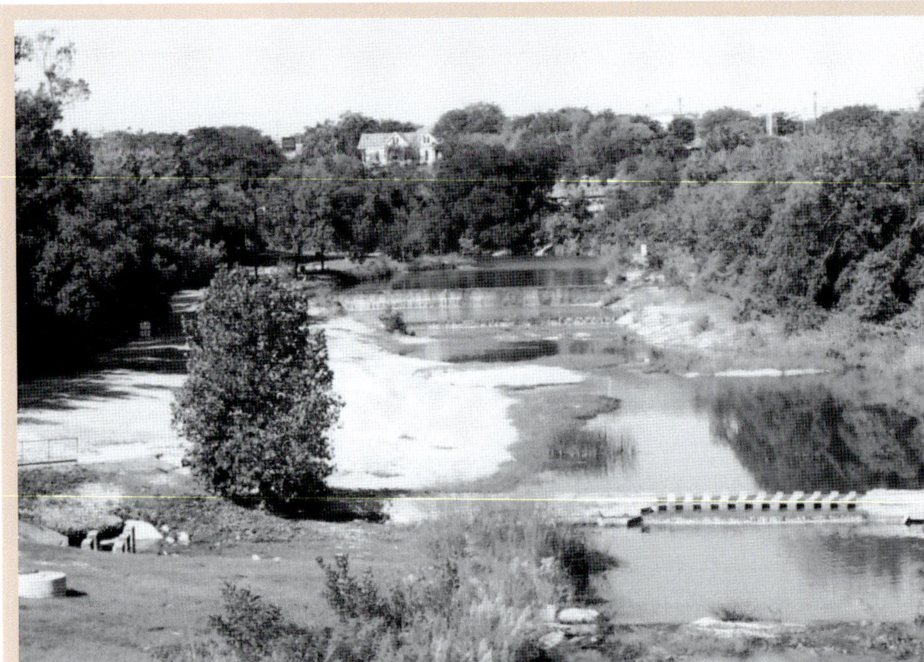

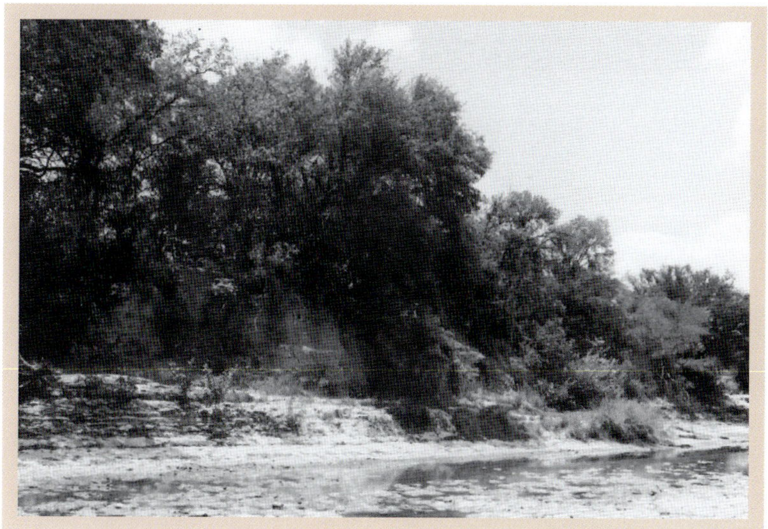

The old Water and Light Plant, photographed in the early 1900s, was perched on the east bank of the South San Gabriel River near the confluence with the river's north fork. It was built by Georgetown Waterworks, which pumped water from nearby springs for Georgetown customers. The facility was purchased by the city in 1911. Today, only faint clues point to the exact location, which was off College Street, near today's Winfred H. Bonner Trail sign. (Then image courtesy Johnson/Ellyson Estate.)

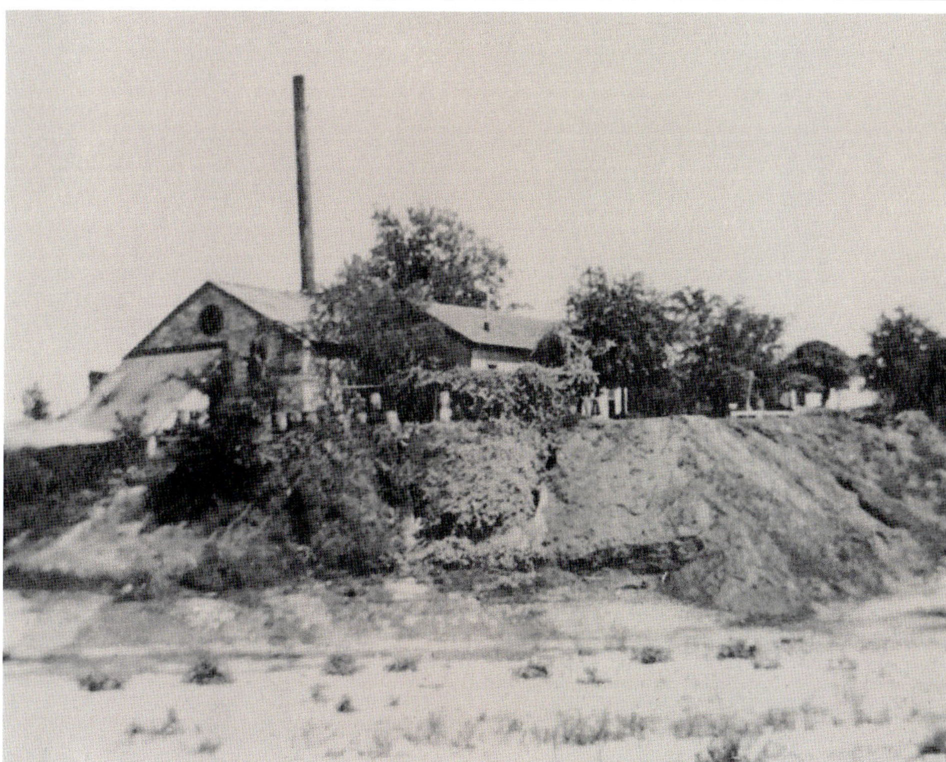

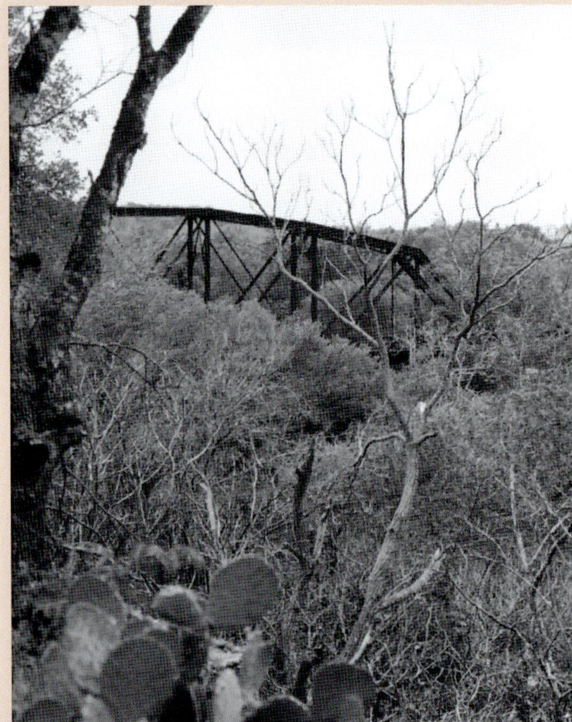

The Missouri-Kansas-Texas (MKT) Railroad completed the Granger-to-Austin line in 1904, crossing the river a short distance below San Gabriel Park. This 1926 photograph clearly shows the two sections of the bridge from upstream on the north cliff. The south end of the bridge at right is on city property, not accessible to the public. Several homeowners in the Katy Crossing neighborhood can enjoy this view of the bridge today. (Then image by George Price Jr.; courtesy John S. Lesesne.)

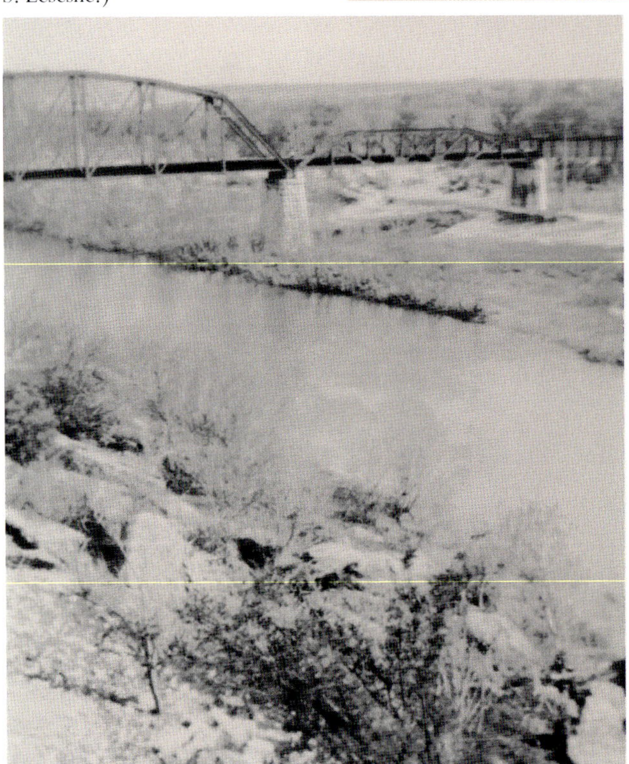

CHAPTER 4

Old-Town Neighborhoods

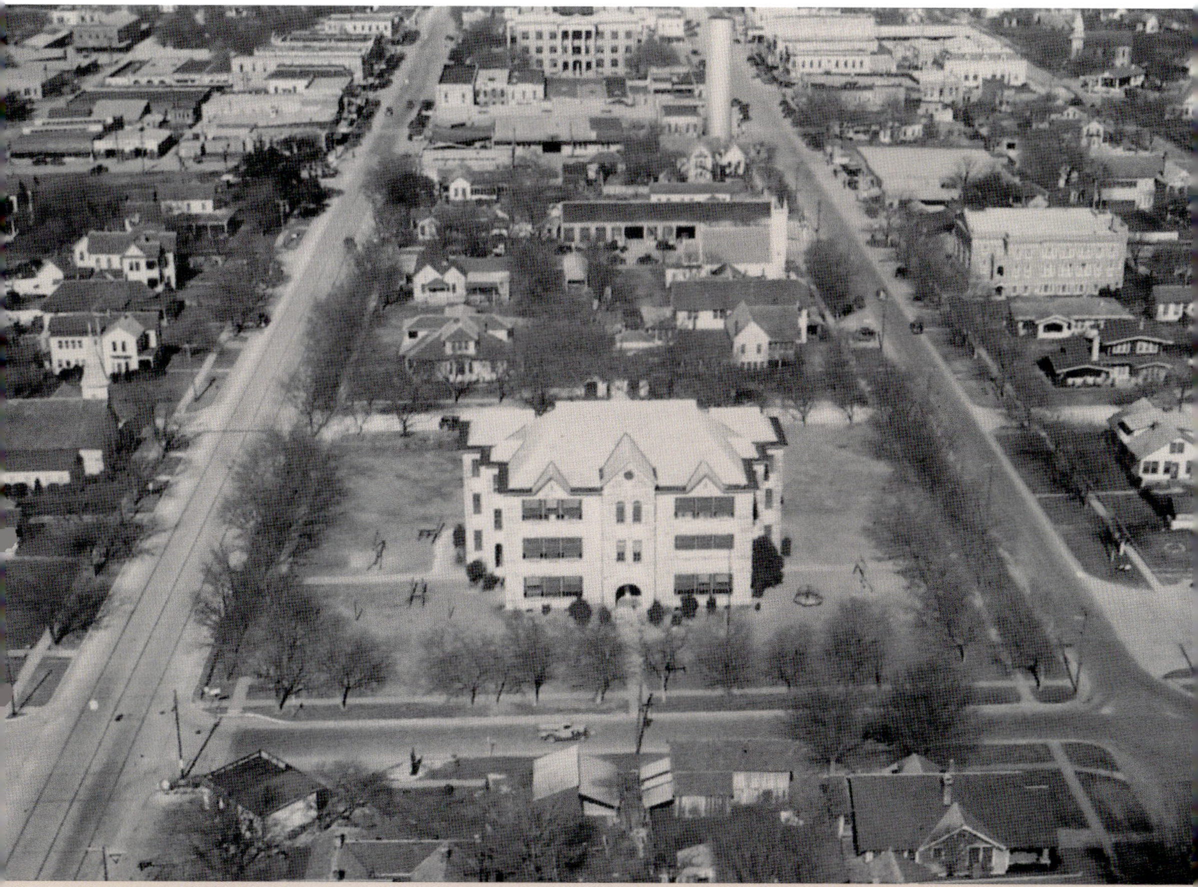

Dating between 1931 and 1955, this wonderful aerial view of Old-Town clearly shows the handsome architecture of the Georgetown Grammar School bordered by Austin Avenue and Main Street, with a truck passing eastbound on University Avenue. Note the beautiful symmetry of this structure with the courthouse at the top of the photograph. (Southwestern University, Special Collections, Georgetown, Texas.)

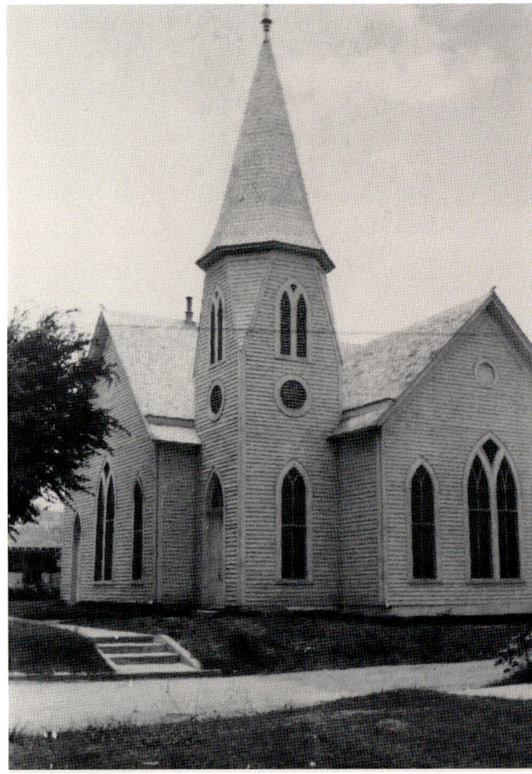

Pictured is the Christian Church, which later became the Church of Christ. This mid-1920s photograph shows a typical design used by several churches in early Georgetown. The building, at 1102 South Austin Avenue, was replaced by a new church in 1972. Today, a commercial building occupies the site. The Georgetown Church of Christ has relocated to 1525 West University Avenue. (Then image by Luis W. Atlee; courtesy *Williamson County Sun*.)

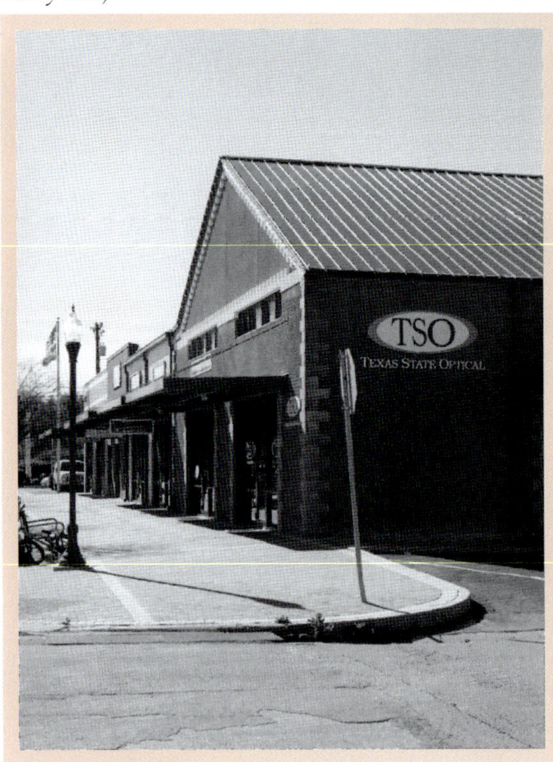

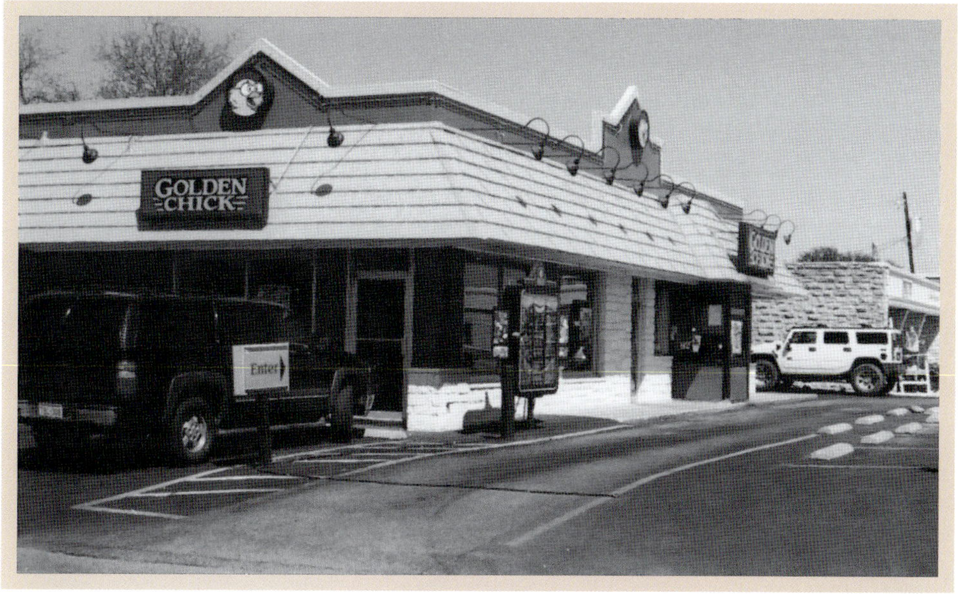

Standing in front of a residence on South Austin Avenue, Charlie McMurray and his horse, Dolly, look equally stylish. The home was a typical one-story Victorian design with a rounded side bay with shingled siding. Numerous homes on Austin Avenue, including this one, were lost to a growing business district between the river and University Avenue. Today, Golden Chick Restaurant sits immediately south of this lot. (Then image courtesy Johnson/Ellyson Estate.)

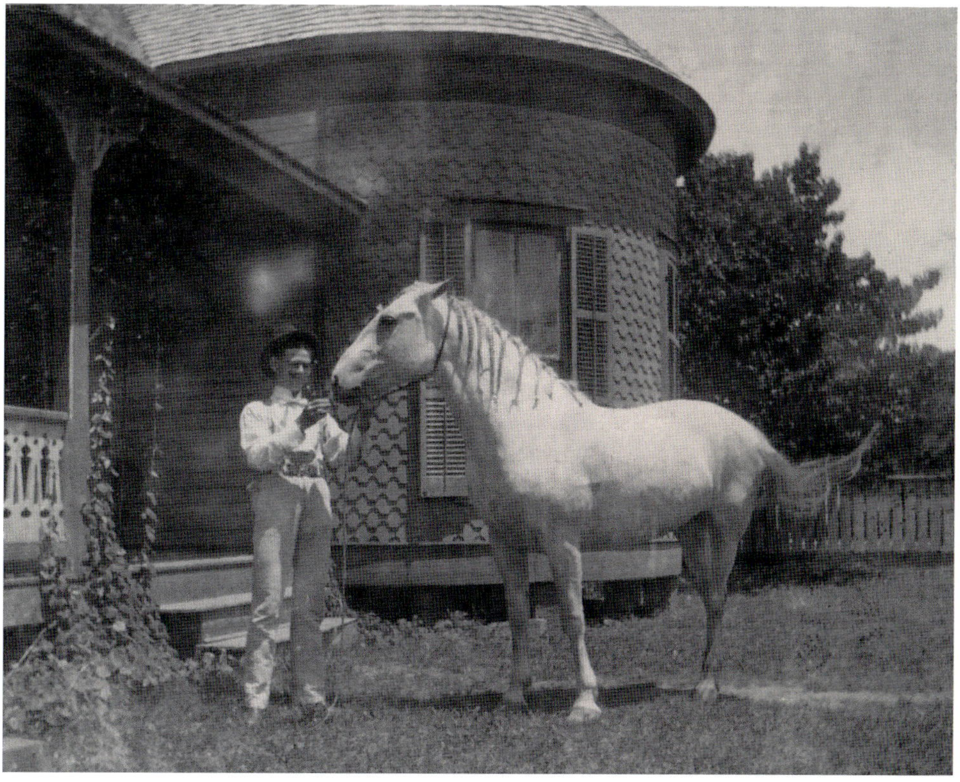

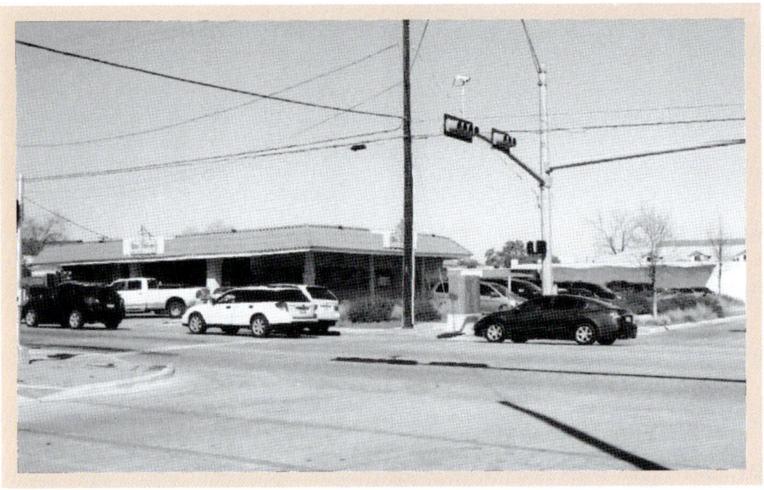

From 1895 to 1957, the Georgetown Public School occupied the 1100 block between University Avenue and Main Street. Several generations attended, loved, and told stories about the school. Donnell Bishop, who was an elementary student around 1920, remembered a rat infestation during which children were paid a penny per rat tail brought to school. Bishop's memory of the smell when the teacher tossed them into the coal-burning stove was still vivid after 90 years. This block today is home to commercial establishments. (Then image courtesy author's collection.)

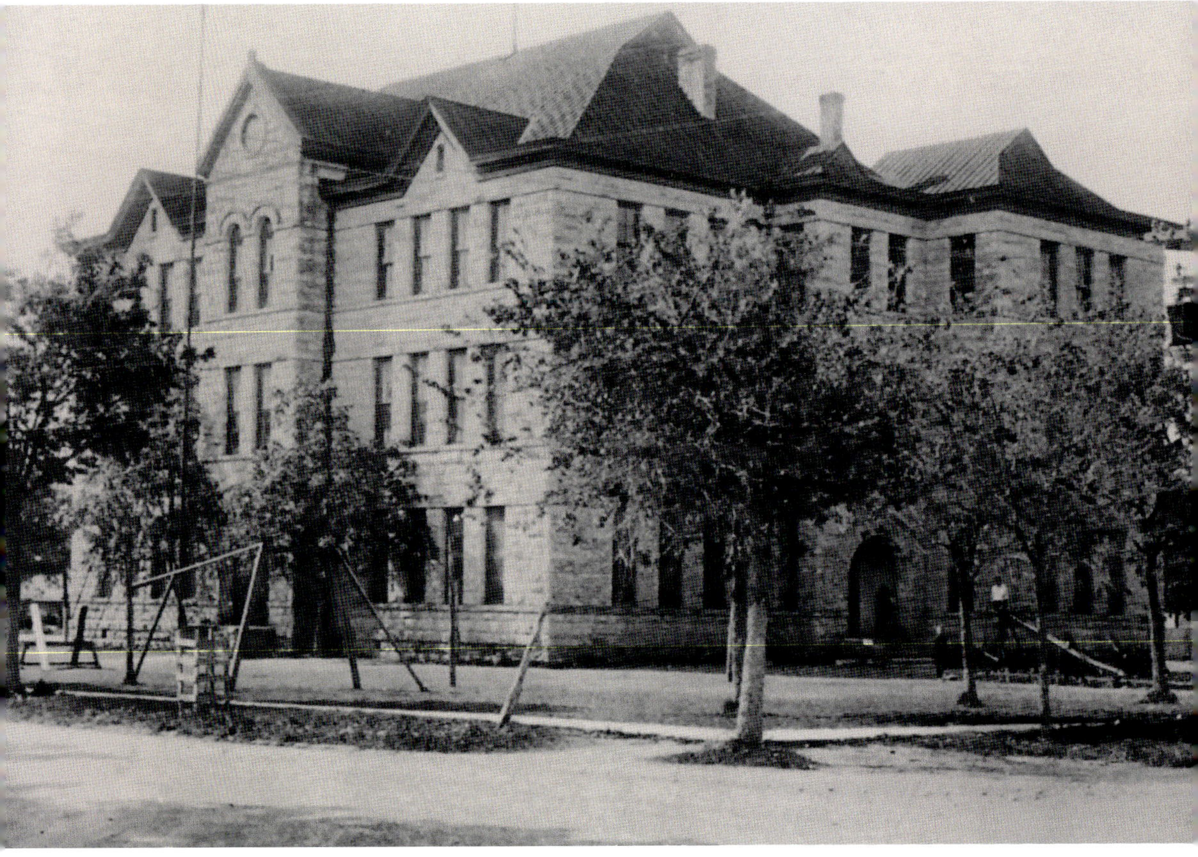

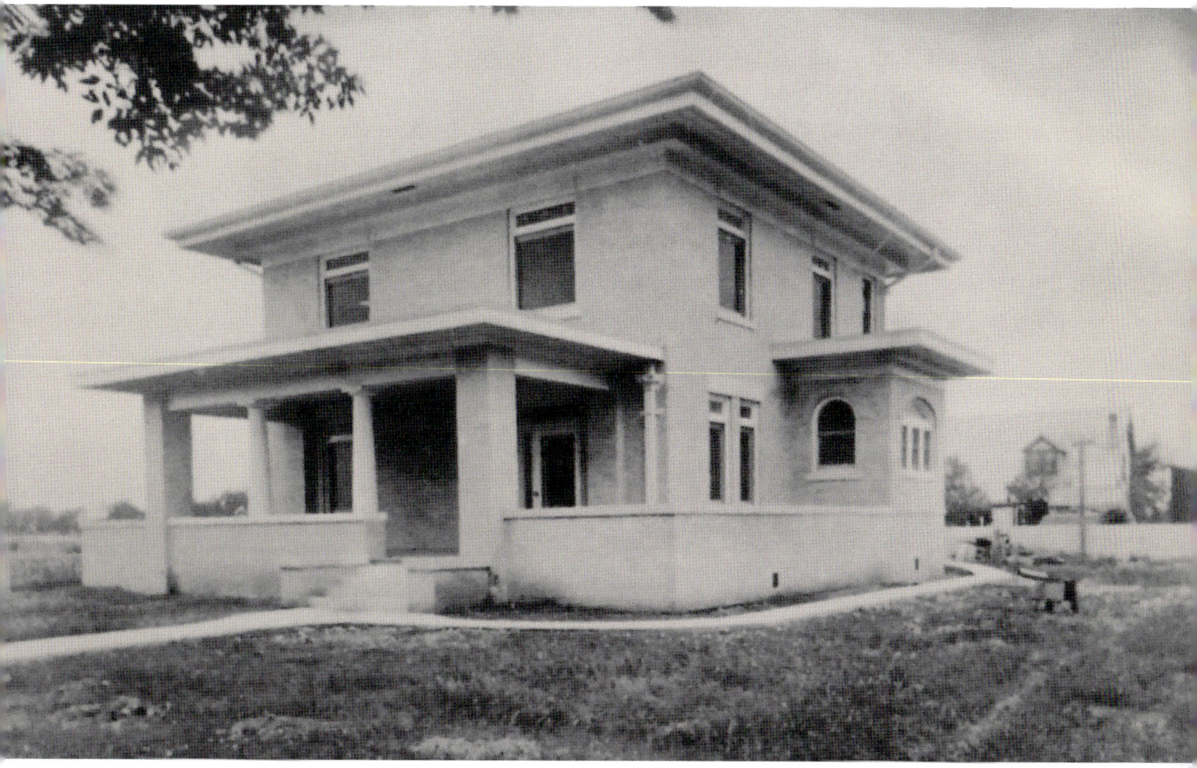

This handsome Prairie-style home was constructed in 1910 by master builder C.S. Belford for Judge Cooper Sansom at 1252 South Main Street. The home is included in the Belford National Register Historic District. Of the 81 homes in the district, over 30 were built by Belford Lumber. Sansom was a prominent newspaperman, attorney, state representative, and district judge. Today, Main Street shows an interesting progression of early-20th-century residential building styles. (Then image courtesy Georgetown Heritage Society.)

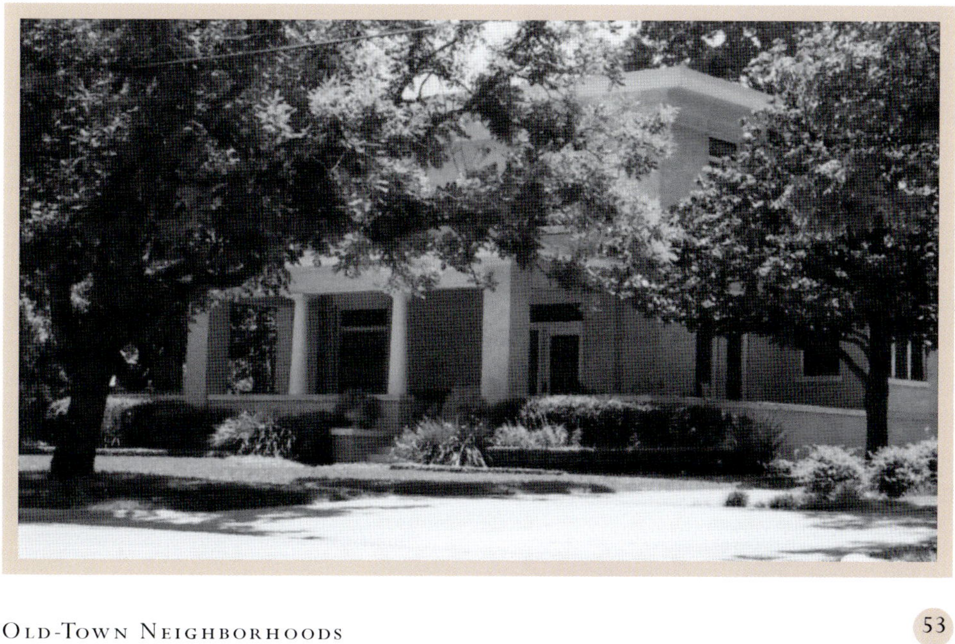

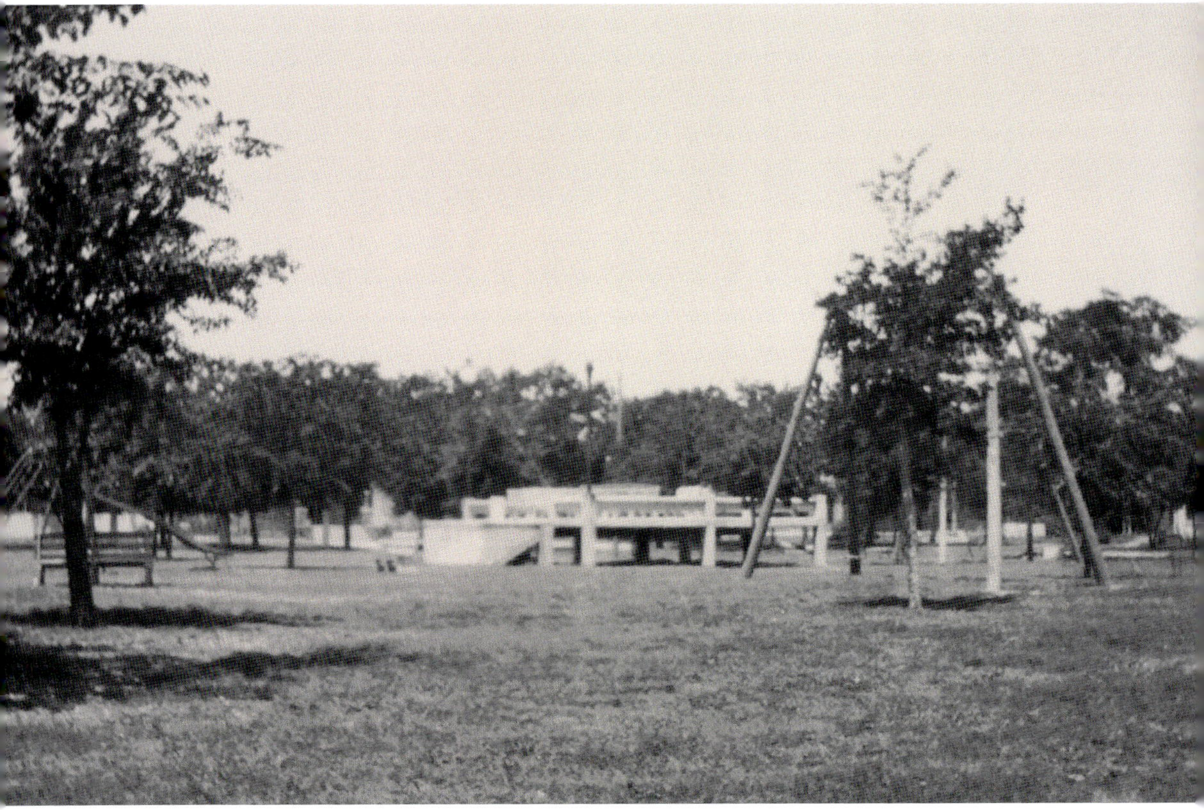

The north side of the 200 block of University Avenue was owned by the City of Georgetown for many years. A temporary school occupied the northwest corner in the early 1900s. Later, the entire block became a beautiful city park with play equipment and bandstand, pictured in this mid-1920s photograph. The large lot then became the site of the Wesleyan Retirement Home in 1962. Today, the same building houses offices. (Then image by Luis W. Atlee; courtesy *Williamson County Sun*.)

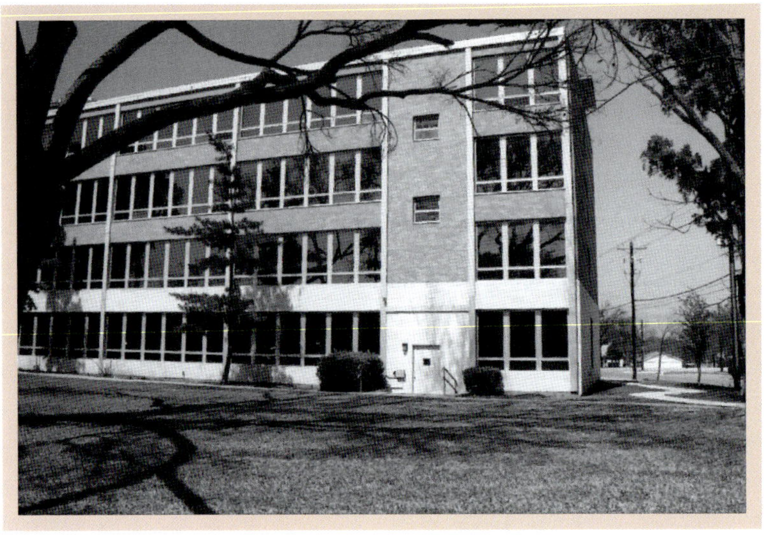

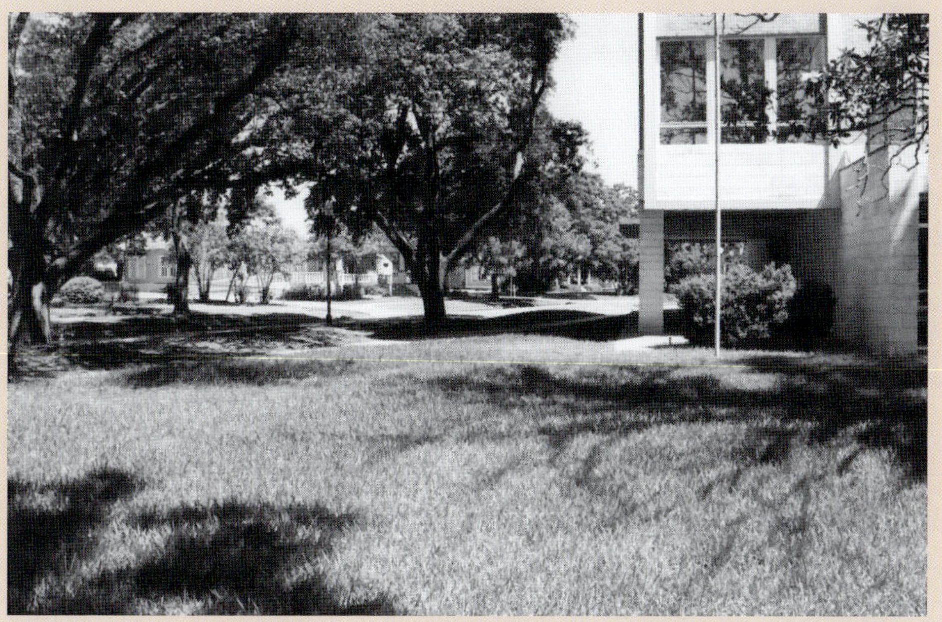

One very interesting installation at the City Play Park was this World War I vintage cannon, presented to the City of Georgetown by the local Abe Harrison American Legion Post, which was organized in 1926. The cannon occupied the southwest corner of the park, and its plaque read, "Dedicated to the boys that died." Today's view shows the corner where the cannon stood. (Then image by Luis W. Atlee; courtesy William Atlee.)

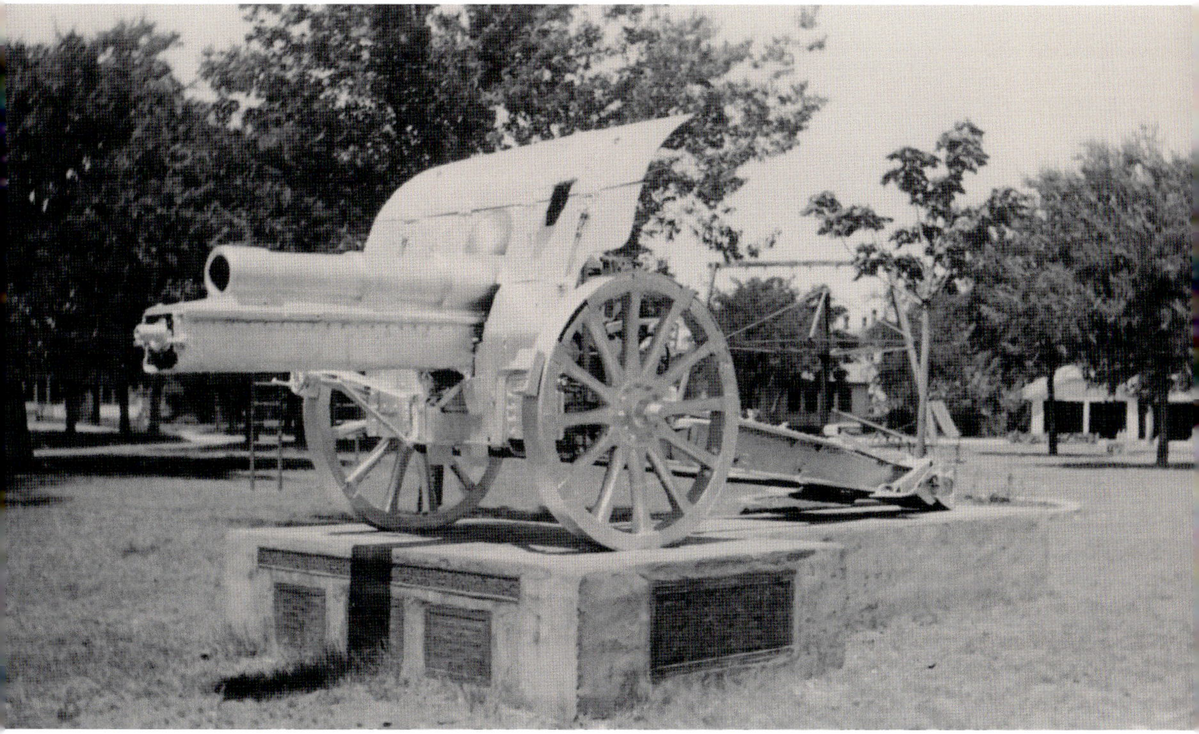

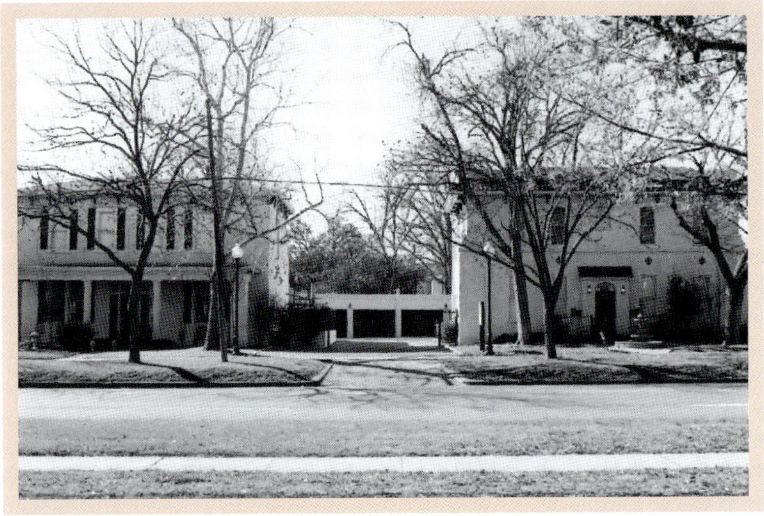

The two handsome homes at 514 and 516 East University Avenue were originally one structure: the home of Dudley Hiram Snyder, built around 1880. Dudley and his brother John Wesley Snyder ran a huge cattle operation and stock farm in Georgetown. They and their brother Thomas, in Liberty Hill, gave generously to Southwestern University in its formative years. The home was split into two residences in 1925. (Then image courtesy Georgetown Heritage Society.)

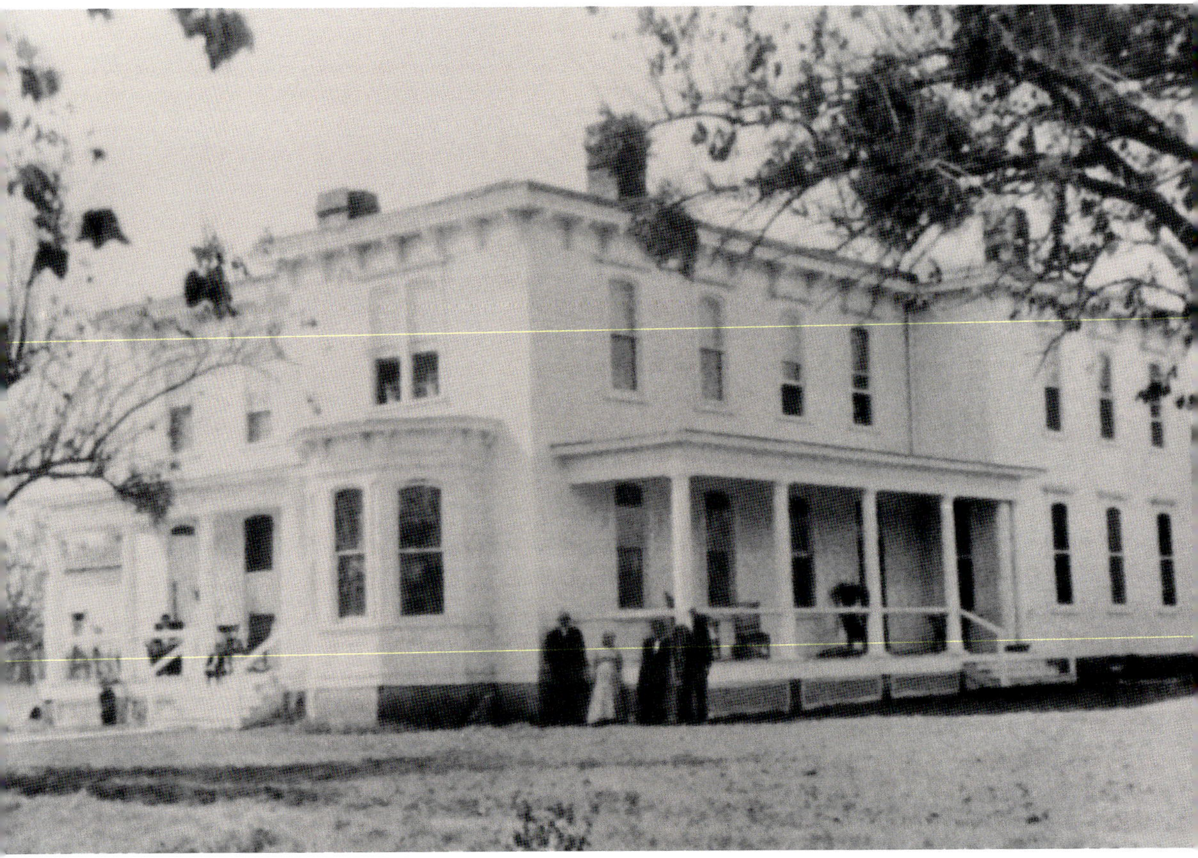

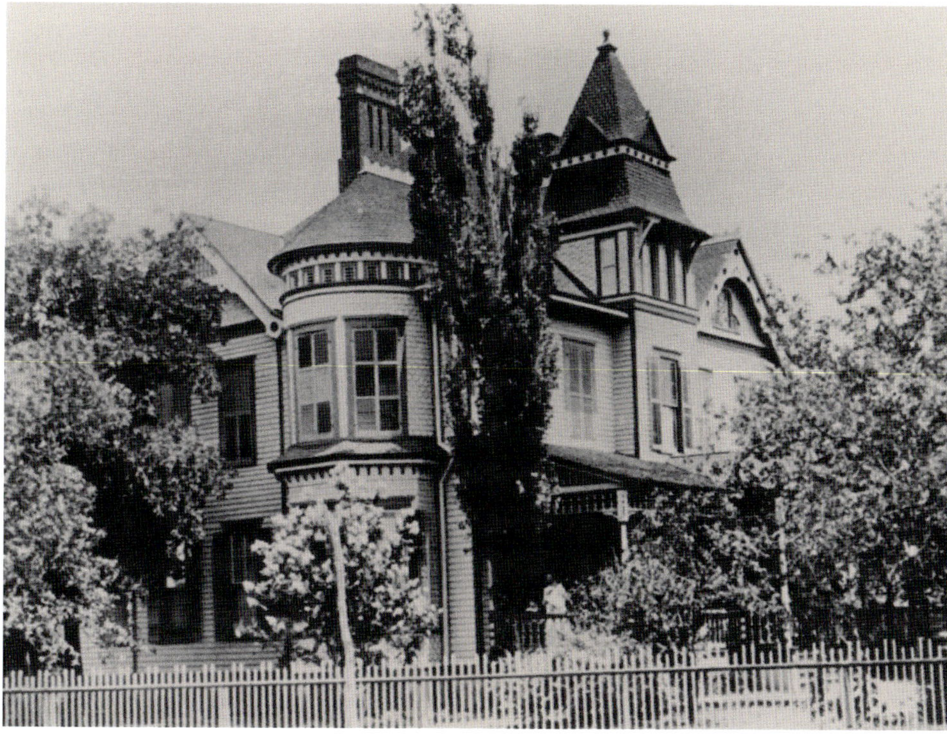

Early Georgetown merchant John Leavell built this elaborate Queen Anne home at 803 College Street around 1880. Visible all the way down Eighth Street from the square, it seemed to keep watch over both downtown and the old Southwestern campus, to the west and south. In 1893, Lula Holland Leavell and two daughters began a literary club here, which eventually became the Woman's Club and is still active in Georgetown today. The home was remodeled extensively in 2010. (Then image courtesy author's collection.)

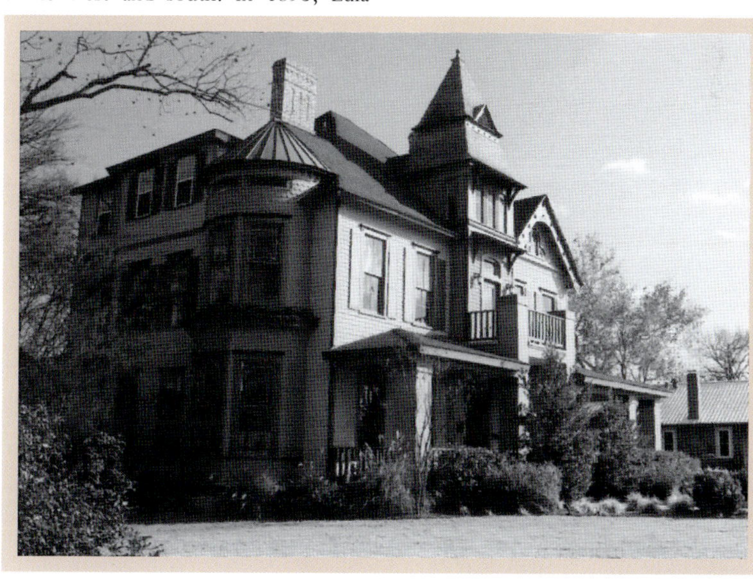

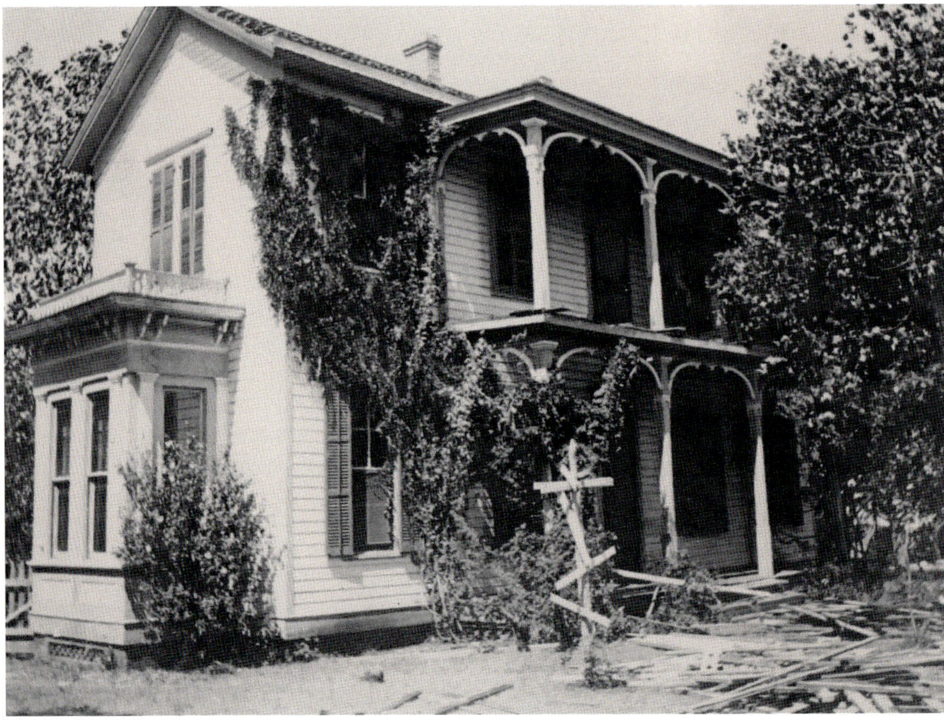

This home at 303 East Ninth Street, built in 1879, is shown in this early image during a 1911 remodeling by Belford Lumber Company for a new owner, John N. Ellyson Sr. Living elsewhere during the remodeling, Ellyson passed away before ever residing here. Ellyson and, later, his son John N. Jr. were owners of Guarantee Abstract, now Georgetown Title Company. The home is still owned by descendants of the Ellyson family today. (Then image courtesy Johnson/Ellyson Estate.)

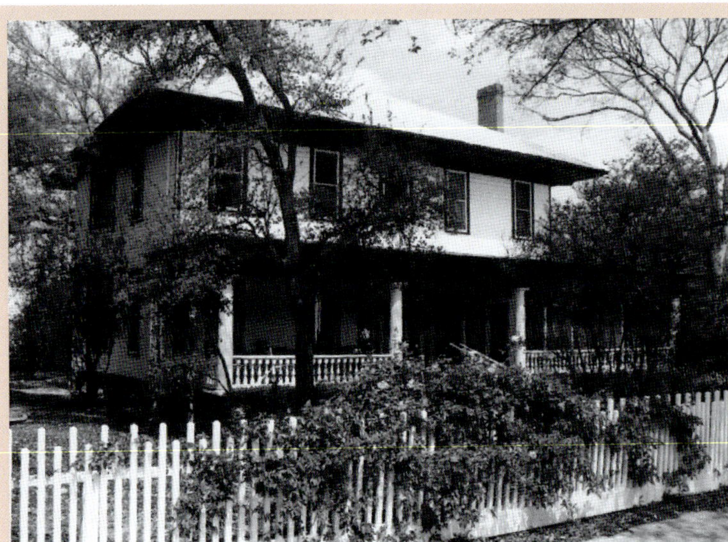

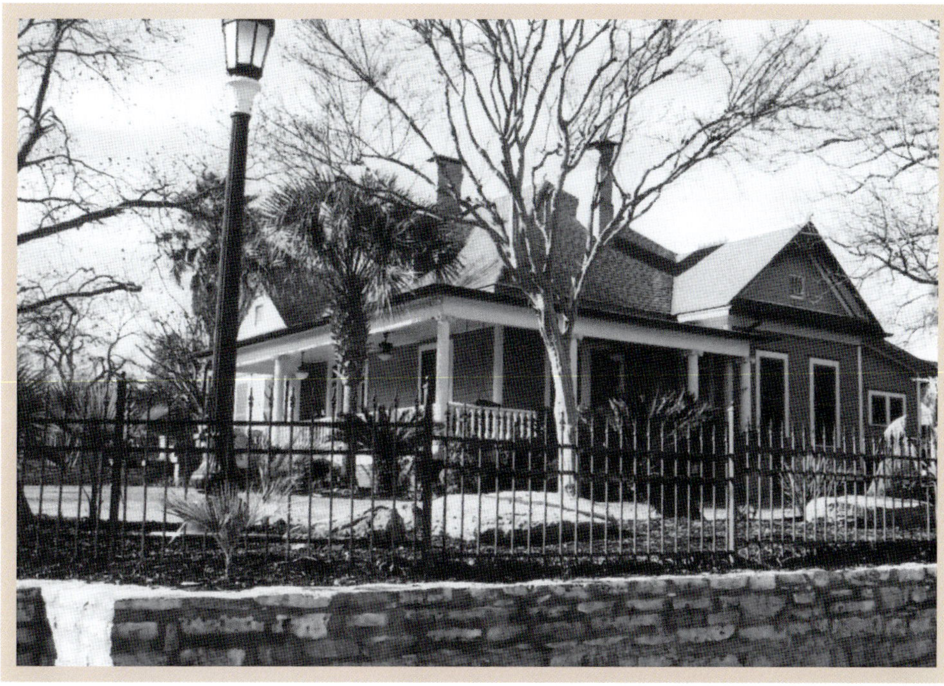

This historical photograph shows the Will and Mary Leake home at 313 East Seventh Street. The image was used in a c. 1910 promotional booklet, which described Georgetown as "the ideal residence town of the southwest." The homes featured in the booklet were examples of the finest in town. This home blended Victorian and Neoclassical Revival styles. In recent years, two successive owners have done comprehensive renovations, making this a truly stunning residence. (Then image courtesy author's collection.)

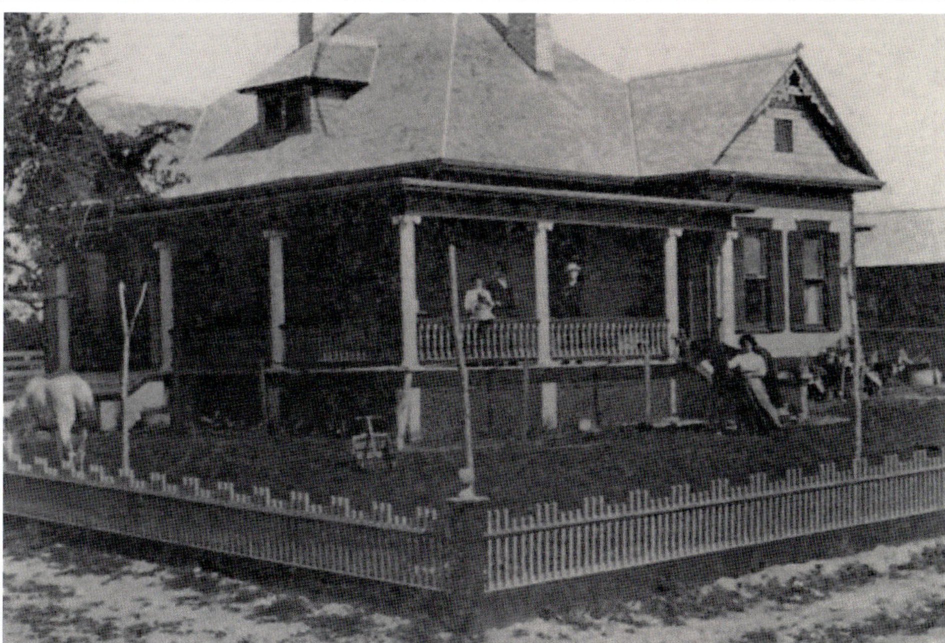

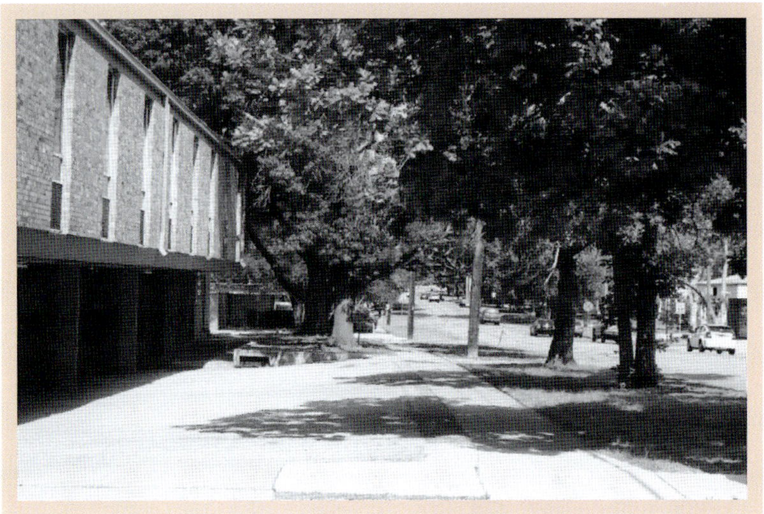

In 1918, local women opened Georgetown's first hospital, King's Daughters Sanitarium. Martin Hospital opened in 1923 and is shown here with its distinctive front steps at 605 East University Avenue. Southwestern University's main building is visible to the east. In 1957, Drs. H.R. Gaddy and Douglas Benold partnered as owners. Later, a new clinic and hospital wing were added to the facility. Today's view shows the former hospital wing attached on the west side of the original building. (Then image courtesy Johnson/Ellyson Estate.)

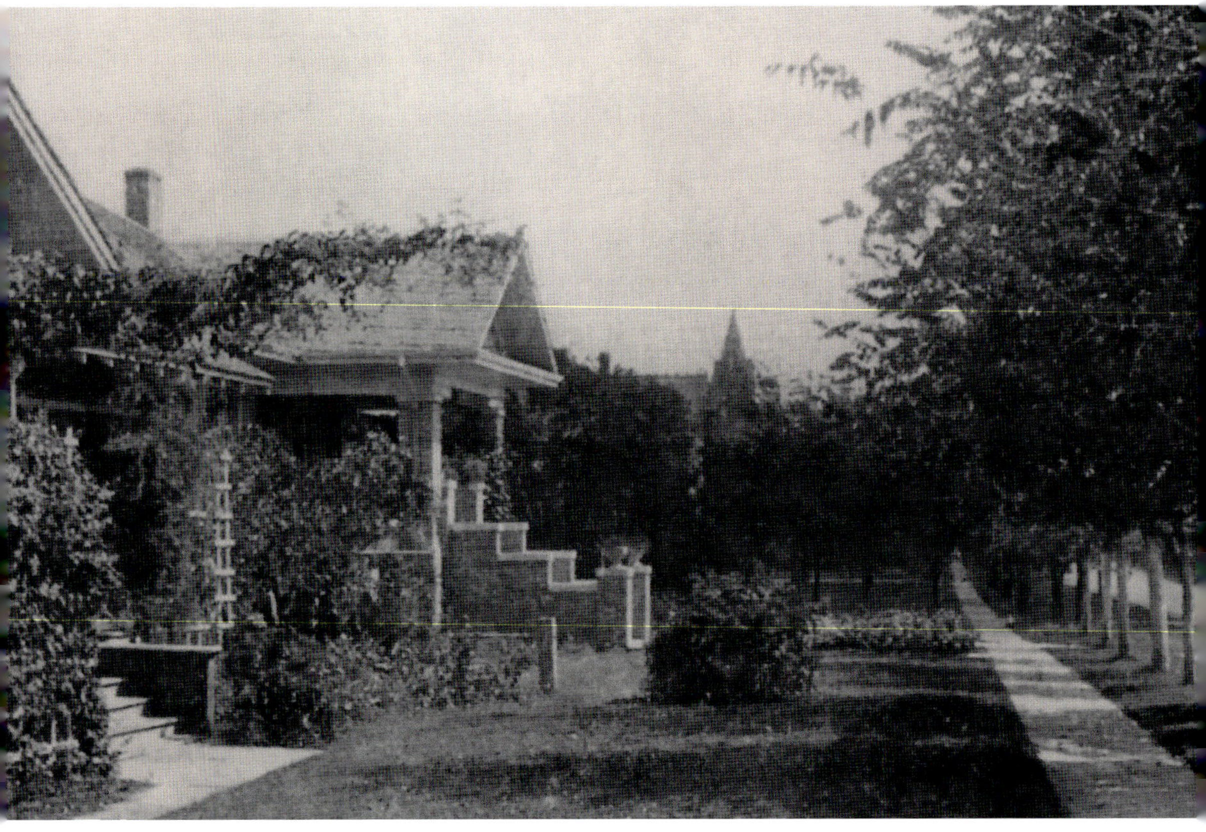

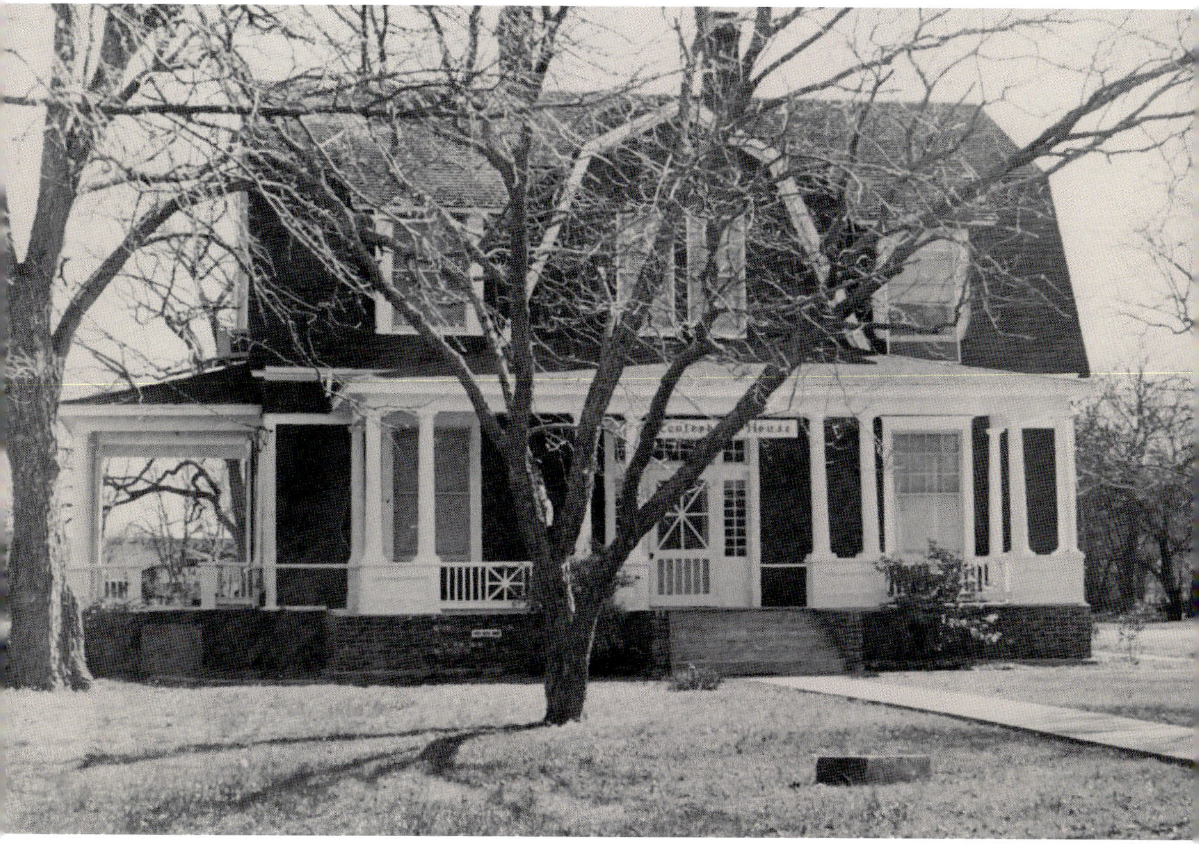

The striking 1910 Daughtrey House at 1316 East University was purchased by the Episcopal Church, which moved its sanctuary just west of the house in 1955. They called the home the Canterbury House. The 300-pound concrete block out front may have been a "mounting stone," allowing riders to more easily mount their horses. The home was moved off the site so the church could build a larger sanctuary, shown in today's photograph. (Then image courtesy *Williamson County Sun*.)

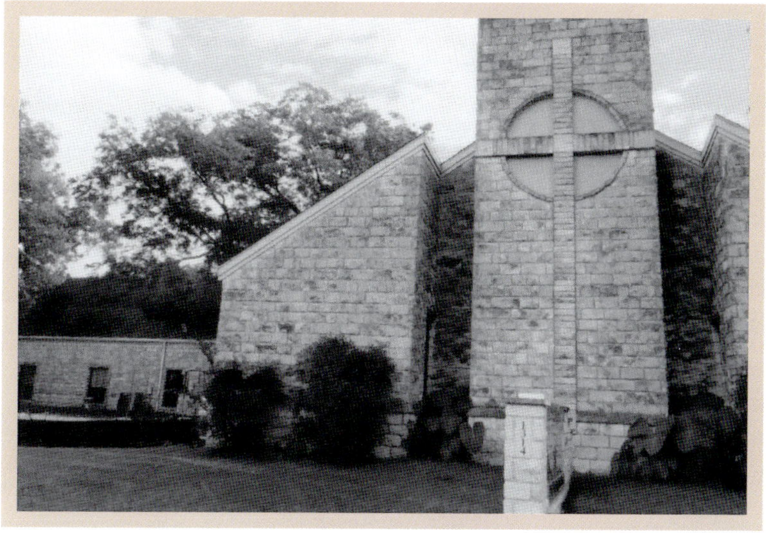

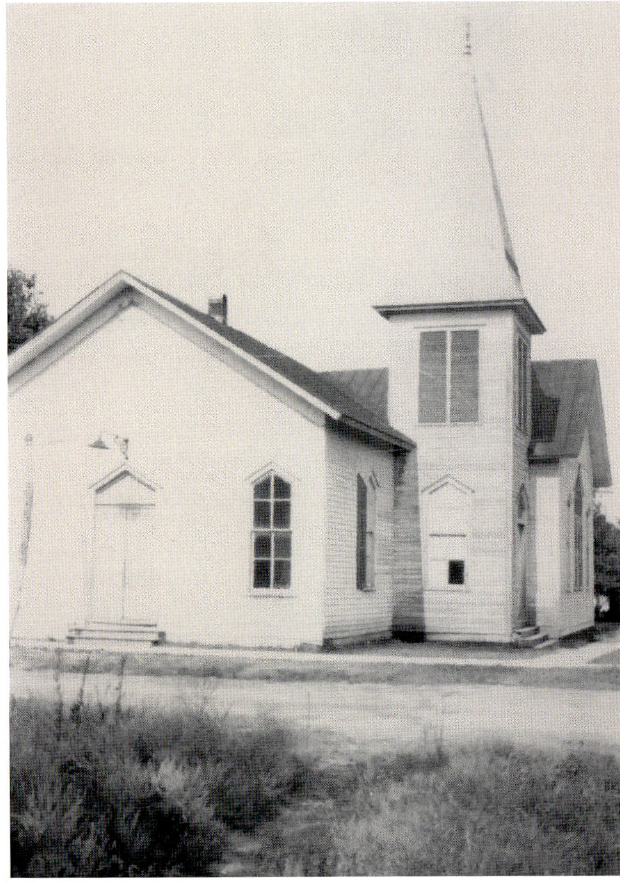

The Baptist Church was organized in Georgetown in 1866. In 1879, Baptist evangelist W.E. Penn claimed 447 conversions at a two-week camp meeting at today's San Gabriel Park. This Missionary Baptist Church was built in 1880 on the northeast corner of Sixth and Church Streets, pictured in the mid-1920s. Today, the lot is residential. A new church was built in 1926, now known as Main Street Baptist Church. (Then image by Luis W. Atlee; courtesy *Williamson County Sun*.)

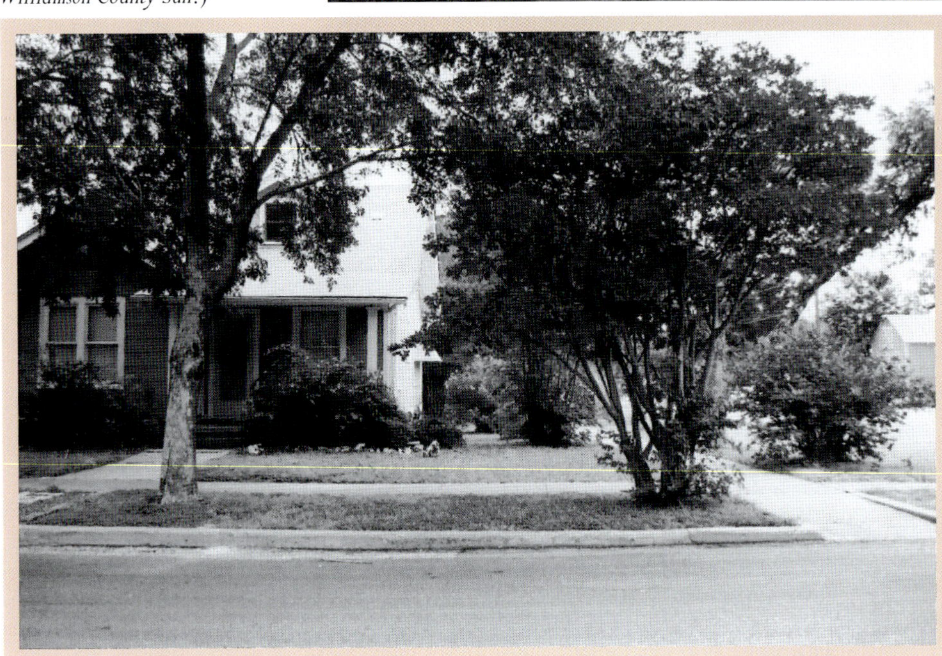

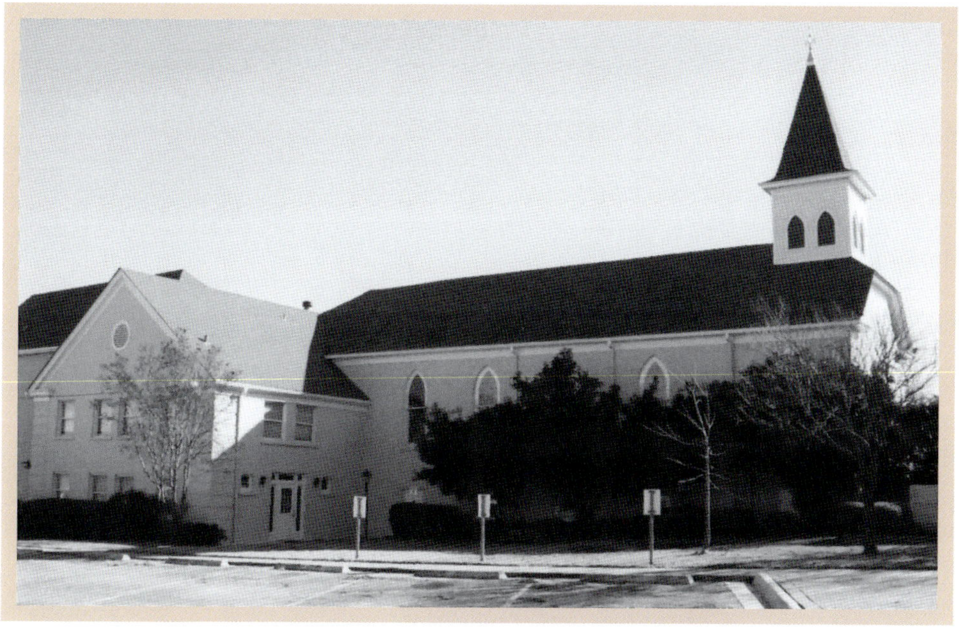

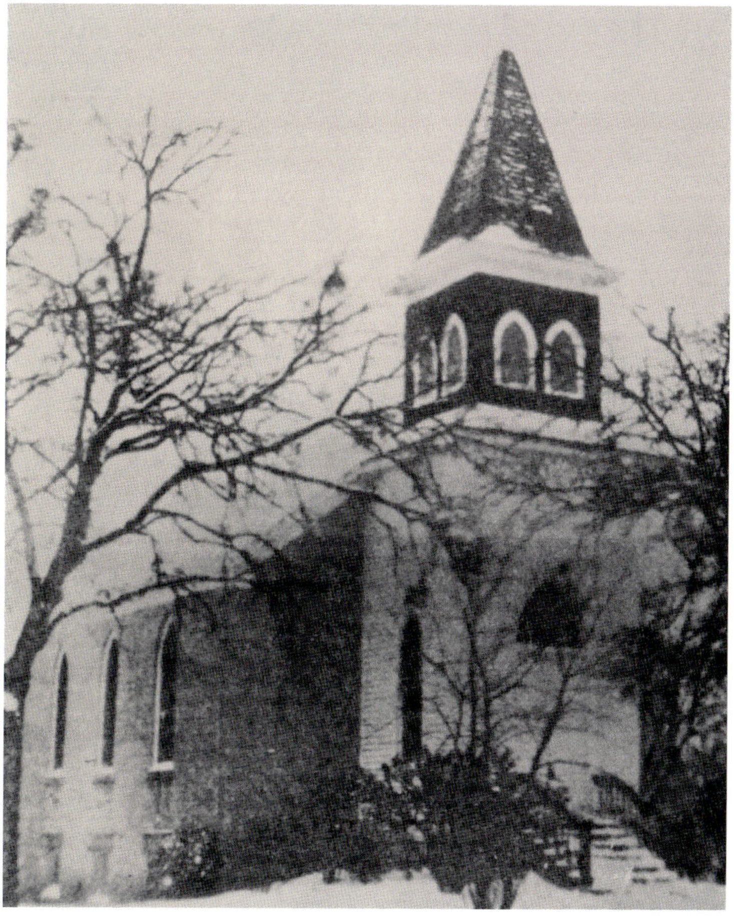

First Presbyterian is Georgetown's oldest church, organized in 1854 and pictured here around 1950. Their first building was also used by the Georgetown Male and Female Academy, which is believed to be the town's first school. Wood from the first building was used in constructing this church, completed in 1873 at 703 South Church Street. Enlarged several times, the original part of the structure has been preserved. (Then image courtesy *Williamson County Sun*.)

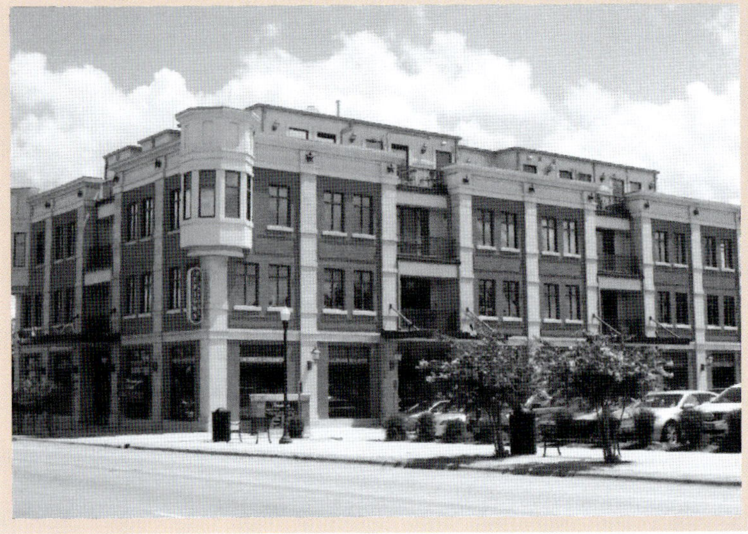

Austin Avenue between the square and the South San Gabriel River was primarily residential until the mid-20th century. In 1958, Bennie Draeger bought into this Ford dealership owned by Bud Fowler (earlier owned by Grogan Lord). Draeger and his sons James and Ron continued to use this c. 1940 building at 501 South Austin Avenue as part of their growing business. The dealership was sold in 2001. Today, the Tamiro Building occupies this site. (Then image courtesy *Williamson County Sun*.)

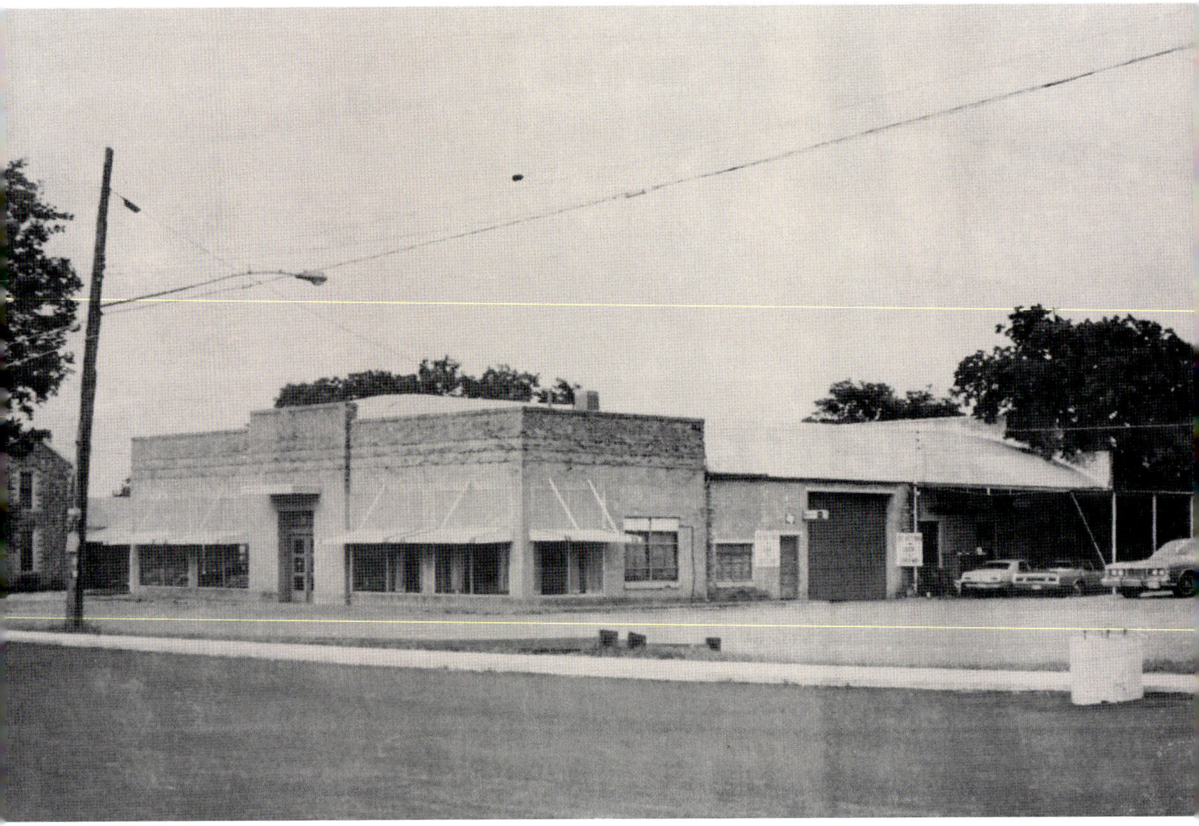

CHAPTER 5

SOUTHWESTERN UNIVERSITY

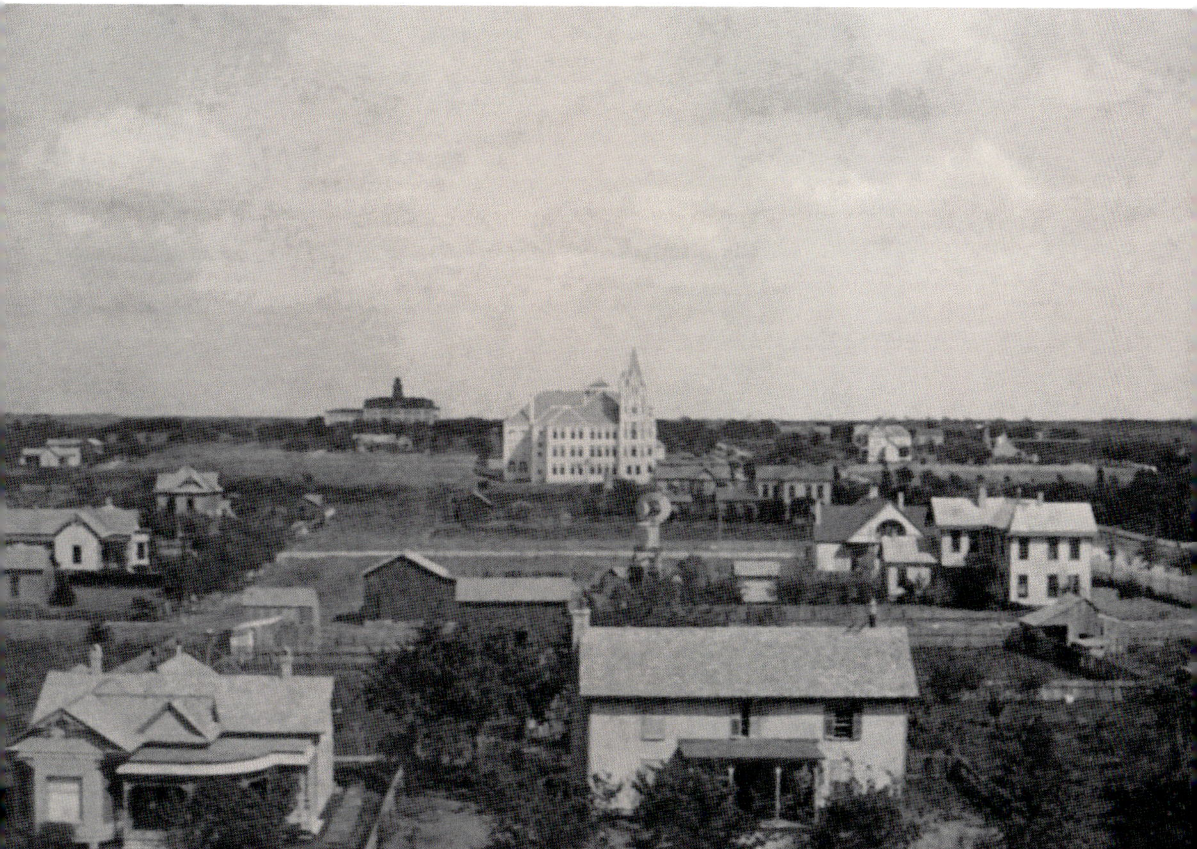

Photographed from the top of the original Southwestern University building around 1900, this view of the campus shows the Main Building shortly after its completion and the 1889 Ladies Annex in the background. These structures set the standard for the new campus with their fine architecture and impressive scale. (Courtesy Mike and Genie Vogler.)

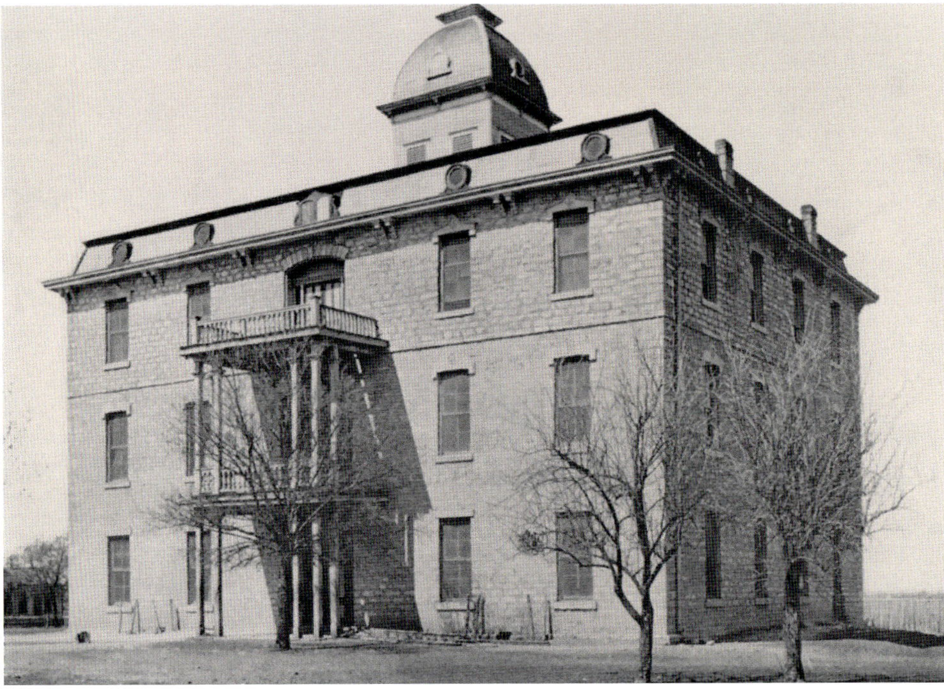

Southwestern's first campus opened in 1873 on the site of today's Williams Elementary School on University Avenue. Intended as Georgetown College, the 1870 building was offered as incentive to the Methodist Church to locate a college here. The campus grew to include numerous buildings, and two Methodist Churches built sanctuaries nearby in 1893 and 1906. The city purchased the property and constructed today's school in 1923; it served as Georgetown High School for five decades. (Then image courtesy author's collection.)

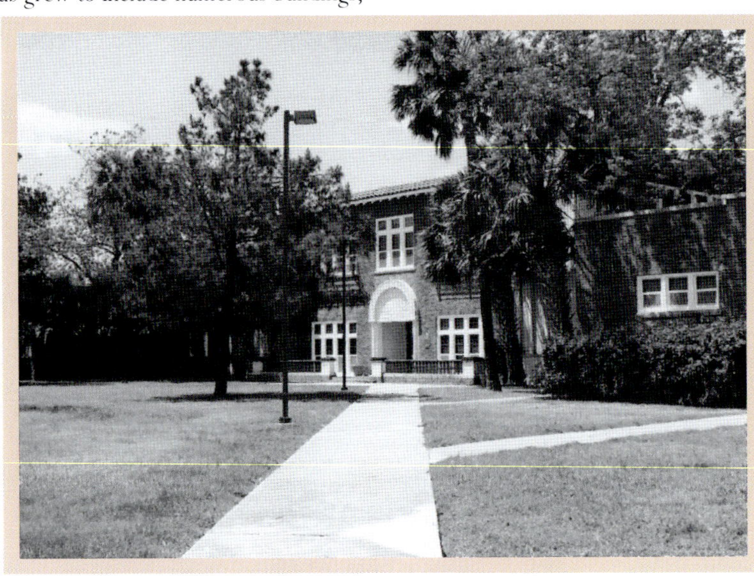

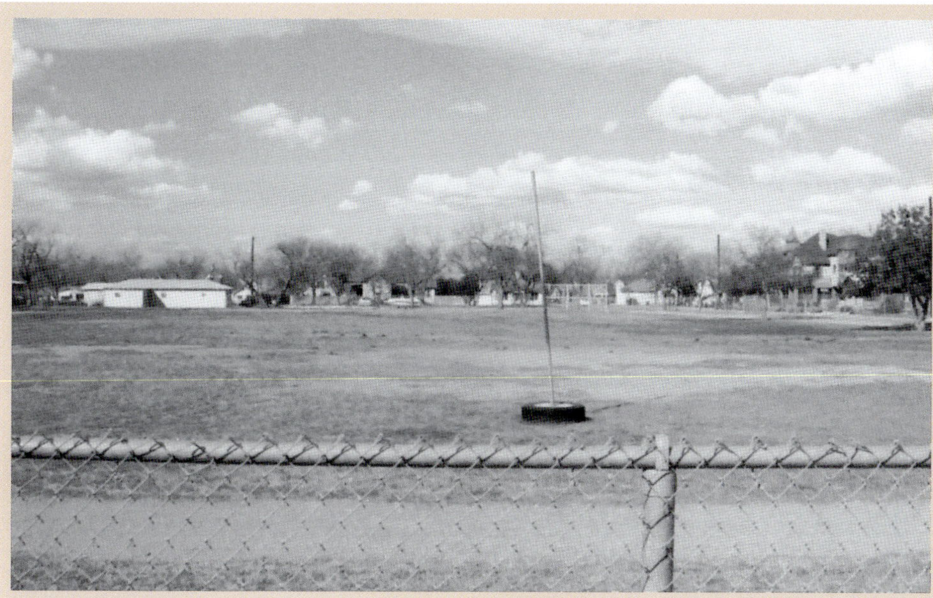

In 1885, Ann Giddings of Brenham donated funds to help build a dormitory, shown at center, offering free lodging for ministerial students and others needing financial help. To its left was a dining hall, and six cottages added still more student housing. In the background, at right, is the Leavell house, still standing today at Eighth and College Streets. Williams Elementary athletic field and outbuildings have replaced the university's structures. (Then image courtesy Southwestern University, Special Collections, Georgetown, Texas.)

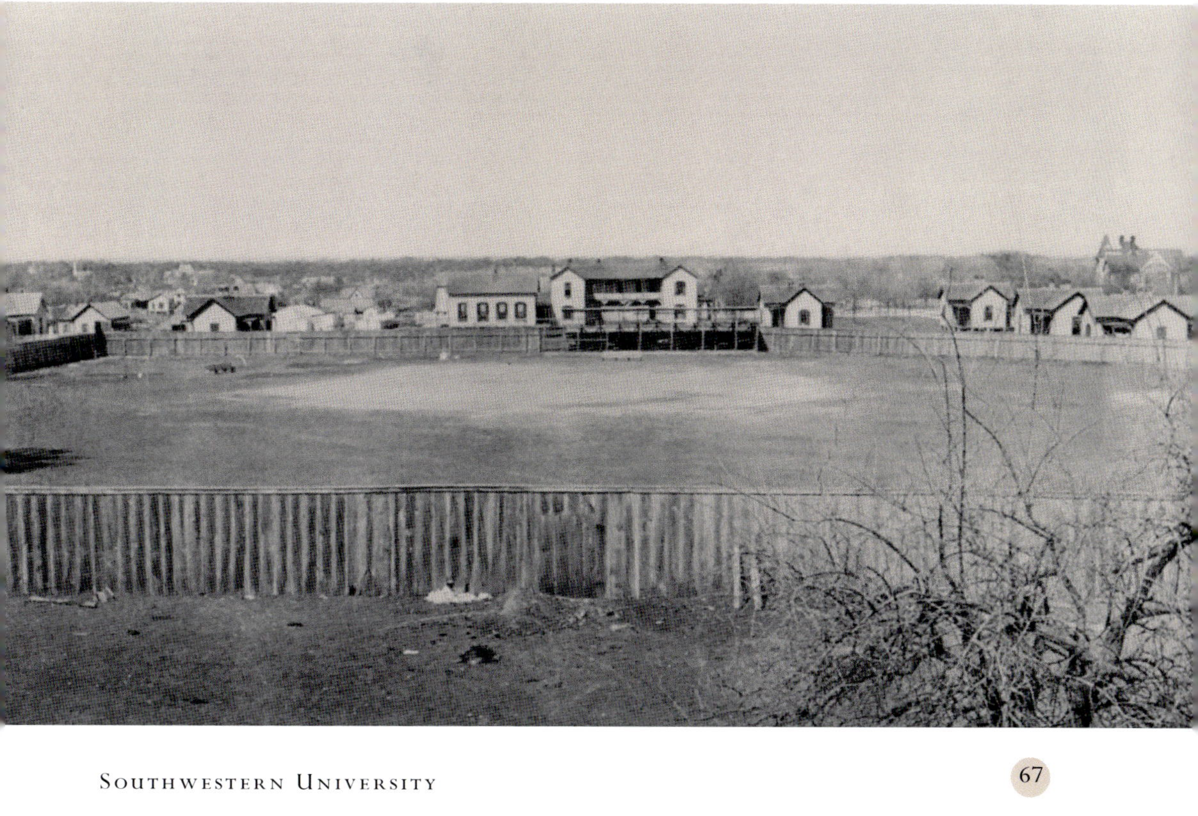

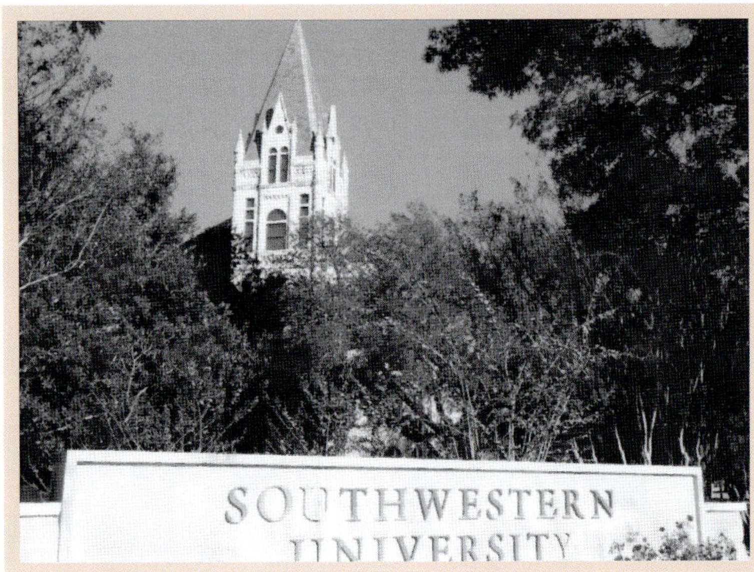

The new Romanesque-style Main Building opened on Southwestern's present campus in 1900. In a town of just 2,700 inhabitants, this elegant, solid structure was truly impressive. The corner tower literally holds history on its walls. In the early 1900s, students often climbed secretly to the top of the tower to sign their names on the interior walls. In recent years, seniors have added their names on "Tower Signing Day" alongside those of their historical counterparts. (Then image courtesy Johnson/Ellyson Estate.)

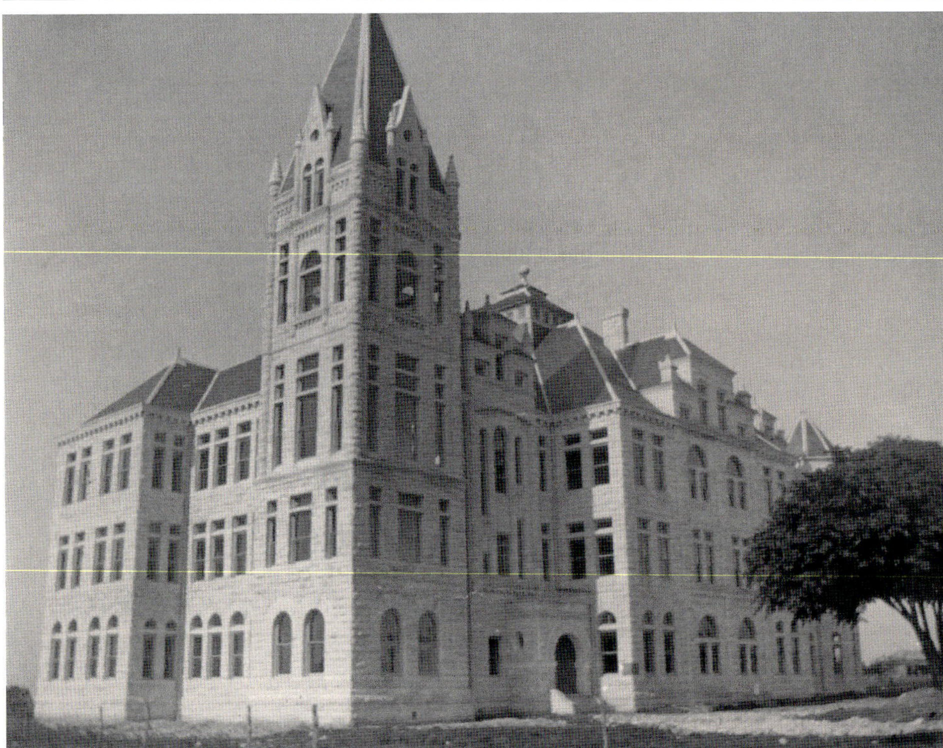

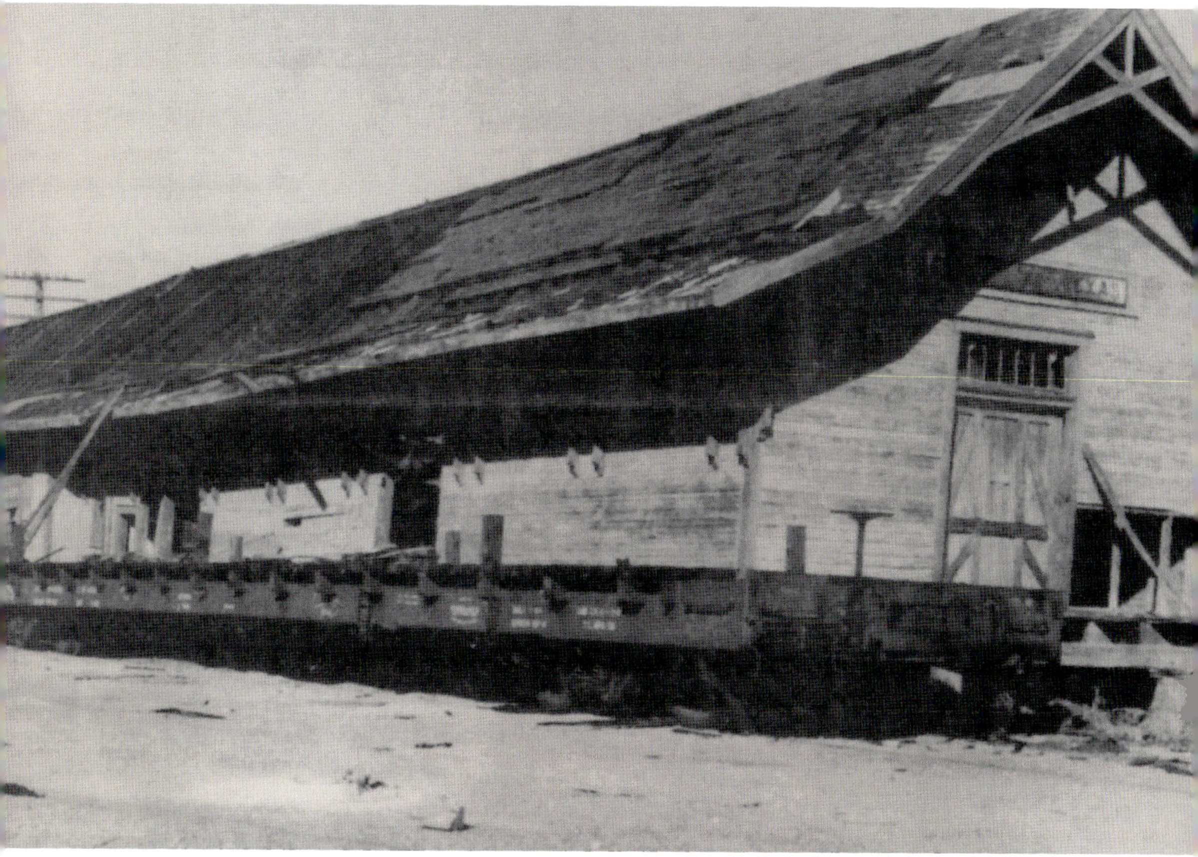

Though not a part of Southwestern's campus, the close proximity to the Missouri-Kansas-Texas (Katy) Railroad station greatly impacted campus life. For about half a century, passenger trains transported students, families, sports teams, and tourists to and from Georgetown over the rails. This old photograph shows the depot being removed in 1971. Its location south of Seventh Street and west of Maple Street is now vacant. (Then image courtesy *Williamson County Sun*.)

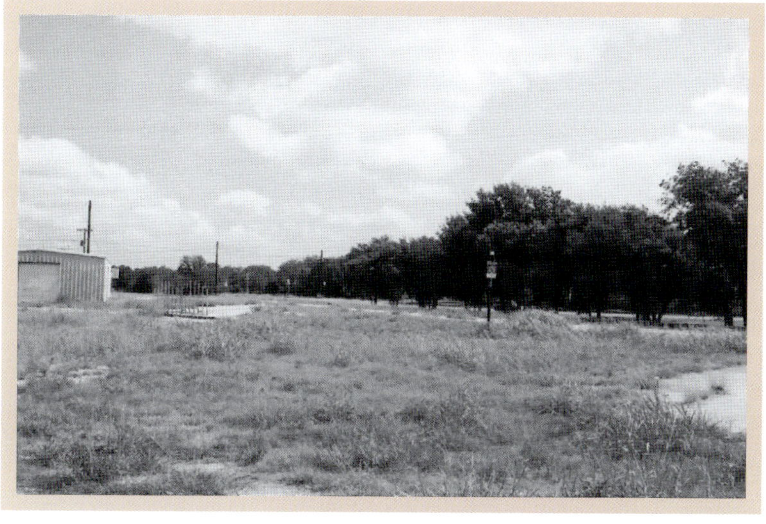

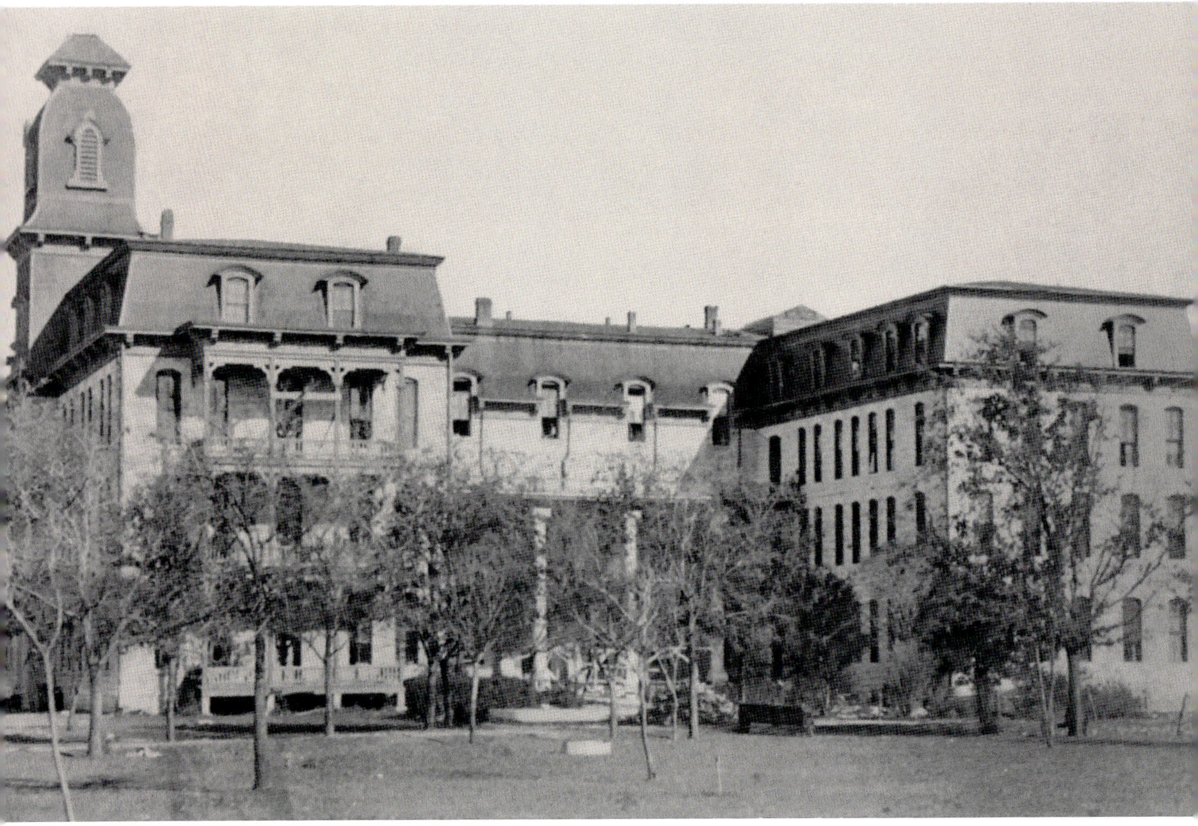

In 1878, Southwestern began its Young Ladies School. Replacing a smaller women's building, the very impressive Ladies Annex, pictured, was the first university structure on the present campus, opening in 1889. Sadly, the building was destroyed by fire in January 1925. All 200 girls escaped, owing to the composure and leadership of Laura Kuykendall, dean of women, who directed them to safety. The building was located close to today's Brown-Cody Residence Hall. (Then image courtesy author's collection.)

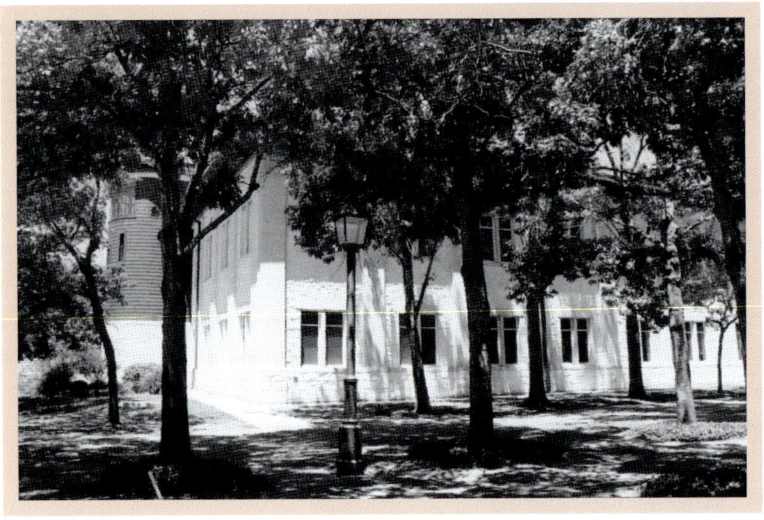

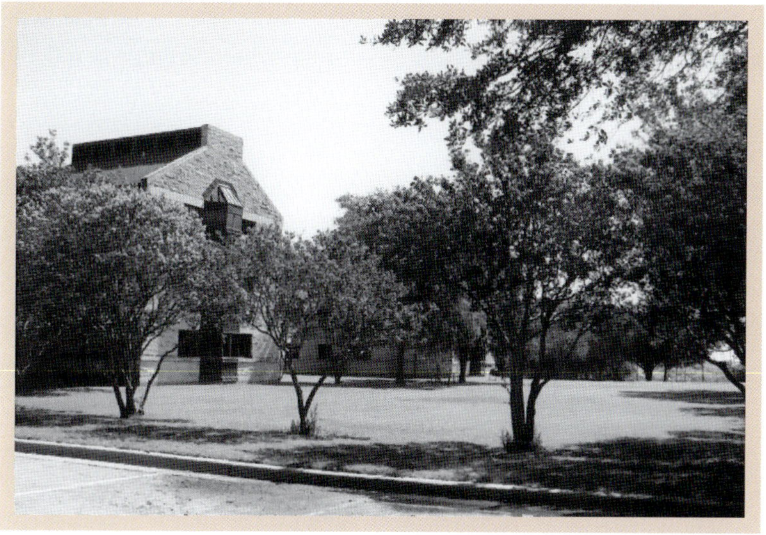

Within days of the disastrous fire at the Ladies Annex, plans were under way to immediately replace it. The emotional impact of the fire brought forth monetary donations from townspeople, students, and other donors, so Laura Kuykendall Hall was finished posthaste. It was a lovely building, much like grand old hotels, with an airy, expansive lobby filled with large windows and comfortable furnishings. Today's photograph shows Maybee Residence Hall in approximately the same position. (Then image courtesy author's collection.)

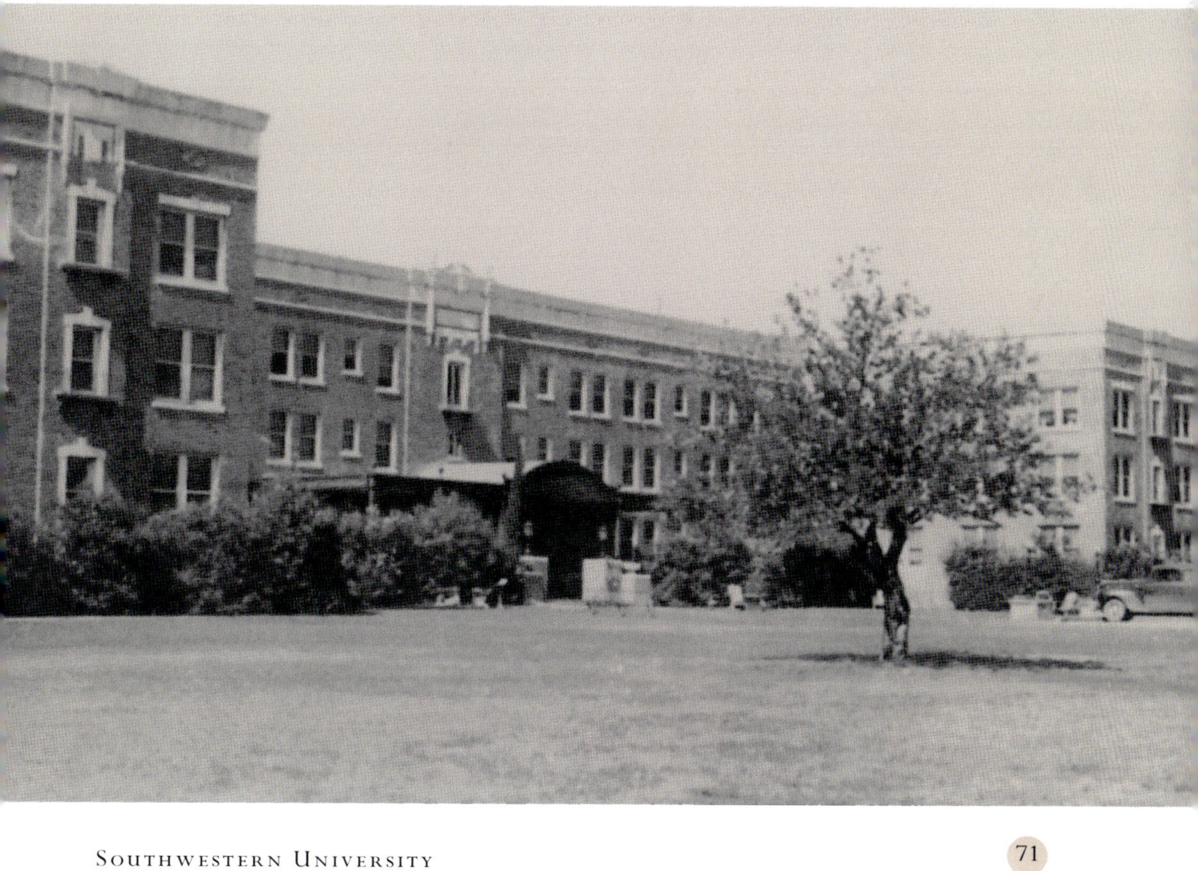

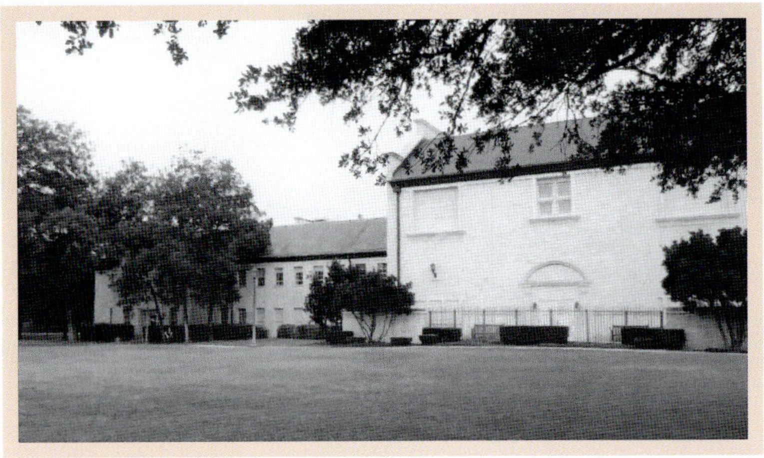

Much of Southwestern's campus is built on land gifted to the university by John Wesley Snyder and brother Dudley in 1887 as the site for the Ladies Annex. The Snyders' large stock farm was located in this area and eastward, and the J.W. Snyder residence, built around 1880, was part of the gift and is today the site of the fine arts building. The home served as the university president's home and then functioned as a student residence until 1955. (Then image courtesy Georgetown Heritage Society.)

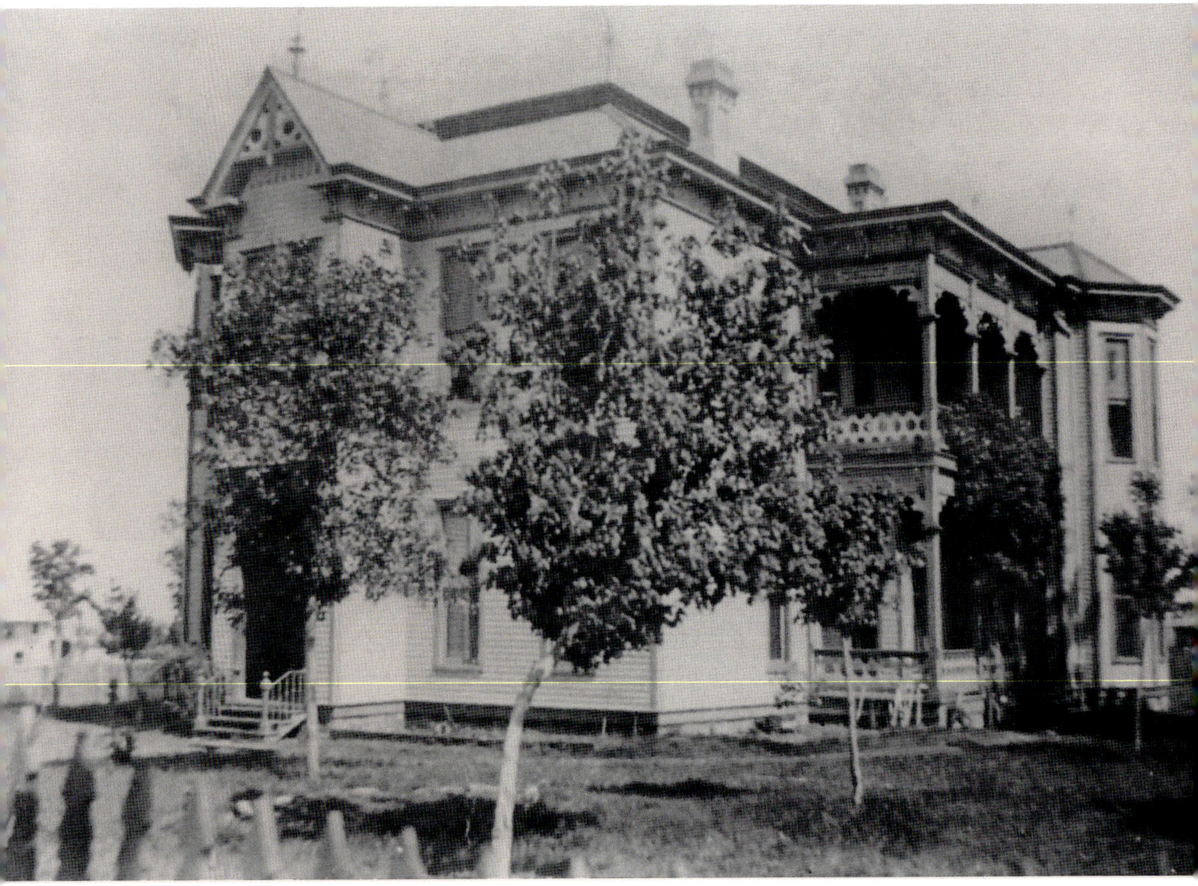

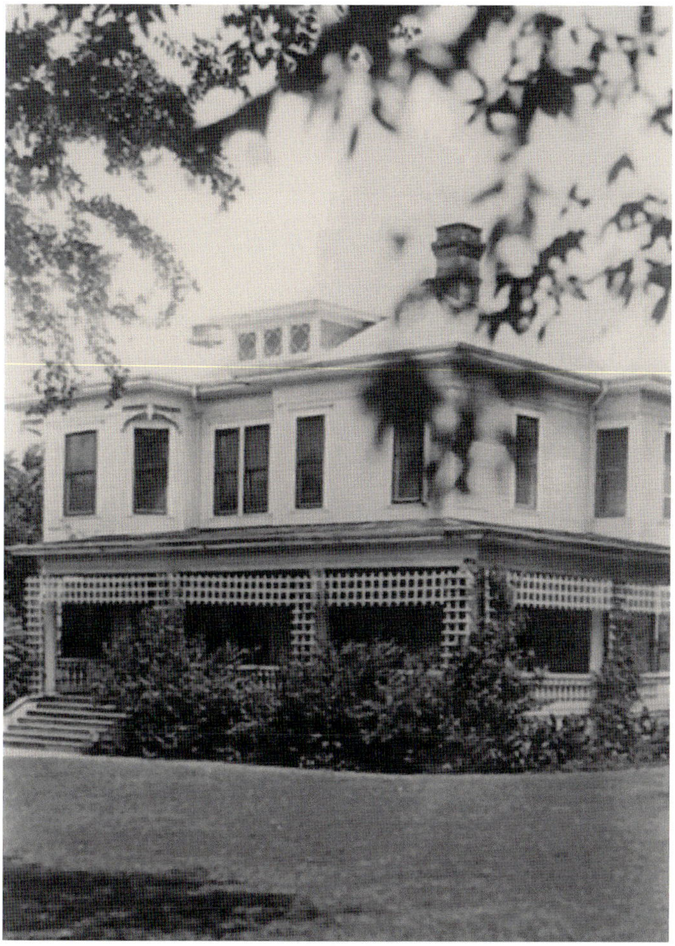

Prominent businessman and Georgetown mayor C.S. Griffith built this home just west of the Snyders in 1905. After the Ladies Annex burned, displaced women were housed at the Snyder house, and Southwestern purchased Griffith's residence as the new president's home. It was moved just east of Kuykendall Hall in the early 1950s and served as the president's home until 1962. It was moved off campus in 1986 but was destroyed by fire soon after. (Then image courtesy Georgetown Heritage Society.)

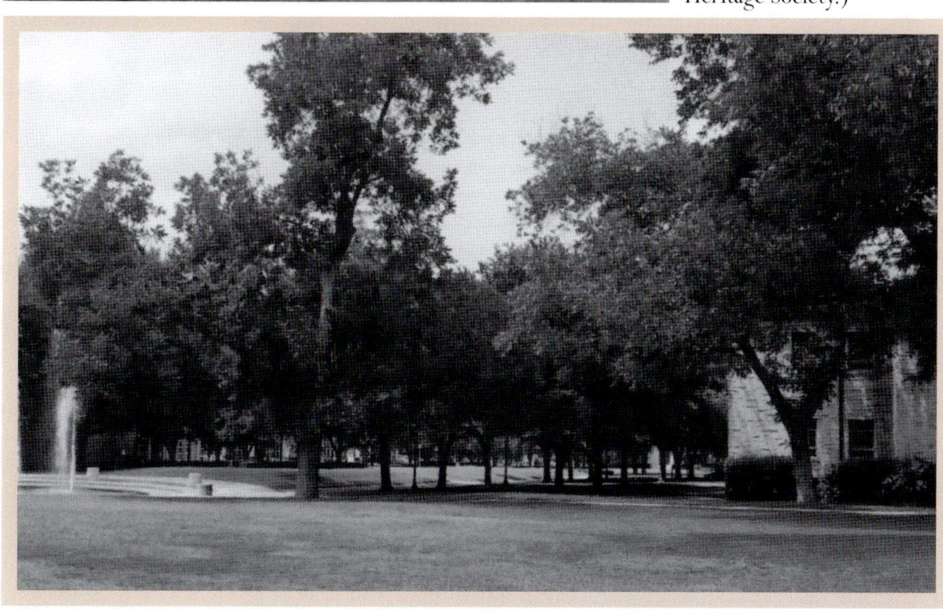

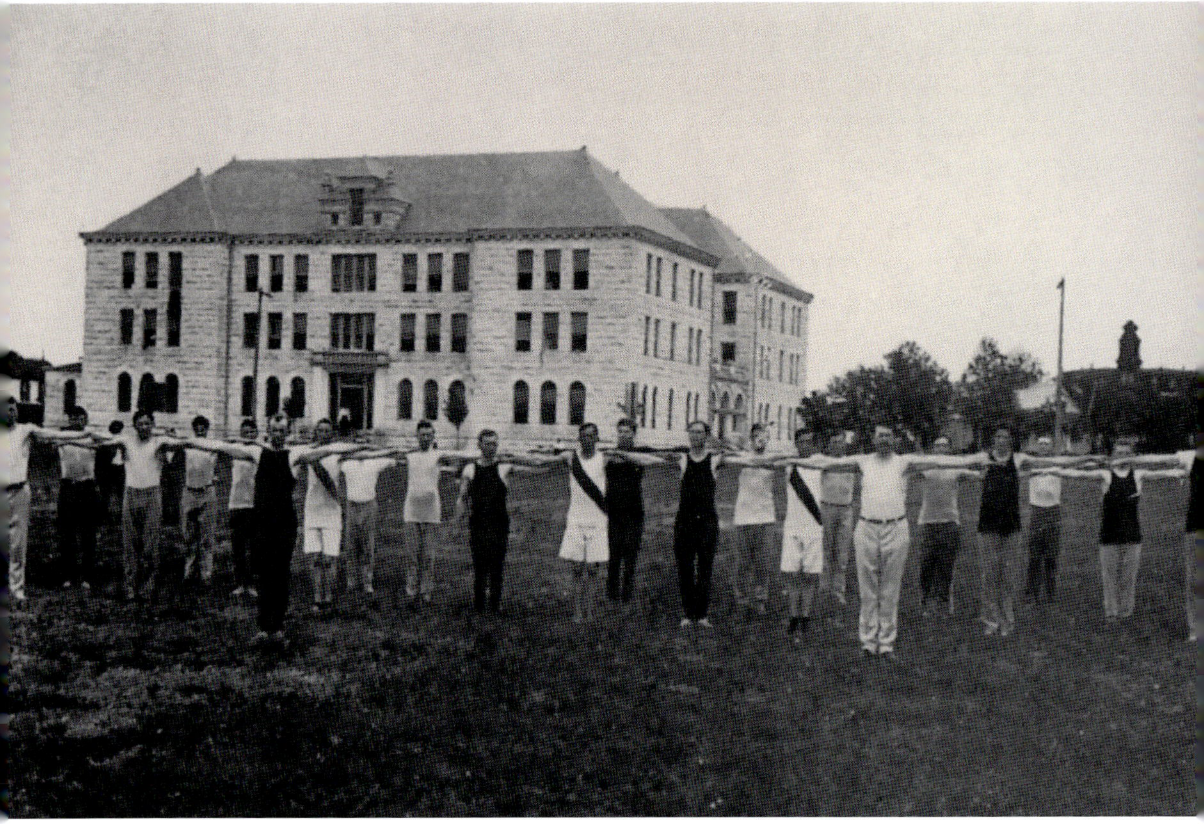

The third building constructed on the new campus was Mood Hall, opening in 1908 as a men's dormitory. According to historian William B. Jones, it was built with modern conveniences, including electric lights, steam heat, and indoor restrooms. This old photograph of a men's "gymnasium class" appeared in the 1911 Southwestern yearbook. Today, this side of Mood Hall is substantially obscured by the Wilhelmina Cullen Admission Center. (Then image courtesy Southwestern University, Georgetown, Texas.)

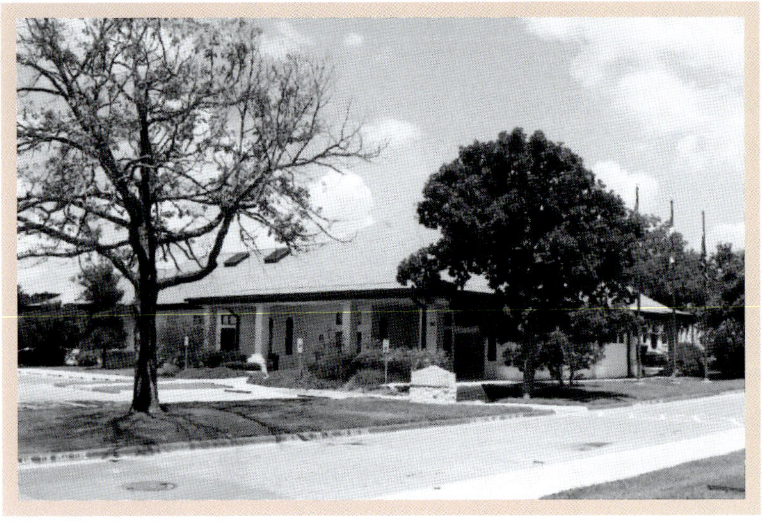

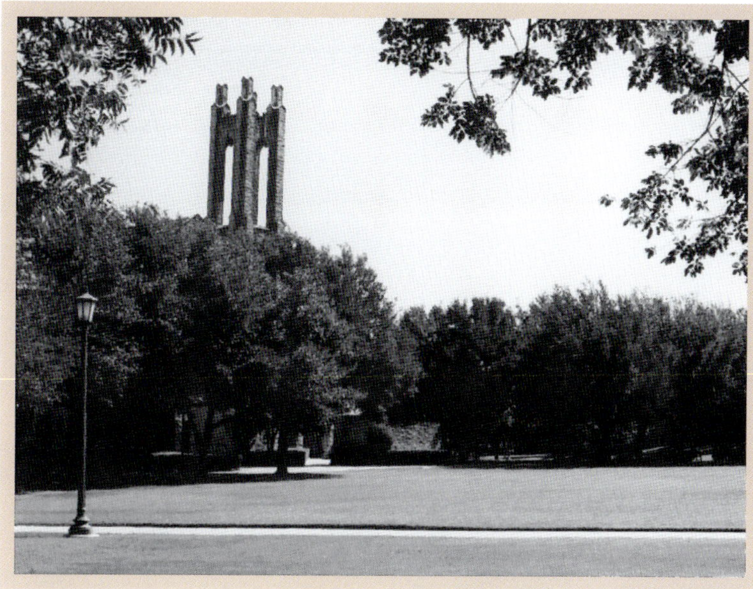

The Williamson County Science Department was built on the present campus in 1918. It was given this name to honor the residents of the county, who initially pledged the entire cost of the building. A truly modern concrete-and-steel building, it was short-lived because of structural defects. Standing just in front of today's chapel, it was torn down soon after the chapel was completed in 1950. (Then image by Luis W. Atlee; courtesy *Williamson County Sun*.)

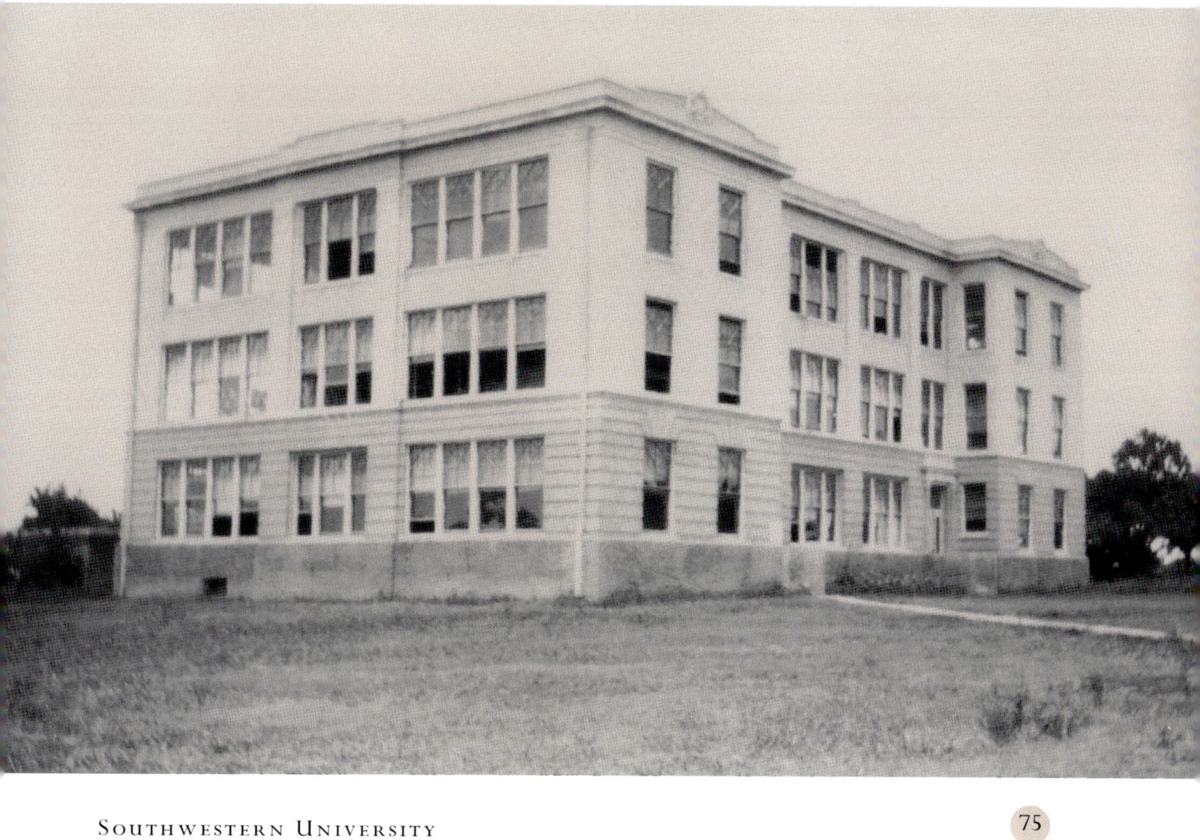

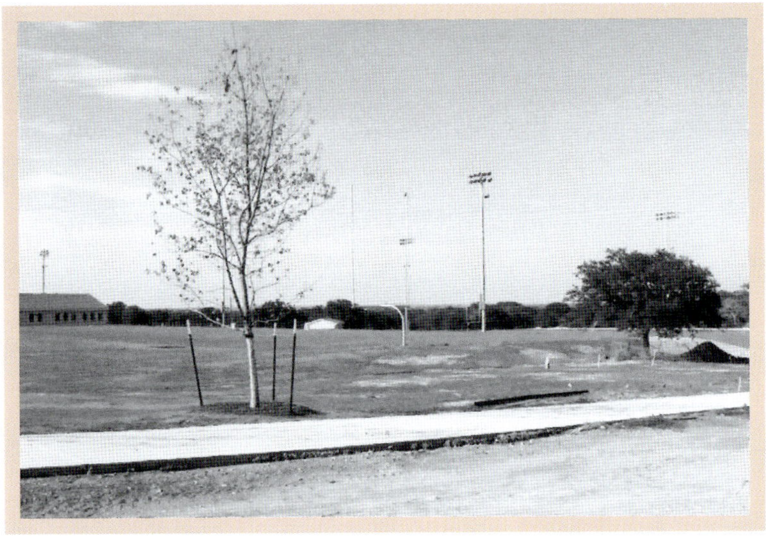

Southwestern's first nine-hole golf course, all par three, stretched across campus from the Administration Building to Kuykendall Hall in the 1930s and 1940s. Dr. Doug Benold of Georgetown remembers just stepping out of Snyder Hall and onto the course. His mother, Nelie Benold, was housemother of Snyder Hall in the 1930s. In 1955, the Kurth-Landrum course, pictured here, opened on the east end of campus. It was replaced in 2013 by athletic practice fields. (Then image by Mark Ashley; courtesy *Williamson County Sun*.)

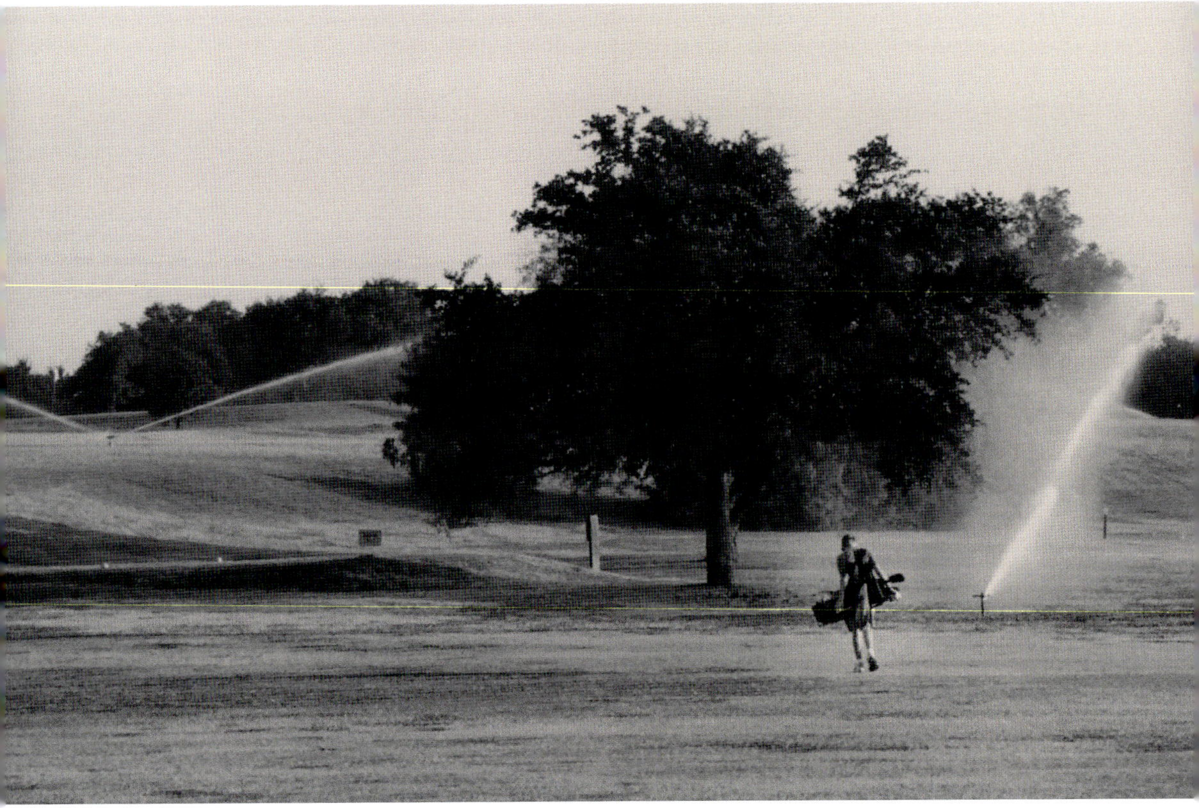

CHAPTER 6

OVER THE RIVER AND AROUND THE TOWN

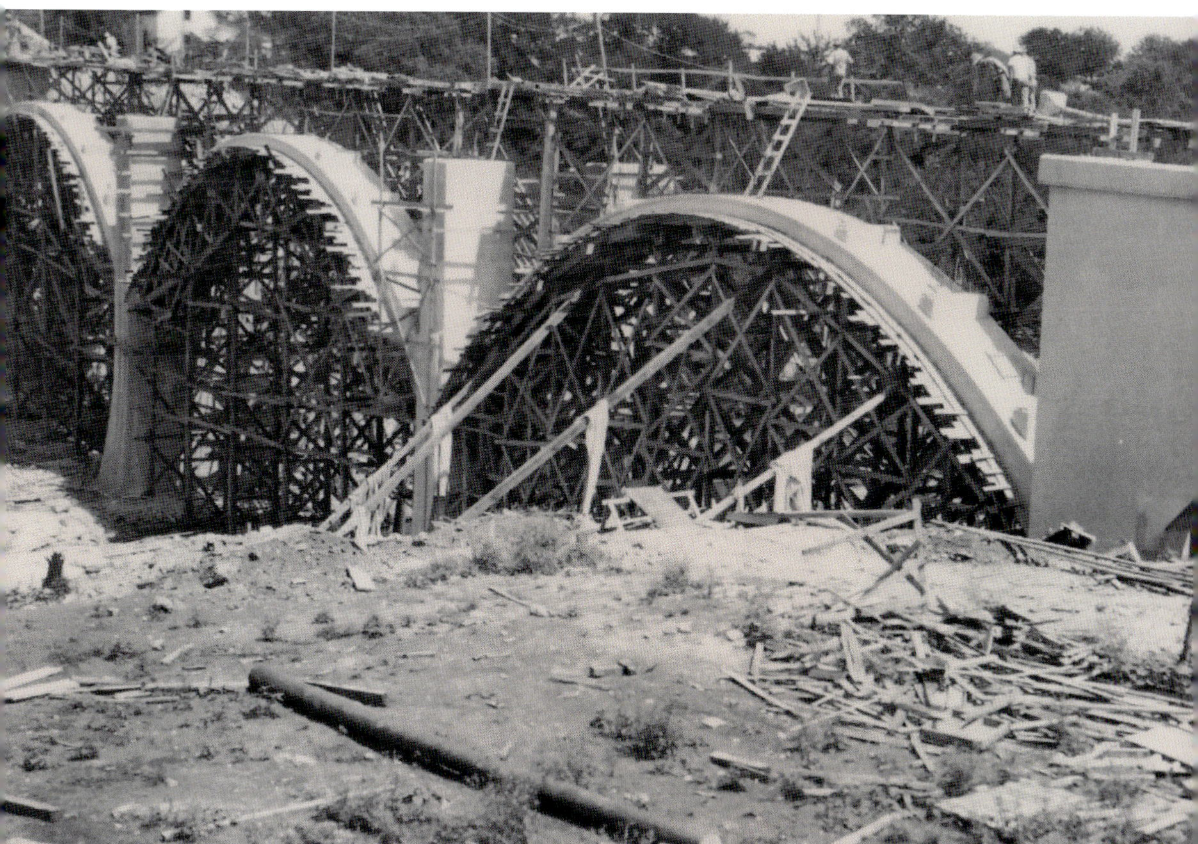

Pictured in August 1938, the construction of the Highway 29 bridge over the South San Gabriel River was well under way. Completing this bridge was the first step in making the Georgetown-Liberty Hill Road a major artery to the west. Until this time, the primary route to the west was the old Booty Road along the North San Gabriel River. (Courtesy Texas Department of Transportation.)

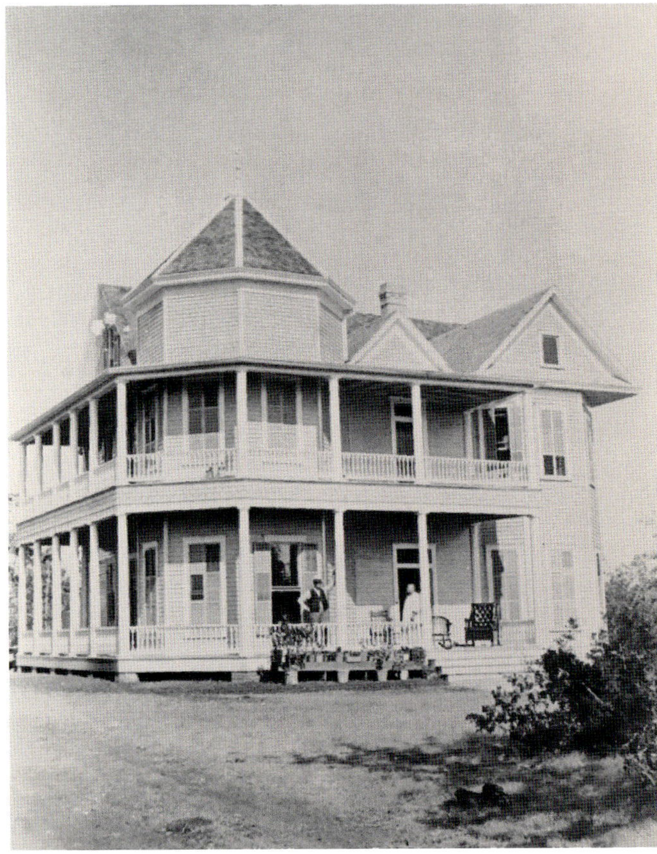

Olivia and J.M. Page are pictured around 1903 at their recognizable home southwest of Georgetown, part of a 500-acre ranch bordered on the east by Railroad Street. Purchased in 1920 by H.M. Weir, it was known in the 1930s for its polo training grounds where Interstate 35 runs today. The ranch gateposts still stand just west of Railroad Street, inside the mobile home park's fence line. The home has been used commercially for several decades. (Then image courtesy Georgetown Heritage Society.)

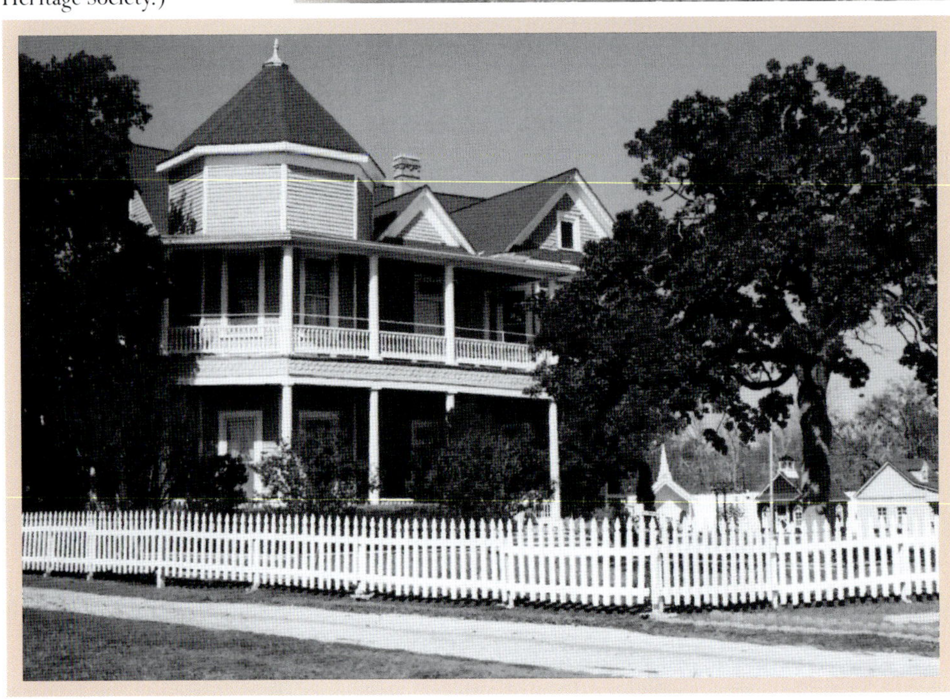

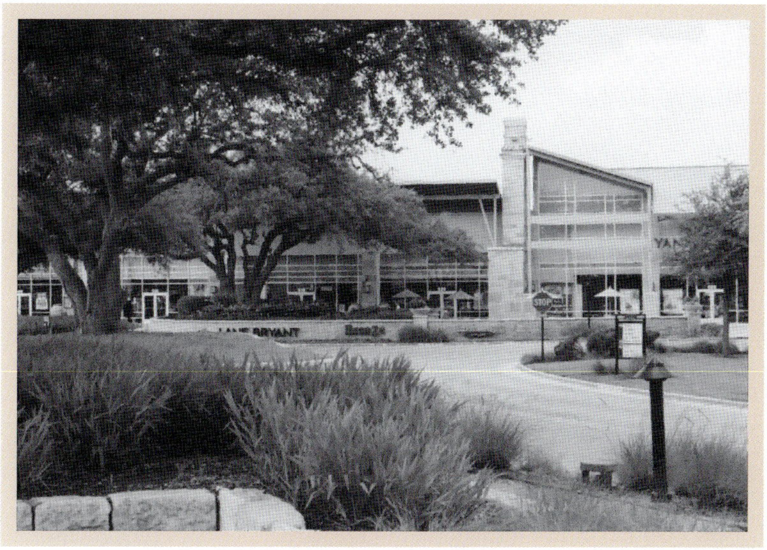

West of Georgetown, rough terrain and sparse population remained the norm until the late 20th century. Today, the intersection of Highway 29 and Interstate 35 is one of the county's busiest. Rancher and businessman Jay Wolf of Georgetown owned the property now developed as Wolf Ranch Shopping Center, which opened in 2005 at this important crossroad. Businesses have now replaced the family's 1969-built home. (Then image courtesy Jo Beth Johnson Carter.)

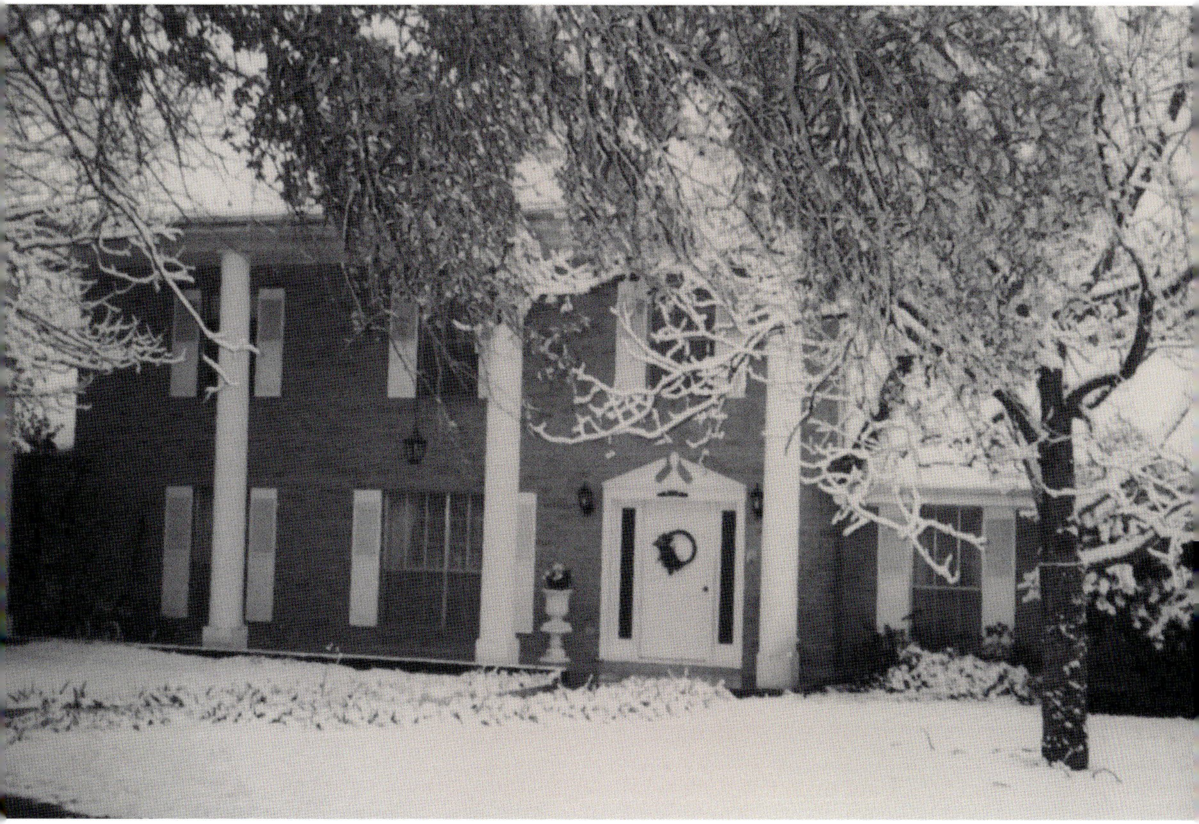

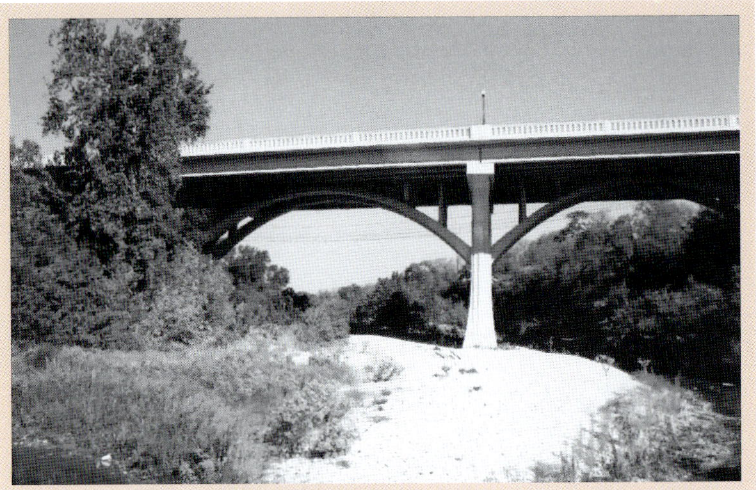

In 1939, the Highway 29 bridge over the South San Gabriel River was completed. At that time, the old bridge at Tenth Street was visible through the arch, two blocks downstream. This rare coupling was only seen for a few years. The old bridge was deemed structurally unsafe and was dismantled by the early 1940s. From this viewpoint today, the "Old West Bridge" has vanished. (Then image courtesy Texas Department of Transportation; now image courtesy Mike D'Amelio.)

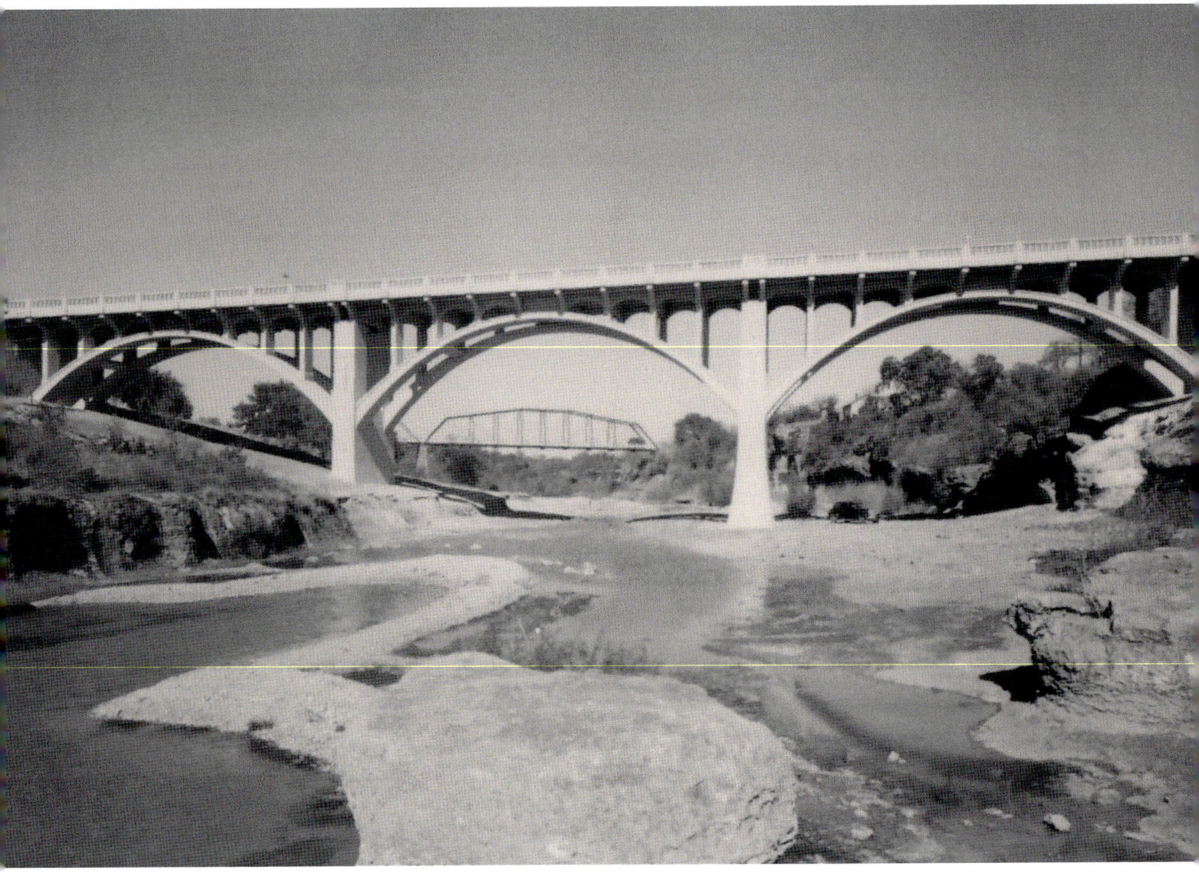

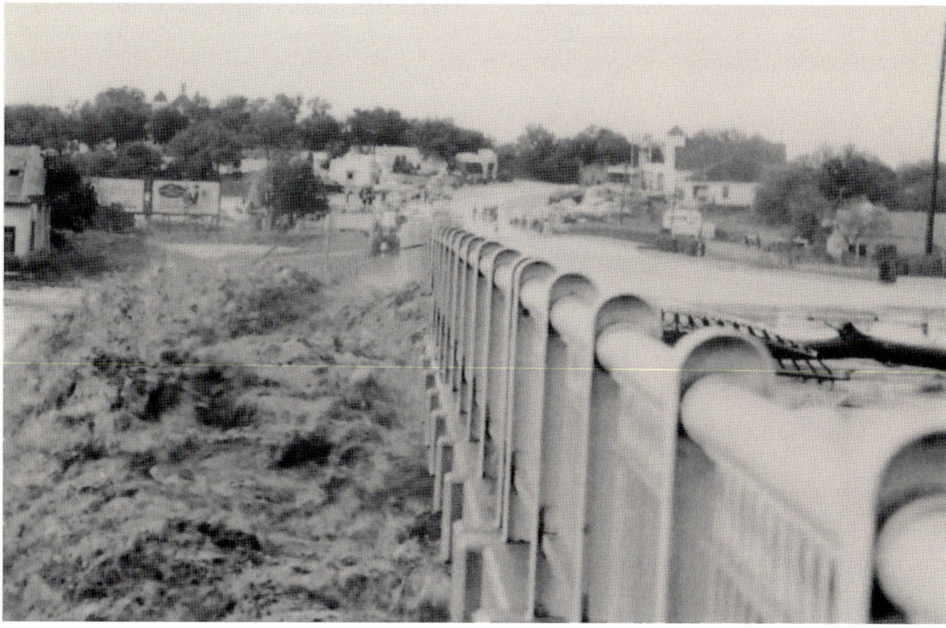

Floodwaters raged on the San Gabriel River in 1957. Looking toward Northtown from the South San Gabriel River Bridge on Austin Avenue, one can see the peaks of the George Glasscock Jr. residence among the trees (above, left). Across Austin Avenue, the old Northside Methodist Church and the home at 607 North Austin Avenue are visible in both photographs. Northtown was a separate community until 1953, when it was incorporated into the city of Georgetown. (Then image courtesy *Williamson County Sun*.)

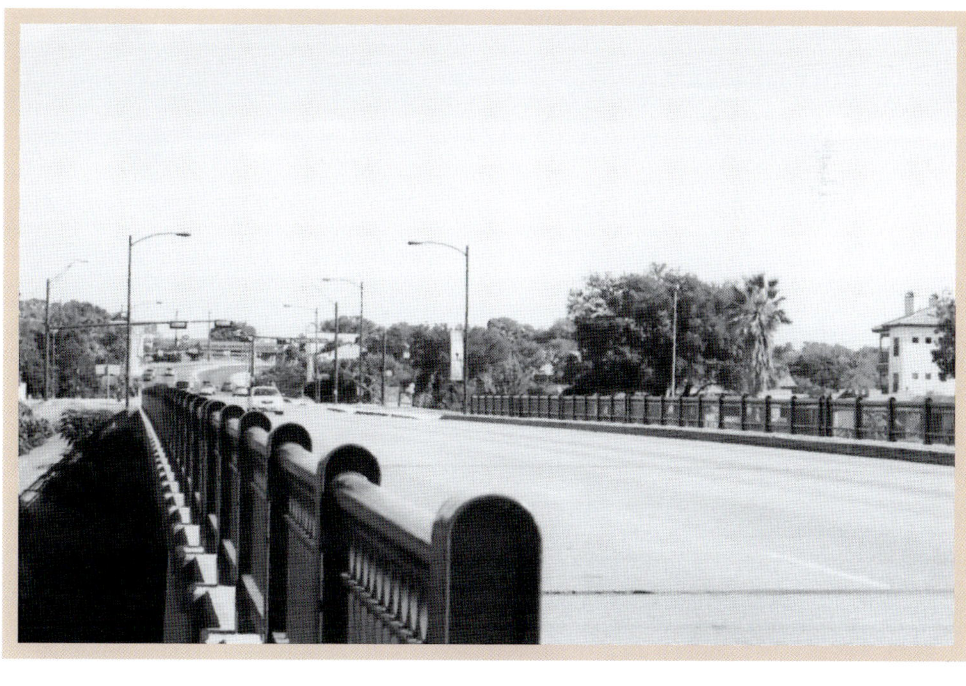

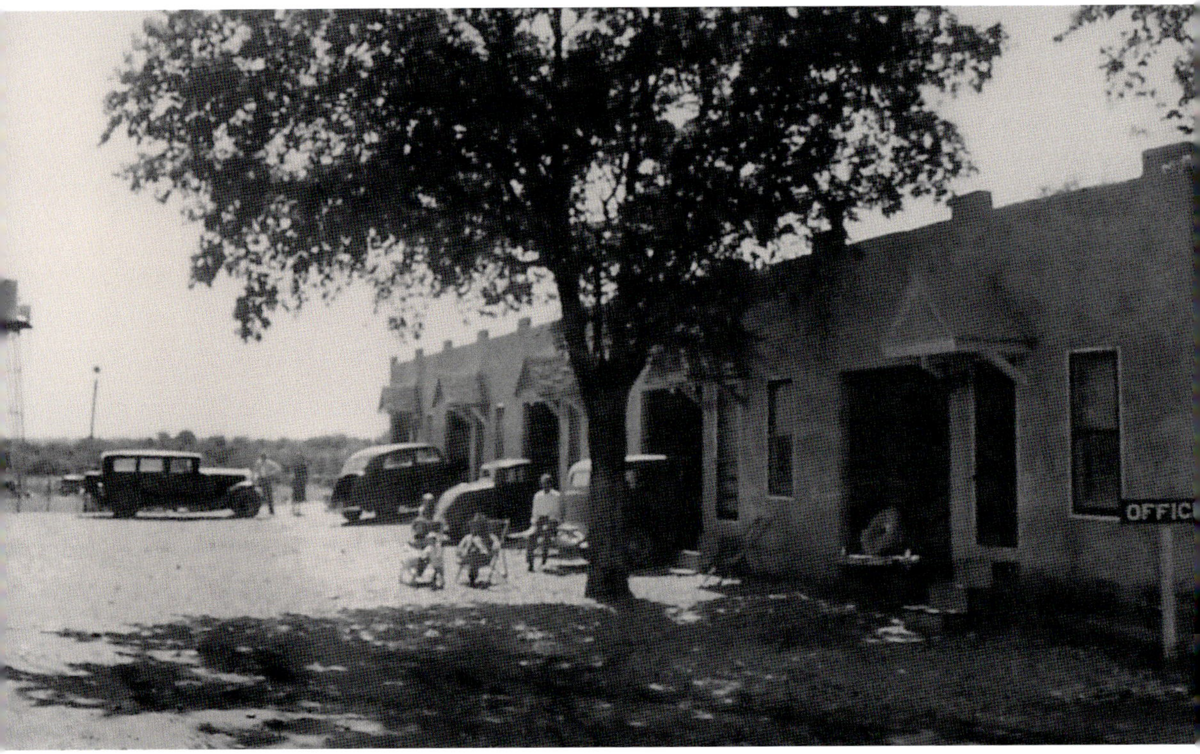

The San Gabriel Courts stood between the two forks of the river east of Austin Avenue for over 75 years. This 1938 image shows the first section, built around 1935 on the South San Gabriel River side of the classic motor court. The baby in the photograph is Johnny Brummett, whose parents built the motel. Brummett remembers both friends and strangers saving motel furnishings from the rising floodwaters in 1957. The Two Rivers apartment community now occupies the site. (Then image courtesy Johnny Brummett.)

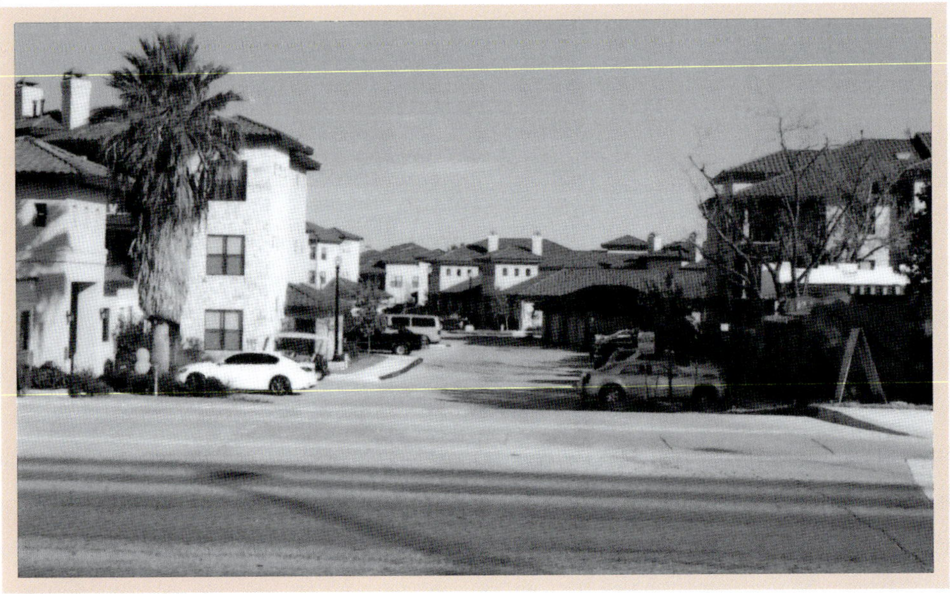

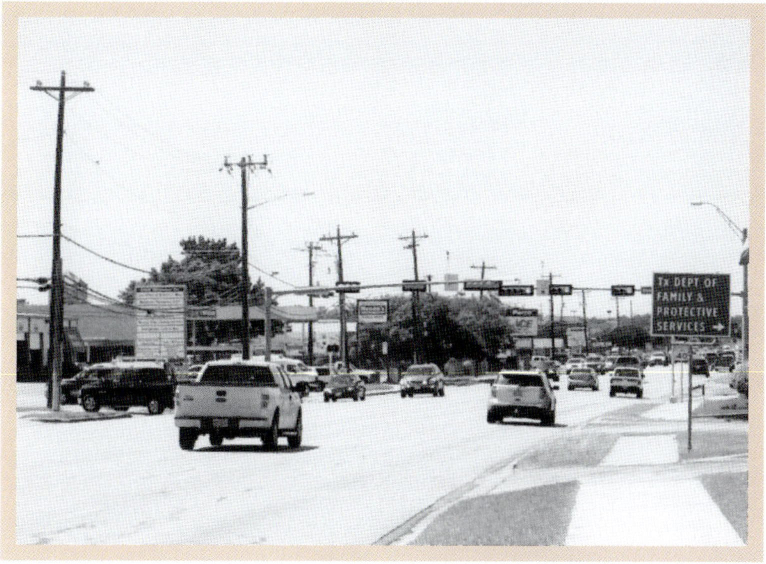

Today's Williams Drive was once a narrow, unimproved country road known as the Lampasas Highway, pictured here around 1910. By mid-century, it was known as Andice Road. Shortly before Interstate 35 was constructed, Andice Road was rerouted near Austin Avenue, and its in-town section named Williams Drive. It was widened in stages as more neighborhoods were developed. Today, Williams Drive is a major commercial street, connecting to the most populated sections of town as well as to Lake Georgetown. (Then image courtesy author's collection.)

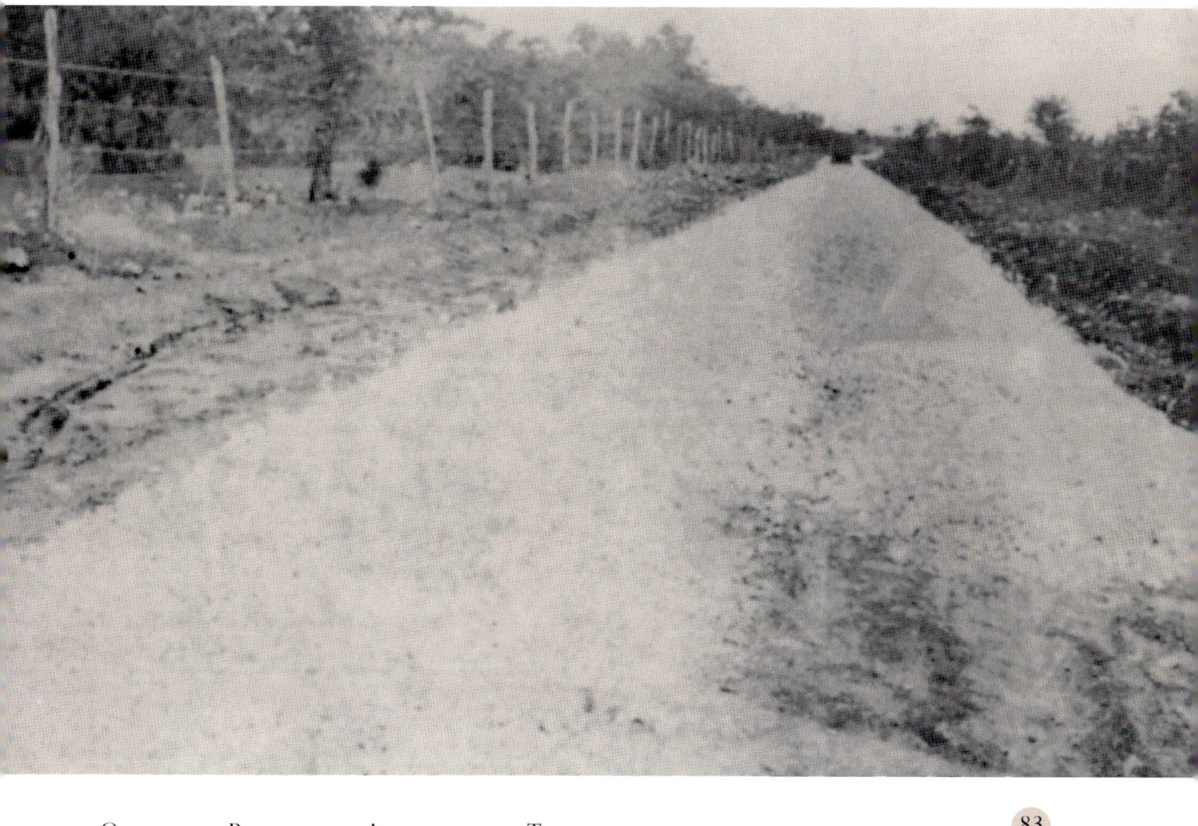

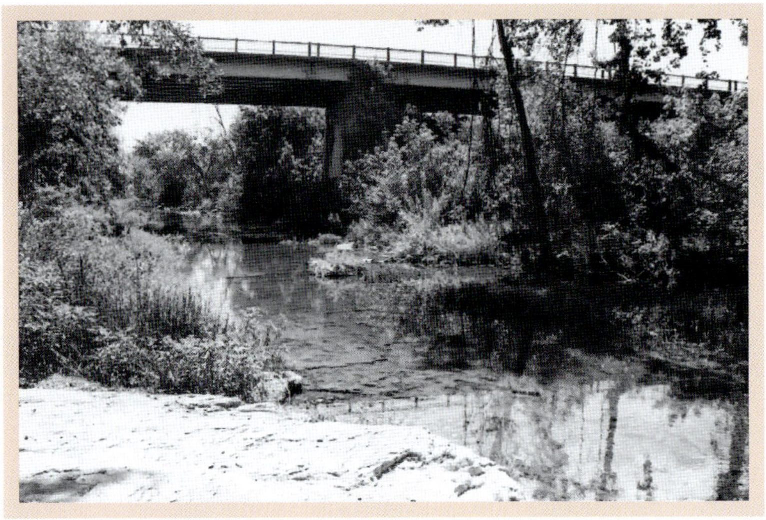

By 1890, according to historian Clara Scarbrough, the need for better bridges became a key political issue. Those over the San Gabriel River in Georgetown were among the most in need. Two iron bridges were purchased in 1892 from Chicago Iron Bridge Company and installed just east of the present Austin Avenue bridges. The North San Gabriel River Bridge, pictured around 1905, was washed out by the 1921 flood. (Then image courtesy Johnson/Ellyson Estate.)

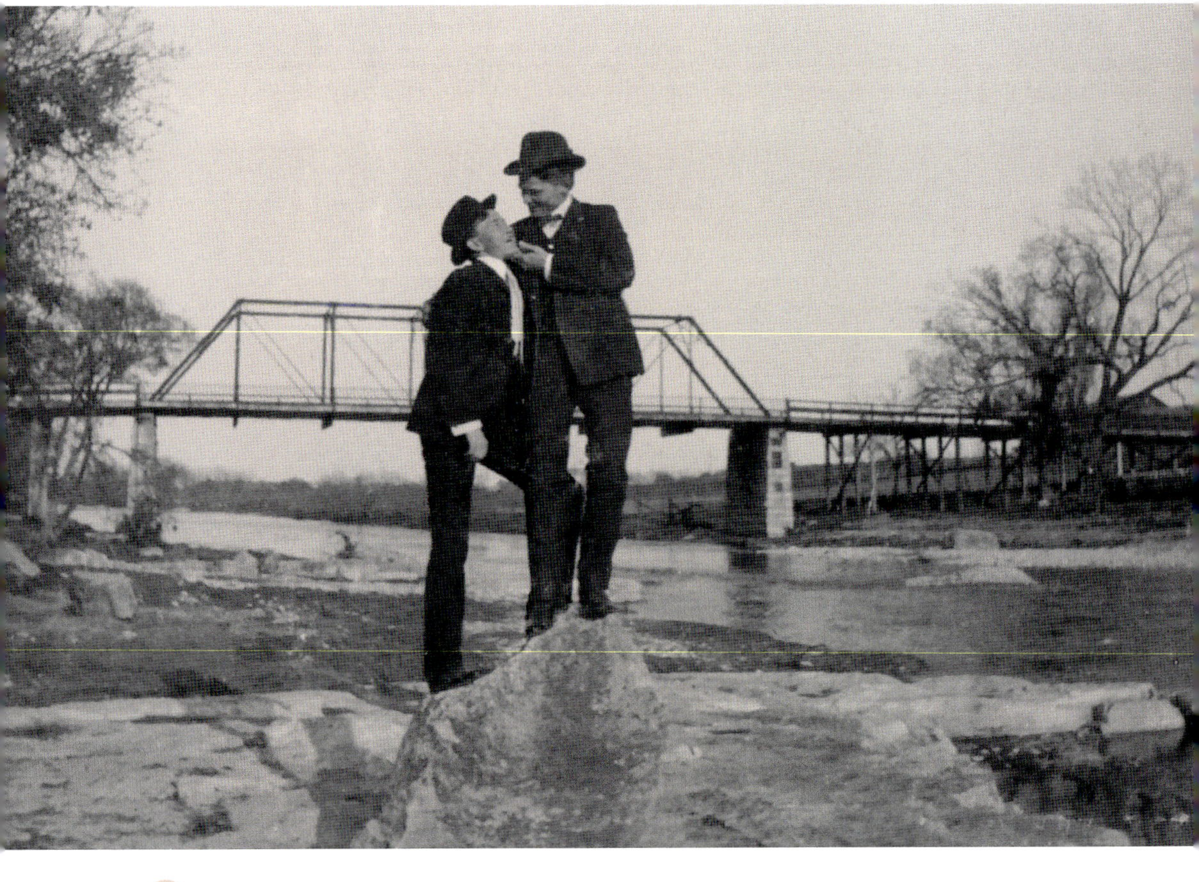

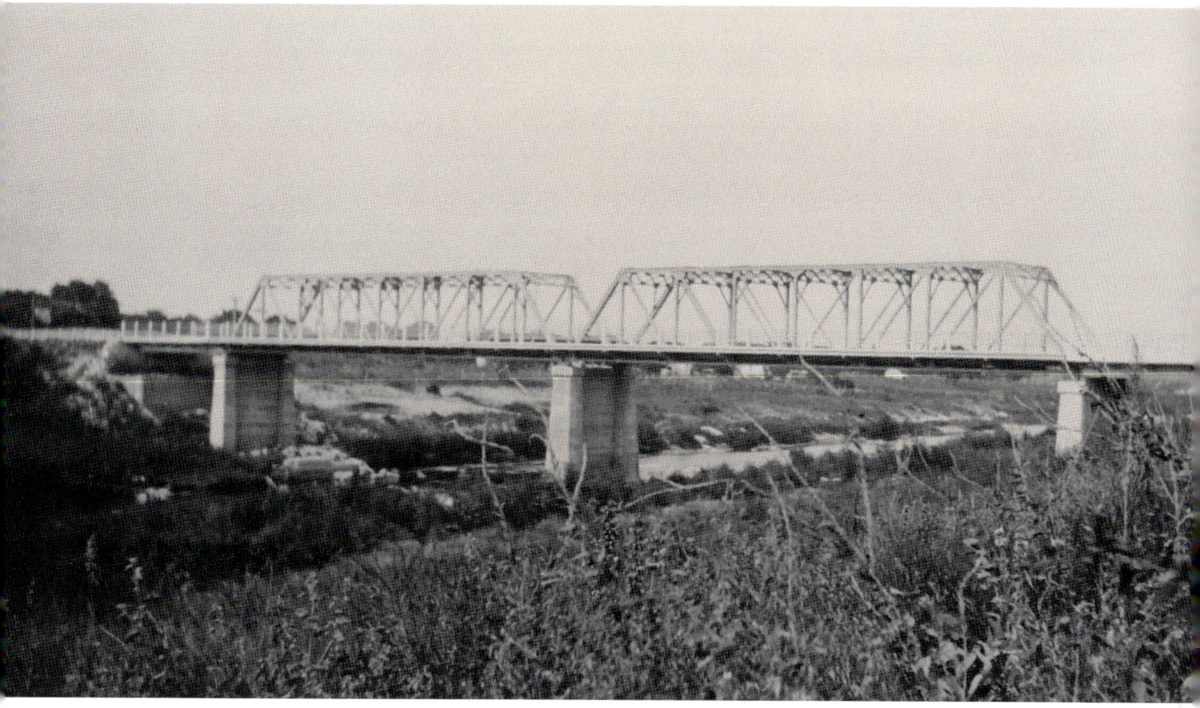

The 1892 South San Gabriel River Bridge below Jail Hill withstood the 1921 flood, but it likely sustained some damage. The *Williamson County Sun* reported that this wood, steel, and concrete bridge was completed by contractor Herman Brown in 1924. The new crossing had moved slightly west to the present Austin Avenue. Today's Austin Avenue bridges were constructed in 1939. (Then image by Luis W. Atlee; courtesy William Atlee.)

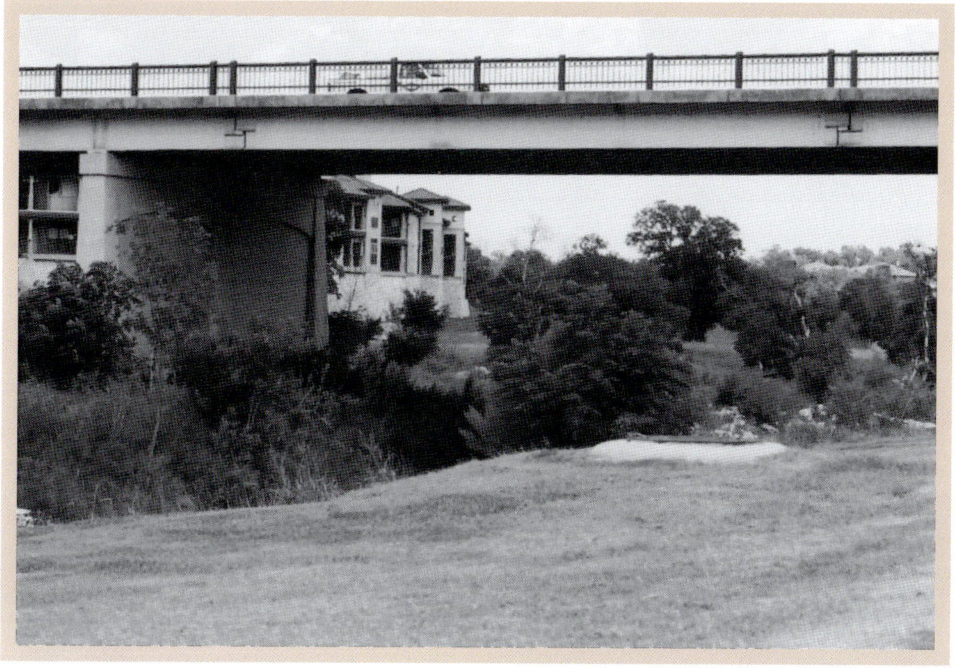

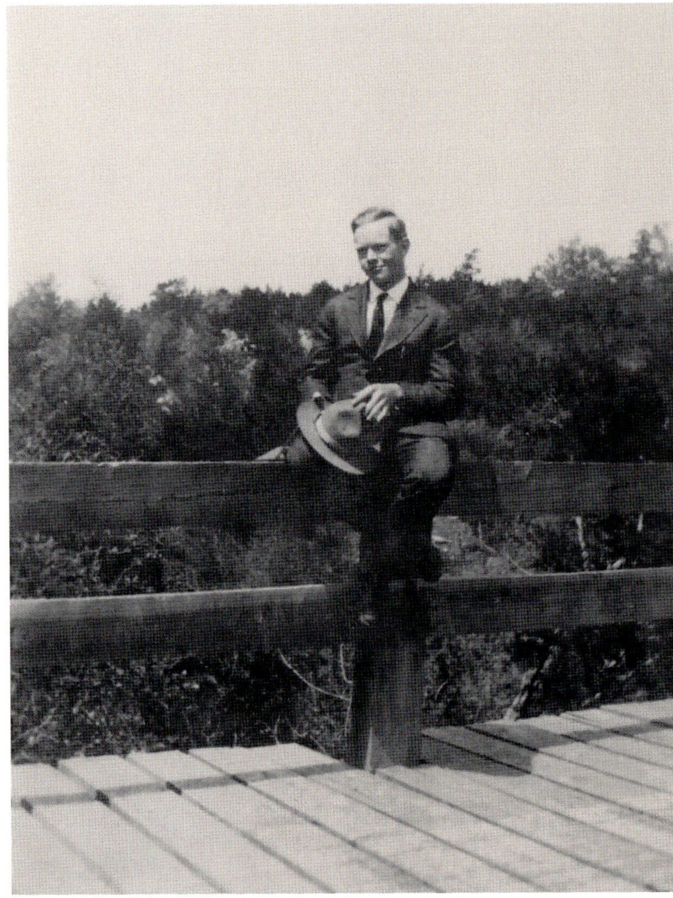

Luis W. Atlee is pictured on a temporary bridge over the North San Gabriel River, just east of today's Austin Avenue. Atlee met his future wife, Mabel Mathews, on this low-water crossing. The couple married in 1917. One of the bridge supports is still anchored into the riverbed, shown in today's photograph. Other pieces of supports are strewn randomly by floods but remain as reminders of the river's history. (Then image by Luis W. Atlee; both, courtesy William Atlee.)

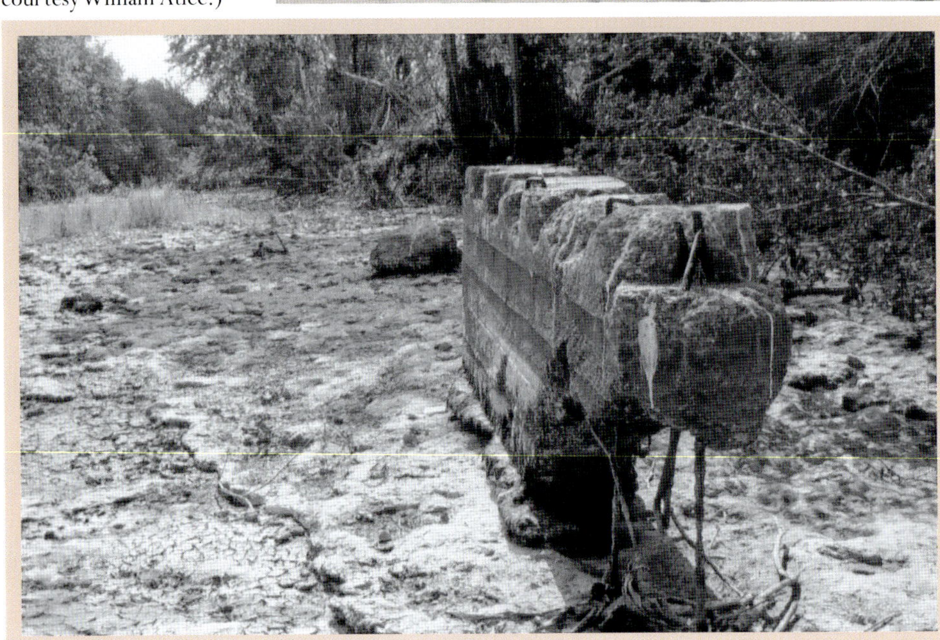

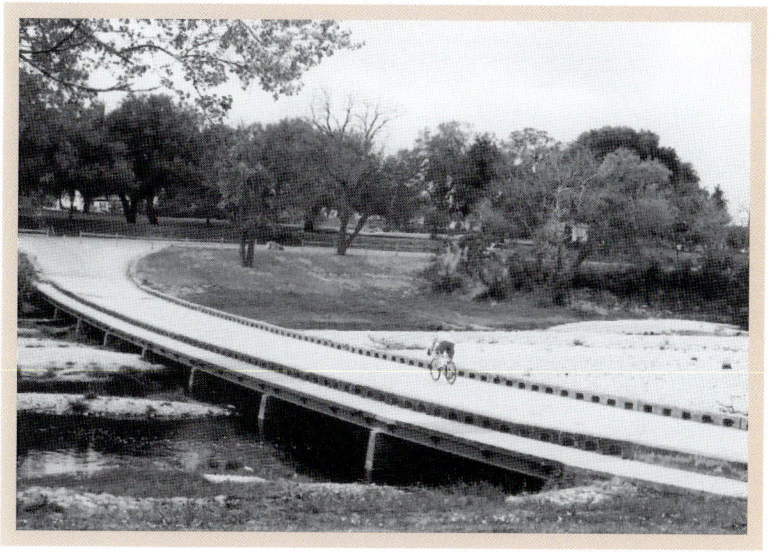

Photographed in the early 1900s, the old causeway in today's San Gabriel Park was built near the Granger Crossing. It was near a stand of giant pecan trees by the river, according to historian Hamilton Wright. Even today, huge pecan trees tower over the north side of the high College Street bridge. The more recent image shows a newer causeway, dating from the 1930s; it is now restricted to pedestrian traffic. (Then image courtesy Johnson/ Ellyson Estate.)

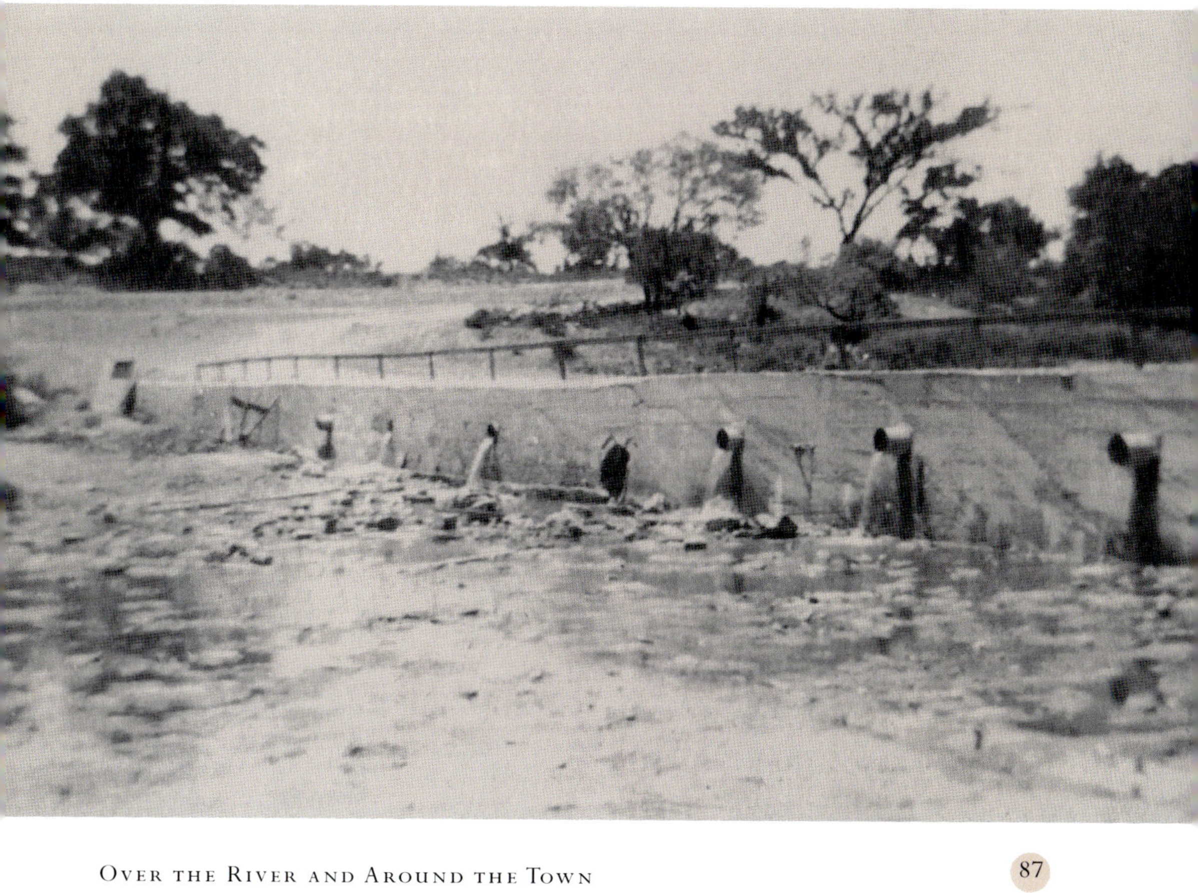

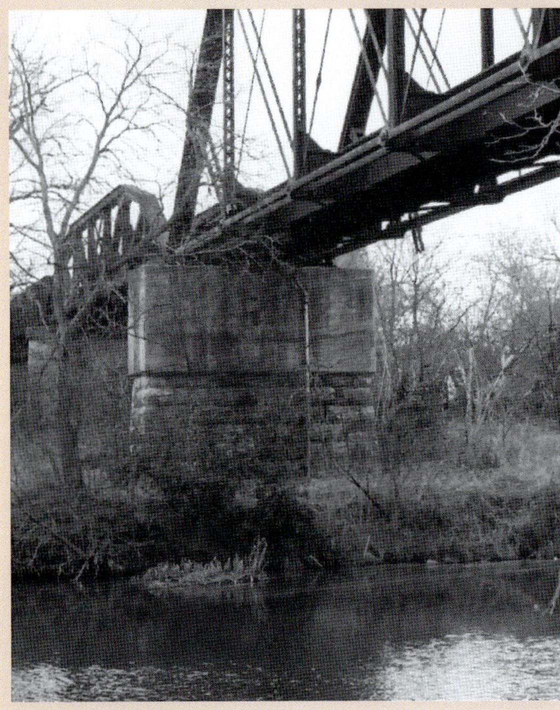

September 1921 brought a devastating flood on the San Gabriel River. Although the greatest loss of life and property was in east Williamson County, Georgetown suffered major losses as well. The North San Gabriel Bridge near today's Austin Avenue washed away, as did low-lying businesses and homes, especially in Northtown. This old image of the Katy Railroad Bridge after the flood speaks for itself. The bridge was repaired, and it still stands today downstream from San Gabriel Park. (Then image courtesy *Williamson County Sun*.)

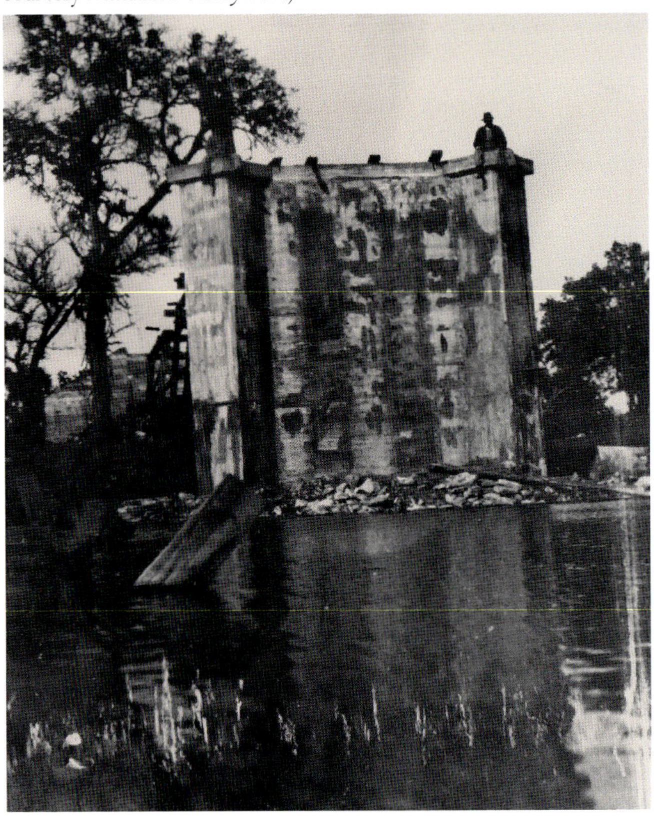

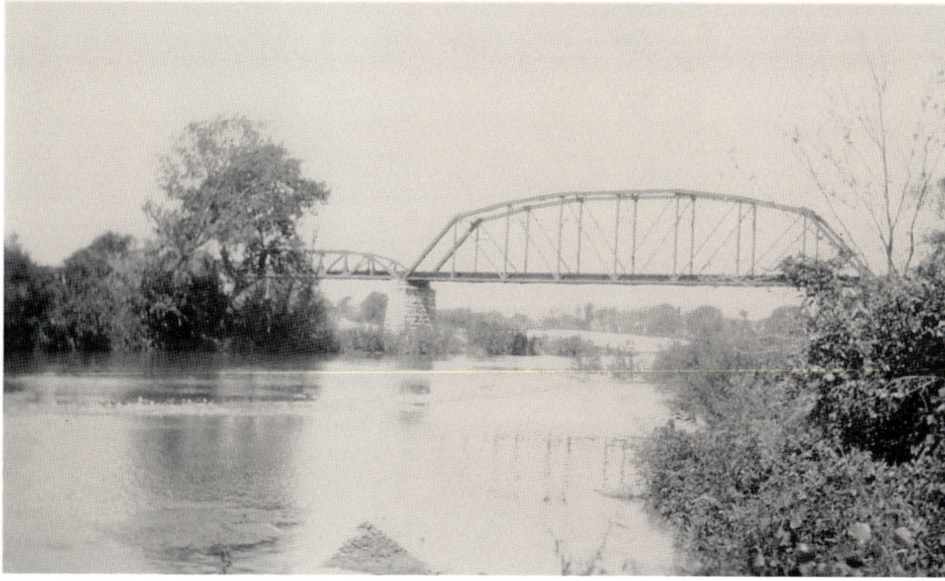

An old image from the mid-1920s shows the railroad bridge from downstream. Floods in 1908 and 1913 ruined the popular Katy Lake near Weir, and many began calling this swimming hole by the same name. Donnell Bishop of Georgetown remembered large crowds coming to swim, barbeque, and picnic here on Sunday afternoons in the 1920s and 1930s. Today, from private property, the same view still looks idyllic. (Then image by Luis W. Atlee; courtesy *Williamson County Sun*.)

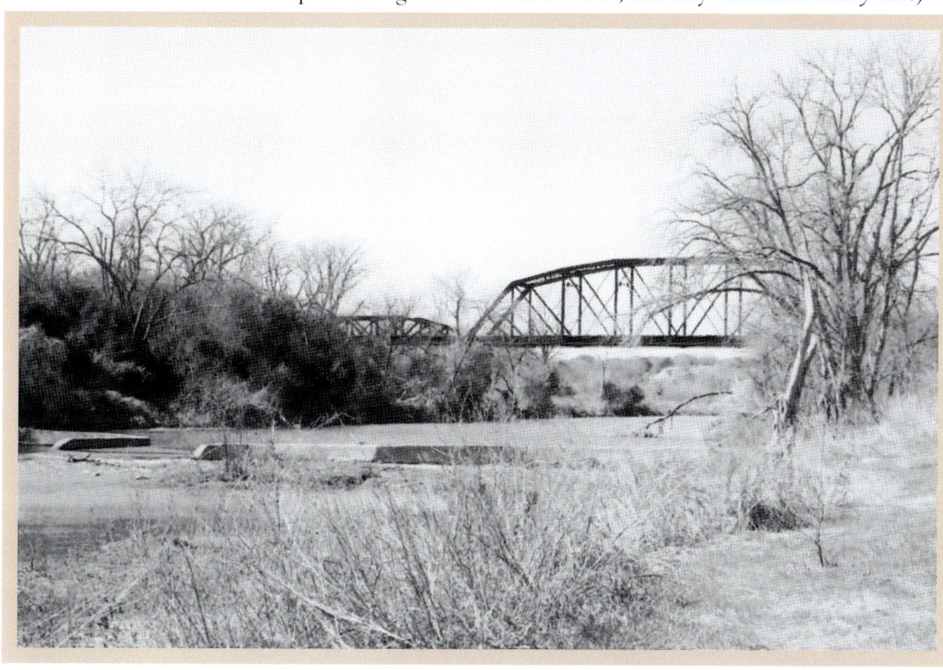

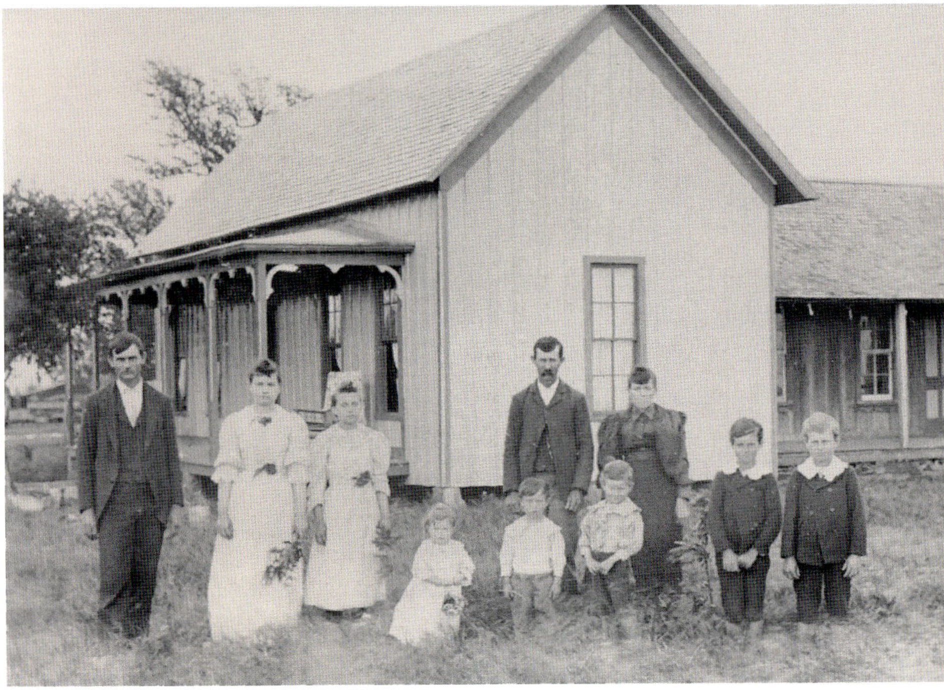

This c. 1895 photograph shows Joseph Benton Bishop, center, and his family in front of their home. Their large Century Farm was bordered by Berry Creek and originally extended both east and west of today's Interstate 35. Some family members attended the old Berry's Creek School that sat near today's Highway 195 crossover to Berry Creek Drive (County Road 190). Today, the home serves as an office for the Live Oaks RV Park at Interstate 35 and Highway 130. (Then image courtesy Bishop family.)

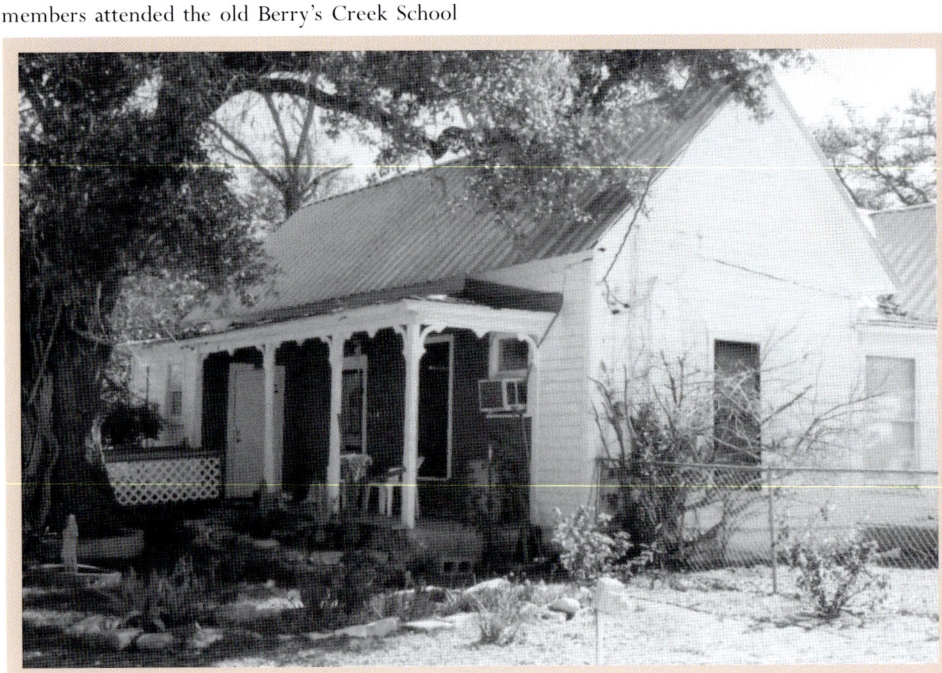

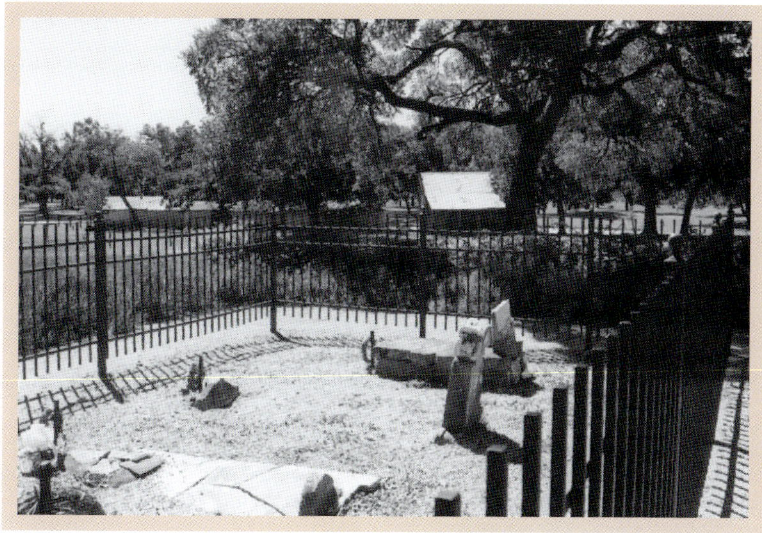

Pioneer and patriot John Berry built his 1846 gristmill north of Georgetown. Today, the 126-acre Berry Springs Park is part of his original tract. In 2010, Hurricane Hermine dumped 15 inches of rain here, breaking the original dam, which was the only part of the mill still intact. Restoration of the dam and millpond was completed in 2013. Pictured in 1948, the Daughters of 1812 visit John Berry's grave, now a part of Berry Springs Park. (Then image courtesy Chamberlin family.)

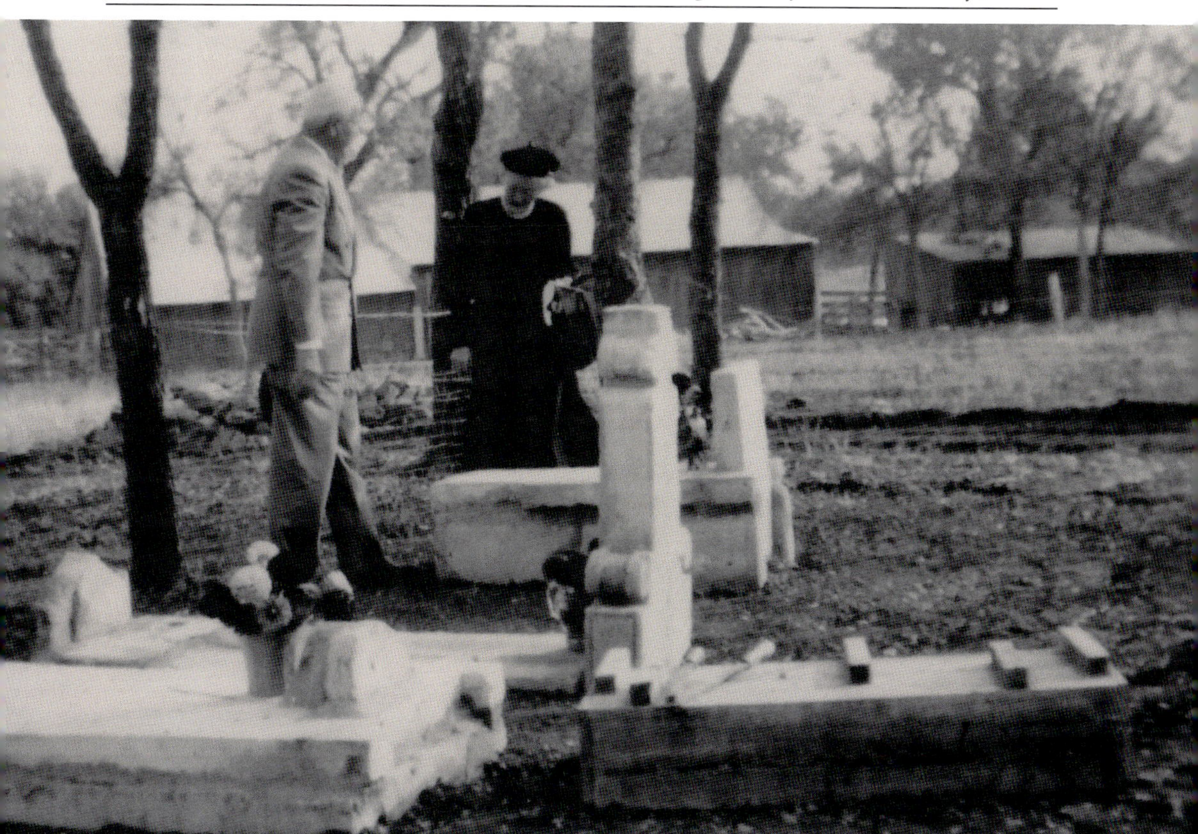

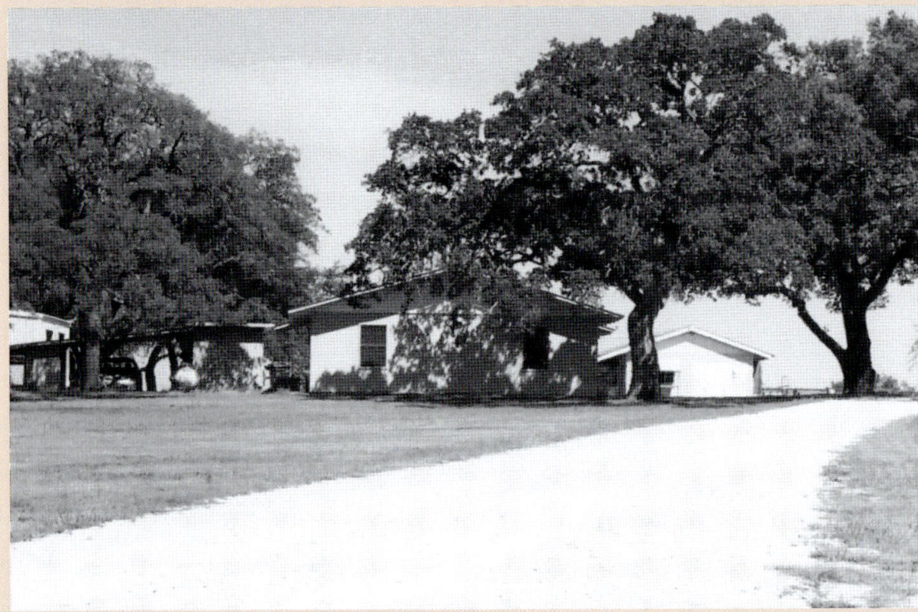

The Williams family started a ranching dynasty around Georgetown. From San Gabriel Park, to north of Sun City, to Berry Creek, Strickland Grove, and Florence, their ranch acreage was immense. Isaac Williams's 1878 home is shown in this mid-1950s photograph. The structure, which burned around 1970, sat among the grove of trees east of Airport Road across from today's River of Life Church. (Then image courtesy Tommie Williams.)

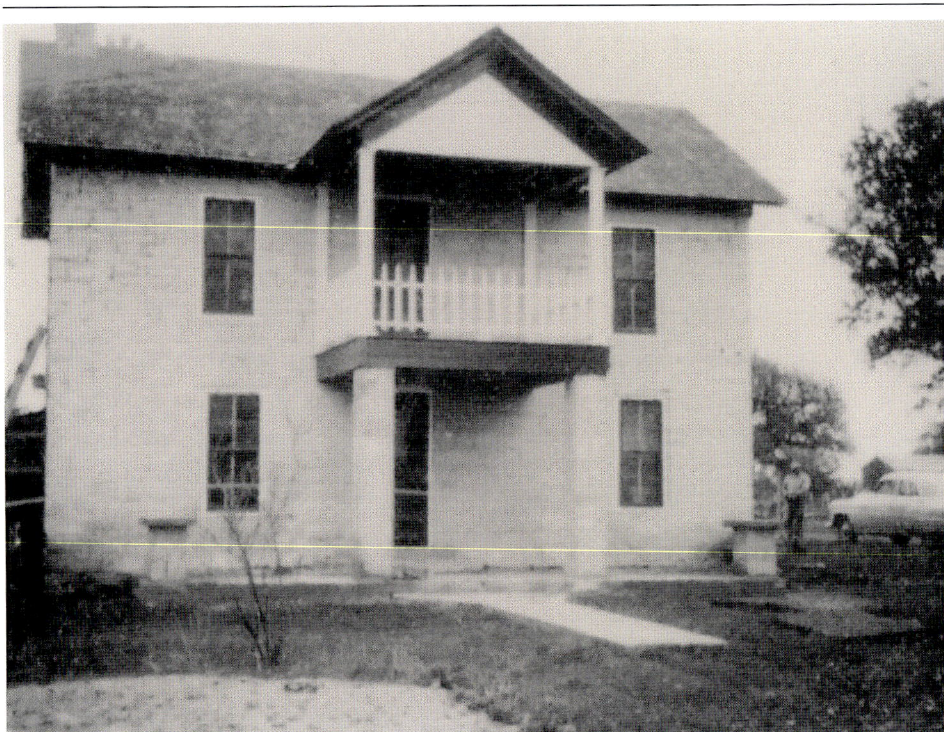

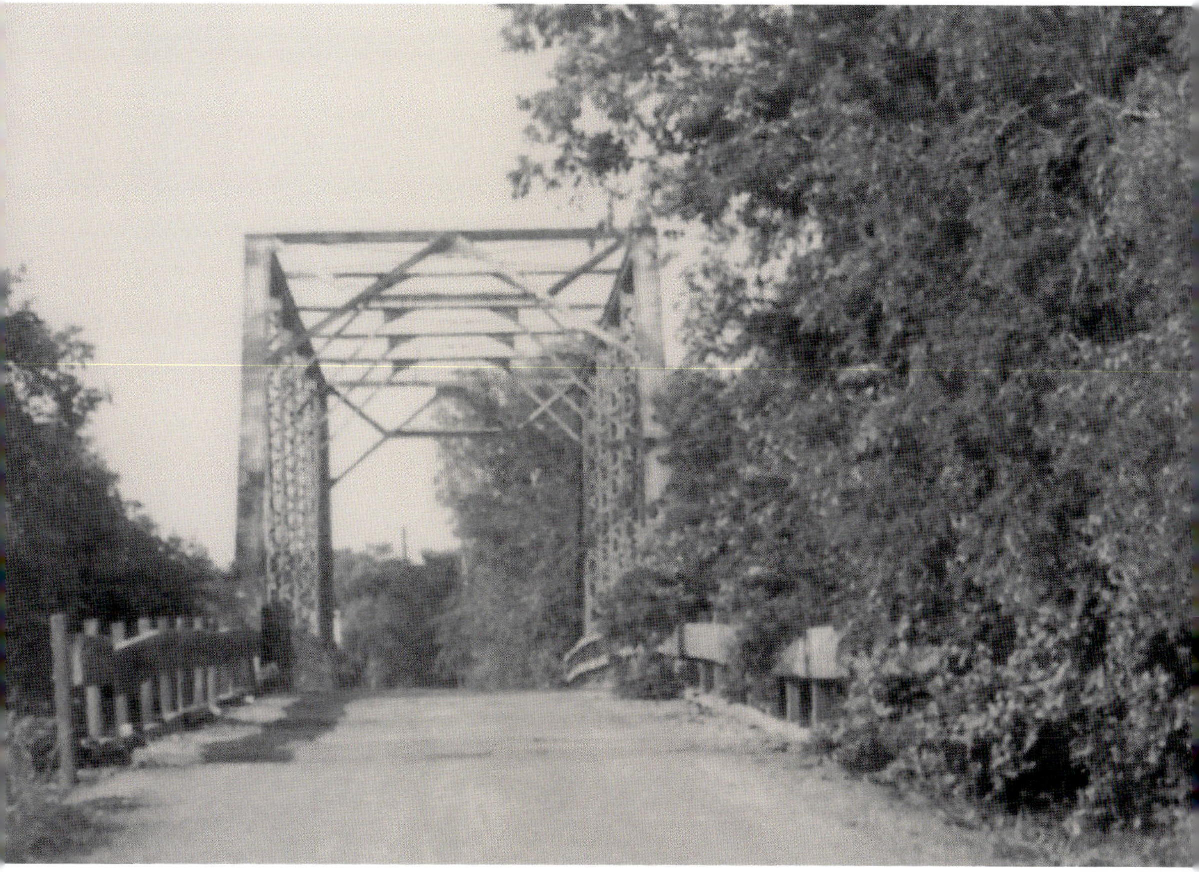

Bridging Berry Creek was essential to travel on the Georgetown-Belton Road, which later became State Highway 81. Historian Clara Scarbrough described the early 1883 truss bridge over Berry Creek as "narrower than the road." The county then "narrowed the road to fit the bridge." Pictured here is the 1891 bridge over Berry Creek on Airport Road. This road was originally the Florence Highway. Today, this bridge survives, unusable, next to the modern bridge. (Then image courtesy Texas Department of Transportation.)

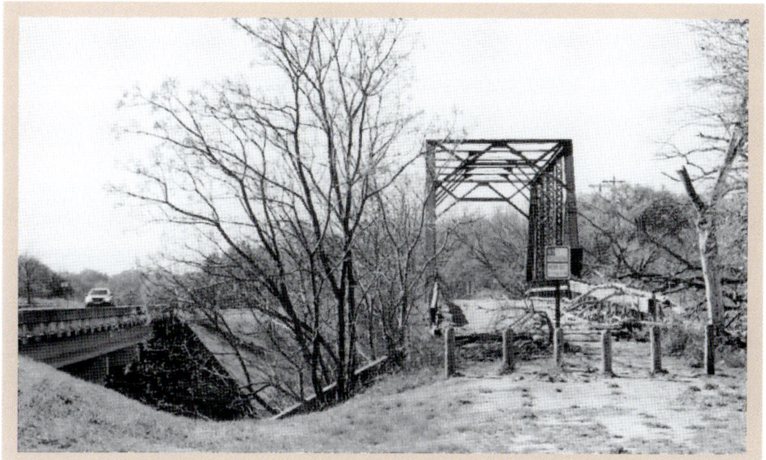

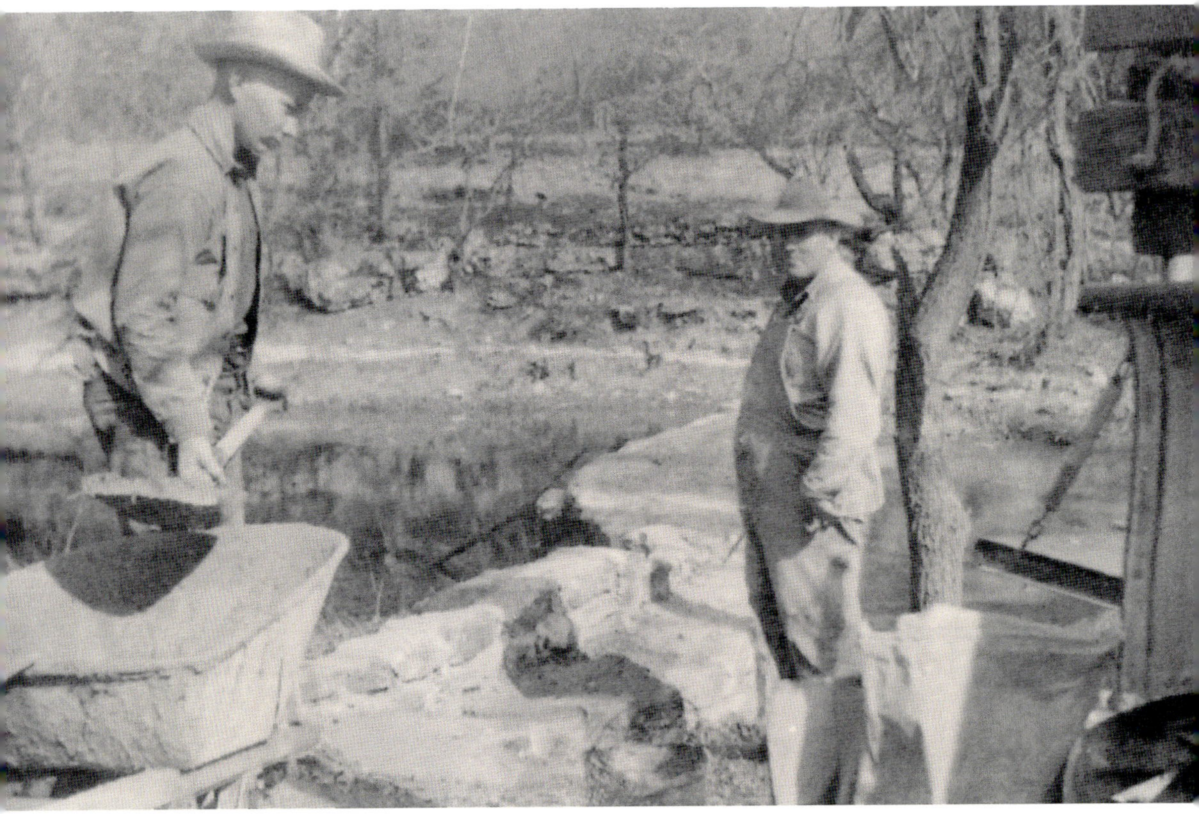

Burness Williams and a brother owned this 700-acre ranch, now part of Sun City, in the 1930s and 1940s. Burness, pictured at right around 1939, built dams on the property, one near the confluence of Berry Creek and Cowan Creek. Williams family history describes this area between the confluence and today's "Bluffs" along the trail as their "fish camp." Today's photograph shows this part of the creek along the nature trail off Great Frontier Drive. (Then image courtesy Tommie Williams.)

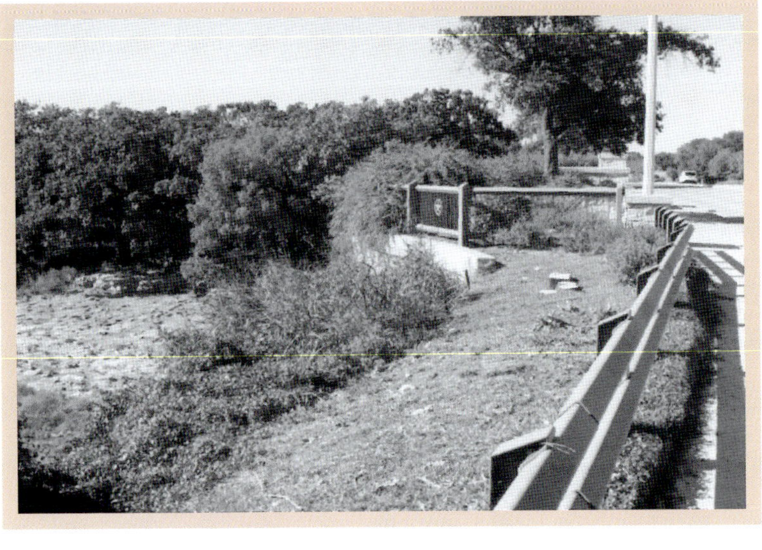

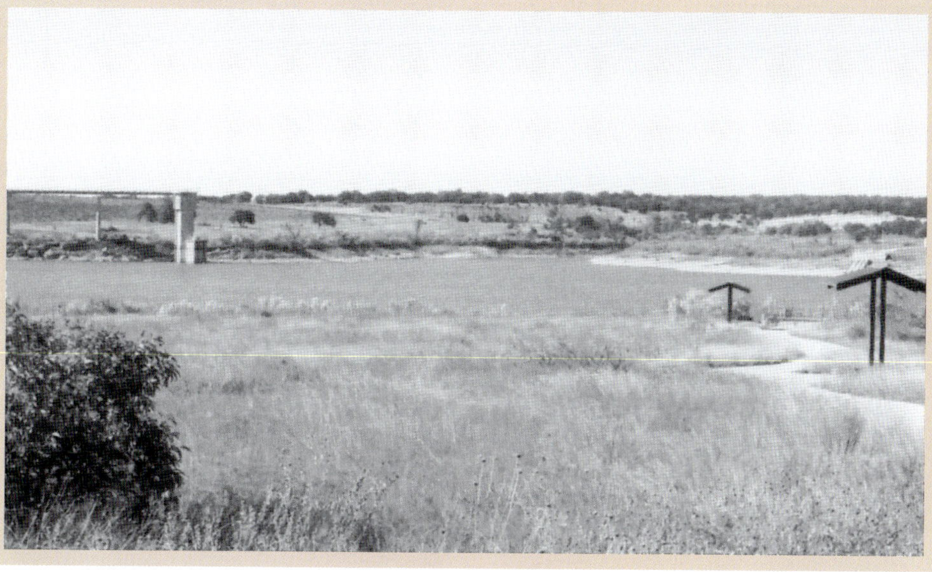

The historic trail that brought pioneers to the Georgetown area along the North San Gabriel River is now covered by Lake Georgetown. The dam and control tower are pictured in 1979 just before the lake was filled. The home at center right was removed but indicates the immense scale of the excavation beyond the original riverbed. Today, the dam and lake provide flood control, recreation, and needed water resources for the future. (Then image courtesy *Williamson County Sun*.)

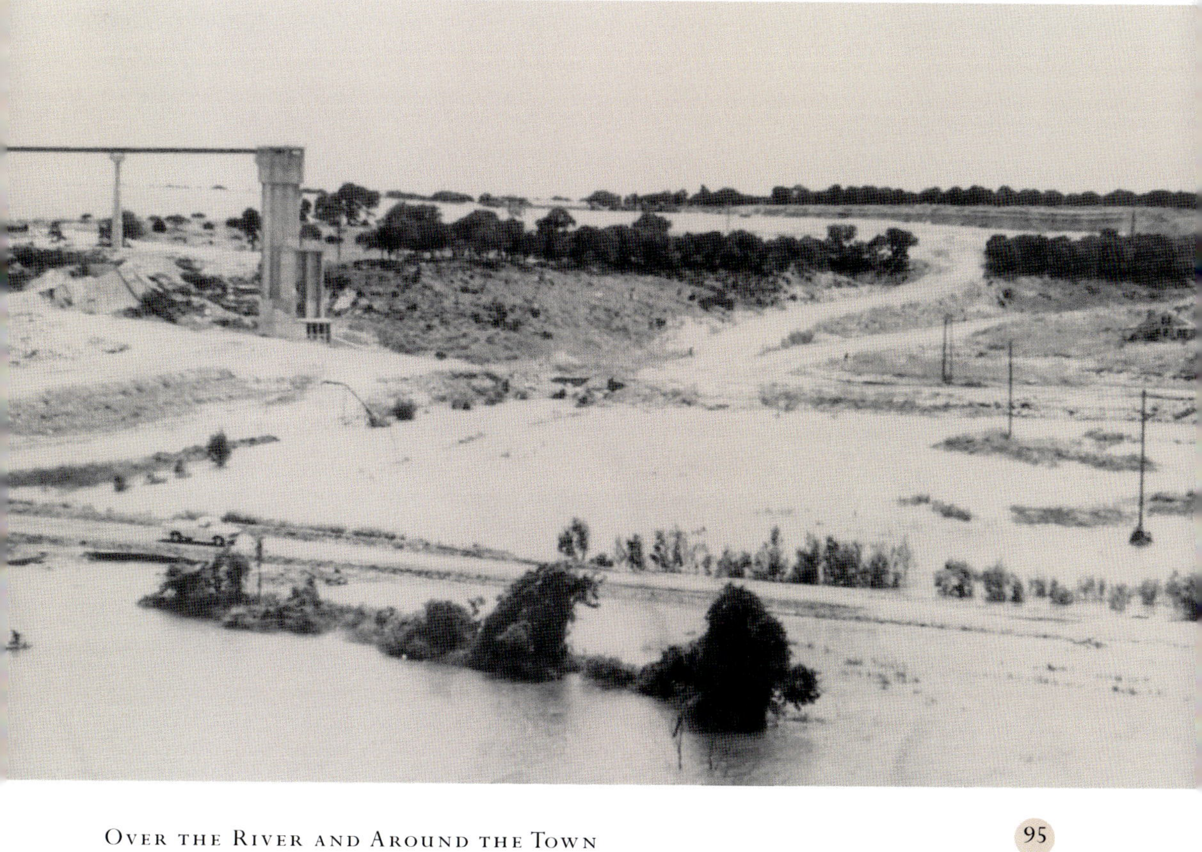

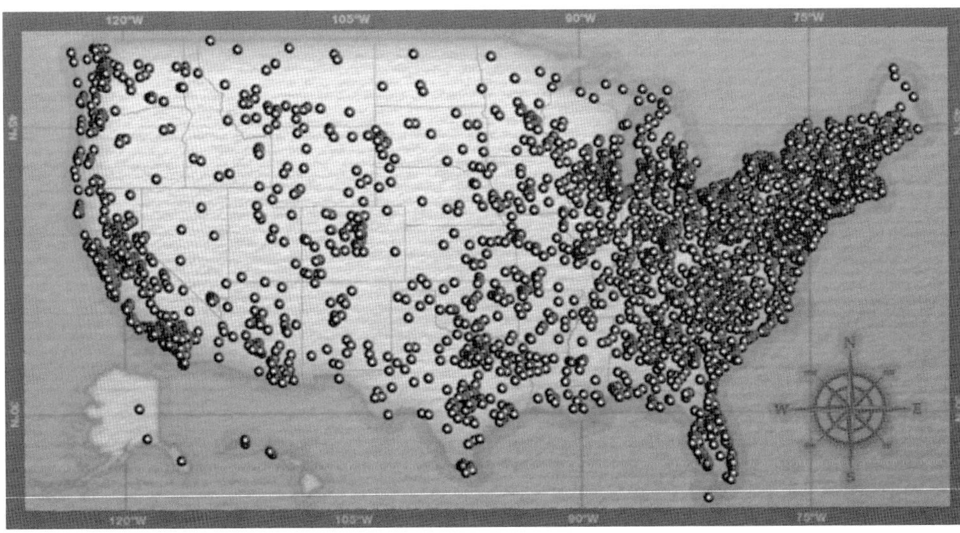